DON'T SAY CRAZY TO ME

From the Woman Who Danced With Frank Sinatra

A Memoir, to the best of my knowledge

Marion Hoffman Koenig

For my Daughter, Erica Nicole
For our adventures across the globe and the humor in good times and bad.

Mostly, for your capacity to love.

For My Mom, Florence Lilian
For loving everything equally. For doing your best.

For My Brother, Alan Charles Hoffman
Honored to have known your gentle soul.

"Everyone you meet is fighting a battle you
know nothing about. Be kind, always."

Quote originally attributed to Ian Maclaren (pen
name for John Watson)

Reignited by Robin Williams

Contents

Chapter 1

My Dad, Charlie

At six years old, I was rushed to Westchester Square Hospital in the Bronx by a stranger named Roy. My seven-and-a-half-year-old brother, Alan, was dragged along, too. The stranger yanked us through milky green hallways into an elevator without a word. I had never been in an elevator. I held my chest, trying to breathe as the elevator doors slammed shut and the space darkened. I screeched.

Frowning at me, Roy said, "Stop your nonsense."

I gasped as the elevator doors opened.

We paused in the doorway of a small room that smelled like Mom's medicine cabinet. I saw men in white coats talking in a circle. Florence, my Mom, was in the middle, clinging to every syllable of their every word. While I could not understand what they were saying, I saw it upset her. My older sisters, Alice and Nancy, were with her.

My Dad, Charlie, was lying in a bed with metal sides like a crib. There were tubes in his arm and nose. I wanted to tell him that his tomato plants had yellow blossoms and that Mom's June roses were blooming.

"Dad," I whispered.

Dad did not turn his head.

Mom stepped out of the circle and whispered, "Dad wants to see you."

I bit Roy's hand and pulled free, tugging on Alan's striped brown and yellow polo shirt to join me, but he gripped the doorway.

I tried to jump on the bed, but my feet slipped on the metal bars. I pulled my shoes and socks off. My bare feet quickly managed the ascent into Dad's bed. Straddling his body, I knelt on both sides of his chest. Dad's big, calloused hands held my face. He pulled me close. Then, I felt his breath on my cheeks. I took his face in my hands. Dad needed a shave.

Brushing my bangs back, he stared into my eyes. I laid my head on his chest, holding my Dad for the first time.

Dad placed his weakened hands around my waist and whispered, "Marion, take good care of Mother. Can you hear me? Look after Mother. Do you hear me?"

I raised my face to Dad's almost shut eyes. I nodded yes and frowned with strength.

"I will. I'll take good care of Mom, you'll see," I whispered.

Dad kissed me, and I kissed him back. Roy took me off the bed.

I grabbed Dad's hand, screaming, "No, I have to ask my Daddy a question."

I was not allowed.

Mom pried Alan's hand from the doorway and whispered, "Dad knows you love him."

My three older siblings walked ahead. They were on the fringes of my life. The stranger I met yesterday for the first time was my 24-year-old brother, Roy. He had joined the Navy before I was born. Mom never mentioned him. Alice, at 21, was in her final year of Nursing at Bellevue Hospital, and Nancy, at 15, moaned whenever she was told to babysit Alan and me. By the time I was ten, these three ancients would all be gone, married or otherwise. This led to a fierce, unbreakable bond between Mom, Alan, and me.

At home, I worried that a recent shaving incident caused my Dad's illness. On March 7, my sixth birthday, I was honored to be Dad's helper on Saturday mornings as he shaved. This tradition was passed down from sibling to sibling.

I arrived late for that duty in May and hurriedly opened the bathroom door. Dad had begun to shave, and the door banged his arm, causing him to cut his chin.

"I'm sorry," I whispered, climbing onto the toilet seat cover.

Dad held a piece of toilet tissue to the cut. It immediately turned red. The red dripped into his white foam. I was too frightened to do anything but grip the towel rack and blink back tears. Dad took a deep breath as he wiped the pink foam with a blue washcloth.

I had no idea I'd see much more blood in a few innocent years.

Eventually, Dad sharpened his razor on the leather strap with his face full of fresh white foam. Looking at me, he whispered, "Find Alan and wait in the garden for me."

"Sure, Dad," I mumbled, crying as I obediently climbed down.

Alan and I played catch in the narrow gravel alleyway next to our home until we heard the screen door stretch open.

"Children, come with me," Dad hollered, heading for his vegetable patch.

The rare times Dad swung open the Holy Gate to welcome us into his well-manicured patch of veggies was sheer bliss for me. Squirming to contain my excitement, I grabbed Alan's hand before he bolted.

Pointing to the tomato plants, Dad described how to pluck the tiny shoots at the bottom of the stem so the soil's nutrition would go to the baby tomatoes. Alan showed his lack of interest by stepping back and nudging me forward. I knelt as I did for my nightly prayers. I stared at the plants before aiming, as I had already hurt Dad's chin, so this had to be perfect to make up for that. I tweaked the tiny leaves and laid them on the ground. I continued until Dad rustled my hair with approval.

Sundays were Dad's day of rest, so he didn't shave. He also did not attend church. Every Sunday, he would say he didn't need church to be good, avoiding Mom's weekly invitation.

Instead, my Dad would pull a fresh sleeveless undershirt from Mom's outdoor clothesline and head to his patch of heaven.

When we returned from the First Presbyterian Church of Throgg's Neck, Mom placed a brown bottle dripping with condensation and a thick glass with a handle next to Dad. He sat in his kitchen chair and sipped his one weekly beer. I looked at Dad's back against the afternoon sun as it shot through the square pinholes of our screen door, creating a haze around him. I felt his loneliness, like when no one wanted to play checkers with me. The times Dad would turn around and join us to read the Sunday comics were the sweetest. I would lean against his bare arm. His skin smelled like freshly hoed earth.

I remember how that June sizzled into July without Dad home. There would be more weeds to pull in the flower beds. Alan and I took turns sitting in Dad's chair, still strong with his scent. The Sunday Comics lay untouched inside the newspaper on the side table between the chair and our couch. As I brushed my hand over the newspaper, Mom said we had better wait for Dad, as he would soon be home.

That day, I learned what a lie was.

Then, the unread newspaper comic strips lined our giant metal garbage cans at the top of our alleyway. I caught Alan leaning into the can, trying to read Popeye's cartoon before tossing trash on it. He threw the garbage in with great force.

The avocado-green phone rang as the crickets' racket alerted us to a steamy August day. It was 7 AM. Mom hung up, tears running down her face. Alan and I, still in our pajamas, were rushed to our young, newly-married next-door neighbors, Tony, the artist, and his wife, Gina. Their dilapidated house and garden butted our flower beds to the left.

My begging to go to the hospital was silenced with blurred words and hugs from Gina. She held my hand to fake a goodbye wave to Mom and my family as they disappeared around the corner. I was mad at my family for not taking us with them, but I shut up for Alan's sake. He was already curled in a ball on the floor next to me, pressed against my leg. My brother's skinny arms and knobbly knees made me want to protect him. His brown eyes warmed his platinum blonde hair and pale face. He reminded me of gloomy and bright Eeyore in my *Winnie-the-Pooh* book. I was his Piglet, timid but brave on occasion. Gina helped me pick Alan up and told us to put on our swimsuits as if nothing terrible had happened.

In their garden stood a gigantic, shiny-leaf oak tree. Under this tree stood an old porcelain claw-foot tub, almost invisible due to the surrounding weeds and wild grass creeping up its sides. Tony hurried to fill it with cold water. Then, he placed his easel next to it.

Alan, sweating in his navy-blue wool swim trunks, and I, in my yellow swimsuit tied behind my neck, almost strangling me, stared at the tub.

Tony raised our hands ceremoniously and summoned us, "Join the painting!"

We climbed onto the overturned milk crate and submerged our hot bodies into the tub of freezing water, squealing with momentary joy. Tony watched us like an attentive rooster while ferociously painting on his canvas.

A few hours later, I heard footsteps crunching in our shared gravel alleyway. My family staggered along. Mom was sobbing. Alice held her. Roy's eyes were red, and Nancy hid behind her huge sunglasses.

Alan submerged himself in the still-freezing water of the outdoor bathtub to hide.

Tony said, "I'm sorry, Flo."

Then, he signaled Roy, saying, "Take care of her. I'll bring the children over."

Once inside, still in my soaking wet swimsuit, I savagely dug through my toy chest for my treasure. It remained spotless in its envelope, hidden under my boxes of dusty puzzles.

It was a tattered blackish-and-white photo of my handsome Dad, Charlie Hoffman. He wore a crumpled suit as if my Mom had made him put it on for the photo. His mass of prematurely gray hair was tousled. He leaned one arm above his head onto our garden's grape arbor frame, staring mischievously at the camera. His fragile-looking wire-rimmed glasses did not suit his well-built body and strong hands, but complemented his passive temperament. I remembered his soft gray eyes sparkling when looking at Mom, a statuesque woman with auburn hair, high cheekbones, and hazel eyes. I resembled my Mom, but I wasn't sure if Dad's eyes twinkled when glancing at me.

Alan, in dry clothes and wet eyes, oddly took charge. He steered me, clutching my photo of Dad, away from the hysterical adults, into his room and sat me on his oval rug full of pictures of whales and fish. He left for a few minutes and returned with my pink bathrobe and a new box of tissues.

We whispered our fears. I would never stand next to Dad in his vegetable garden.

Alan said he would never read the Popeye cartoon. Sometime later, with a mountain of soiled tissues stacked so high we could barely see each other, we suddenly stopped crying. Alan pulled pillows off his bed. Exhausted, we fell asleep. I awoke frightened that the cut on Dad's chin had killed him.

Chapter 2

Where's Heaven?

Two days later, on another steamy August morning, Mom, Nancy, Alan, and I, dressed in navy blue, piled into one of Uncle Bill's black limousines. I figured we were dressed in the same color so Mom wouldn't lose us.

The limousine pulled in front of a two-story pink cement building with tall white marble columns resembling a nearby Italian restaurant. The sign read Funeral Home. Roy, dressed in his naval uniform, met us. Men wearing black suits, sweating and red-faced, went in and out with hearts and crosses made of flowers, some bigger than me.

We entered through double doors that creaked open. Mom's perfume was overpowered by an unfamiliar smell that stung my nose. Roy escorted us past empty chairs to the front of a long, dim room.

The second we settled, Nancy asked, "Mind if I sit with Tana?" referring to Mom's best friend, Marion Montana. Tana was Godmother to Nancy, Alan, and me. I was named after her. She showered Nancy with gifts and hugs, but not Alan and me.

Mom looked at Nancy with disbelief and replied, "If that is what you want."

Nancy ran a couple of rows back. Tana began twirling her fingers into Nancy's wavy hair.

Nancy bragged that she was the only one who looked like Dad, possessing his oval-shaped face, gray eyes, and wavy hair, adding that he loved her most. She would tease Alan, a platinum blonde, and me, a brunette, by calling us Day and Night.

Dad taught my three older siblings French songs while bouncing the bow across his violin. He taught them gardening know-how, fort-building, and even Algebra. I imagined him bestowing hugs on them upon returning home from work. But he never wasted his cuddles on Alan and me. We got the leftovers, the scraps of Dad.

Four older men in various shades of gray hair, black jackets, and crooked ties sat one row behind us, bickering. These were my uncles, Mom's brothers, Fred, Bill, Henry, and Frank.

On a platform 20 feet in front of us was a highly polished, dark wooden box encrusted with gold leaves that Mom whispered was Dad's coffin. I understood now why we called our dining table the coffin table.

The room's pale blue ceiling with painted cherubs holding flower wreaths was barely visible above the dimly lit chandeliers. Alan and I sat side by side between Mom and Roy.

"Alan, what does the word 'funeral' mean?" I asked. He muttered, "It means Dad is dead."

Frowning at him, I said, "Dead is the same as being in Heaven, right? Mom said so."

"Guess so," Alan replied.

"Then, if Heaven is a place, we can visit Dad," I said.

"I don't think it works like that," said Alan.

"Marion, you know how I call you Toughie Maroono when we play cowboys and Indians?" asked Alan.

"Yeah," I whispered.

He tenderly said, "You may need to be Toughie today."

The room became darker and smaller as people wearing black filled the seats.

Pulling his clip-on navy blue and red striped tie until it landed in my lap, I pointed to our Mom, wiping her eyes with her soaking wet embroidered cloth handkerchief. Alan looked at me apologetically and bolted. Nancy dashed after him.

Alan dealt with problems by hiding. He slid under his bed at home to avoid folks like our nagging Aunt Augusta, shy Uncle Bill's wife. Aunt Augusta thought Alan was strange. I thought she was.

The scary organ music finally stopped as our Reverend stood behind the podium next to Dad's coffin. I heard heaven, Archangel something, Charles Hoffman, age 56, leaving his beloved wife, Florence, and five children, two of them only 6 and 7 years old. Then, words rushed past me into the dark room.

Dad worked for Borden's Milk Company. Bosses and co-workers praised him as they paraded to the podium one after the other. They shared how Dad, as foreman, worked shoulder to shoulder with his men before dawn on scalding

11

hot days or freezing snow-laden ones. He helped unload massive metal jugs of refrigerated milk and rushed them into the bottling plant.

Their speeches grew louder until they burned my ears. I drowned out their words by slapping my taffeta dress as the pain increased.

I heard my sister, Alice, say she missed having her sunrise coffee with Dad before they left our sleepy home together.

Then, my handsome brother, Roy, explained how he joined the Navy to honor Dad and fought in the Korean War.

After his tearful remarks, Roy returned to his seat, reached for my sweaty hand, and said, "You need to say goodbye to Dad."

"Nah," I said, assuming a position of resistance by clenching Mom's dress and pushing my feet against the seat in front of us. Mom patted my knee to obey. Roy and I walked to the box.

Bending my head back to look up at Roy, I asked, "Why is Dad dead?" Roy said, "Cancer."

"Can you catch cancer from a cut?" I asked.

He didn't answer as he knelt beside the coffin and sobbed, so I imitated him and knelt. I eyeballed the golden circle of leaves on the side of the box. I started crying. I felt something cover my shoulders. Then, I heard a flutter, like when my neighbor Mrs. Garibaldi's pigeons brushed my arm. I looked around but saw nothing. My belly took a deep breath. It felt good.

I stood up with Roy and looked inside. My Dad, in a naval uniform, was in the box. I touched his chest and felt a hardness, unlike the chest I rested on in the hospital. I cried harder. Roy slung me over his shoulder and dumped me in Mom's lap. He returned to the coffin and closed the lid with our minister. The organ music began again as Roy, my four uncles, and one man in black sadly carried Dad's casket.

Holding Mom's mighty hands, Alan and I followed. My taffeta dress sounded like waves crashing on a beach as I kicked my feet forward, imitating the men.

Squashed back in the car, I heard the adults chatter about Dad's death, ignoring Alan and me. I kneeled and gazed out the car's back window. Dad was in the car behind us. Why didn't we ride with him to keep him company?

The limousines slowed down before entering the Long Island National Cemetery. We left the cars and formed a circle around a deep hole in the ground as Dad's casket was balanced on boards over it.

Without warning, soldiers shot three rounds into the air. Alan screamed, and I ducked, covering my ears. The Officer and Roy exchanged salutes. Then, Roy confidently wrapped his strong, tan hand around Alan's tiny, pale hand, showing us how to salute. I stared at Roy's right thumb, black and curled. It reminded me of a monster's claw in a fairytale. Roy saw my fear and quickly stuck his right hand in the pocket of his tight pants.

Mom put her hand over her heart.

Roy and a Naval Officer removed the American flag from Dad's casket and folded it. I watched as one corner of the flag met the next corner until it made a neat triangle. I had hoped they would hand it to me. They gave it to Mom. Her knees buckled as Roy and Uncle Fred grabbed her arms and led her to the limousine. Nancy, Alan, and I joined them. Rubbing the window's condensation, I watched the cemetery grow smaller and fell asleep on Mom's lap.

Chapter 3

The Wake And The Worm

Returning from the burial, Mom and visitors poured into our home through our front door. Our 1,100-square-foot house with one bathroom sat high above its exposed, white-washed cement foundation, almost floating. I thought it resembled a turtle.

I snuck through the back entrance. The green wood-framed, stiff-spring screen door was held open with a piece of clothesline that awful day. Our home was crowded with people. Some faces I knew from the neighborhood. Others were unrecognizable, with loud voices and hard pinches on my cheeks. Mom appeared to enjoy their company. My ancient siblings were bragging about their accomplishments to anyone who would listen. I barely knew Dad, but I felt he would have hated this crowding and noise.

Our yellow metal kitchen table had been moved to the kitchen window to allow people to flow from the living room. The local butcher, Jerry, stood behind the table, cutting chunks of meat as people pushed their plates before him. The sunlight shining through the white ruffled curtains framed this enormous man in a bloodstained apron. I wanted to close the curtains behind him to stop the light.

I squeezed past the hungry strangers searching for Alan in the living room. His bedroom door was shut. I let him be.

My Dad's death introduced me to odd, distant family members and strange secrets. I began mingling with the creatures circling Mom.

I eased into it with my one-eyed Uncle Henry. He wore glasses with the left lens much thicker than the right because when he was nine, a mean teenager hit him in the eye with a rock hidden inside a snowball. I knew Uncle Henry as an orderly at St. Barnabas Hospital in the Bronx. But Mom knew better and assigned his paint-stained easel a corner in the front room. He spent weekends with us, creating fine art. Mom brought these oil paintings to church, where they won awards.

According to the Morse Clan legend, Henry and his younger brother, John, could have been famous artists. Around 1923, Mr. Solomon Guggenheim conducted a tenement talent tour in Harlem. Mr. Guggenheim offered funding for extensive art courses to develop my two Uncles' talents. My grandfather put the kibosh on the idea. He wasn't going to have sissies for sons.

Uncle John lived far away in Harlem Valley State Hospital. Mom said we would visit him together when I grew up. I had a tiny, round, brownish photograph of him. His eyes and wild hair reminded me of Tarzan.

I spotted Uncle Fred, a Merchant Marine, the eldest and funniest of Mom's five brothers.

He never failed to bring back treasures and stories from his travels. Alan's red Fez with a long black tassel was the latest. My presents were jewelry that I would be allowed to wear when I was older. I'd complain older than what?

Uncle Frank, the youngest, was a Fireman. He was more serious and average than his brothers.

Steering through the crowd to the sunny front room, I met Shady. He said he was Dad's friend when they were kids. He told me how Dad played the violin as a boy. Kids ribbed poor Dad. Shady said he suspected that was why Dad became a boxing champion in the Navy.

"I never heard Dad play," I murmured.

Shady wiped the rosin from the violin and laid it in its case. I stroked the fine musical instrument as Shady unwound the bow. I learned that Dad gave the violin to him because he wanted it to be played. I didn't know if fiddling was for me, so I didn't ask if I could have the violin. I left the room mad at myself for not asking.

In the living room, I was head-to-hand with Grandpa Morse's gigantic mitt. Grandpa Morse was among the first members of the International Brotherhood of Teamsters (IBT) at its 1903 inception. Should I look up or push on? Heck, I had to be polite that day.

"H-h-hi, Grandpa," I shouted.

Looking down from the sky, Gramps grabbed me by the waist and lifted me to meet his face. My eyebrows hit my hairline as I stared at his full, bushy mustache.

"How's my little one?" he chuckled, smooching my cheek until his whiskers reddened it.

Gramps continued, "No more H-h-hi, do you hear?"

"Ok-k-kay, Gramps," I sputtered, running before my feet touched the ground.

Since I saw Dad in the hospital, my mouth chopped up words before I could spit them out.

Aunt Augusta touched my shoulder as I was about to escape. She told me how much I reminded her of my Mom when she was a young girl, as they grew up together in Harlem.

I used my plate to hold back the onslaught of frilled crinoline skirts and low-belted bellies determined to reach our garden. As I plopped onto the back stoop, I saw a dry earthworm lying on the cement. I ran to the kitchen sink and filled my blue and white striped cereal bowl with water. I briefly dunked the worm in the water and laid it on the grass to watch it return to the earth. It did not move.

I screamed, "Not the worm, too."

I carried it to rest on the cool earth beneath the tea rose bush.

Neighbors were drifting out as I squeezed through to find Alan. His bedroom door was open. Alan was hiding behind Dad's favorite chair, head bowed against his knees, and his hands wrapped around his calves. I dragged him to our spot under the gnarly pear tree, staring at Dad's vegetable garden.

I told Alan I heard Uncle Fred say Roy was to be the man of the house now. Roy didn't even live with us. He wasn't gentle like Dad. Alan said he didn't know.

I had a bigger problem. I had to unearth the Archangel our minister mentioned at the funeral to find Dad.

"Alan, Marion, where are you? In trouble again?" shouted Roy.

We sauntered past Roy and headed directly to Mom. She said there was a package for me on her bed. The note on top of the violin case read, *Marion, try it. You must return it to Harlem when you are through with it.*

Alan and I spun around our garden that night, catching and releasing fireflies. I told him about the weird being near me in the funeral parlor, and how I thought it might be an imaginary friend like my school chum, Jeannie, had. Her friend appeared when her Mother scolded her. I also believed my friend was a he because he smelled like earth, not sweet like a girl. Alan said it sounded okay to him.

I spent the remaining summer days stretched out in Dad's vegetable patch, trying to spot a cloud that resembled him. I saw dinosaurs, elephants, and giraffes, but not my Dad. Alan played with his new friend, Dennis, whose family had recently moved across the street. He confided he didn't think about Dad when he was with Dennis.

The autumnal start of a new school year stopped my vegetable patch routine. Would I find Dad outside the vegetable patch?

Chapter 4

Pecked By A Hen

Six months later, we were in a different hospital. Mom was visiting her brother, my Uncle Bill. Alan and I sat in its lobby with Nancy and Aunt Augusta. I was going to draw birthday cakes. I overheard Mom say that Bill was "at death's door." Instead, I drew different door shapes, wondering if my Dad was behind one.

Aunt Augusta told Nancy to visit Uncle Bill. I was glad I was not invited. I didn't like the pukey smell of hospital rooms and hated metal beds. A few minutes later, Nancy returned, saying her uncles were making Bill laugh. Mom was helping Bill sip juice through a straw. Aunt Augusta stomped her foot, mumbling that she should be caring for her husband.

Uncle Fred popped into the hospital reception. He informed Augusta that Bill refused to allow her to ask for forgiveness for the years of hen-pecking. Augusta, hysterical, reminded Fred that she had been Bill's wife for over 20 years. Uncle Fred firmly held Augusta and said, "I'm sorry."

Augusta's face turned white behind the heavy rouge.

Suddenly, my imaginary friend started wriggling, weighing on my shoulders. The smell of shoe polish intensified. I was about to ask Alan if he smelled anything, but was interrupted by Mom announcing Uncle Bill's death. Nancy, Alan, and I pulled on our coats as we were rushed out of the hospital into the back seat of one of our uncles' cars. I forgot about the shoe polish odor.

We climbed our home's 13 steps, Dad had constructed over an original coal room. This front entrance was usually reserved for top brass, such as ministers and doctors.

Our home was becoming the stopover for death talks, death preparations, and death itself.

It was a weekday, meaning Alice was at Bellevue School of Nursing. Roy didn't live with us and was out of town in Florida, attending flight training to become a pilot for a new Pan Am aircraft. Nancy went to her friend Olivia's house. Alan grabbed a triangular peanut butter and jelly sandwich off the kitchen table and ran to his room to avoid Aunt Augusta. I waved a rectangular-cut sandwich in the air as Alan returned to trade the triangular one, which, in his estimation, was for girls. He would starve before eating it.

I munched mine at the coffin table, eager to learn where everyone goes after death. Mom passed cups of tea, and the death talks began. Augusta did not attempt to scold her late husband's family for preventing her from seeing Bill before he passed.

Mom started, "Augusta, you live in Lake Ronkonkoma. Bill's limo business is in Manhattan. That would be

21

difficult for his friends and clients to reach, especially in this wintry weather. We'll have his wake here."

Augusta whimpered but, again, agreed.

Like my Dad, Uncle Bill was laid out in our local Funeral Parlor two days later.

Mom had decided Alan and I should not experience another funeral. I was glad not to look at another dead person. Instead, I stared at Uncle Bill's photograph on our coffin table.

As Mom headed to the funeral parlor, Jimmy, our sweet local grocery store owner, arrived to babysit Alan and me. He brought the fixings for Uncle Bill's wake. "Florence, let's not make this a routine," said Jimmy, hugging Mom.

Alan slid under the coffin table to play with the toy soldiers Roy had given him a month after Dad's death.

I remember Roy arguing with Mom about becoming a sailor to honor Dad.

"Instead of the truth?" said Mom as the steam from the iron veiled her face.

Slamming down the iron, Mom met Roy's eyes and said, "You chose to leave this house because you were ashamed I was pregnant. Your old Mom dared to be pregnant. And Korea! Let me remind you that my dream…"

Roy interrupted her with, "You and your premonitions."

Mom continued, "My dream of a trunk overflowing with rubies made me sense you were injured. I spent the next three days aggravating everyone I could reach in the Naval Offices to search for you. Do you know what it took to convince military men that my intuition was more accurate than their soldiers on the ground?"

Mom returned to ironing and said, "Finally, the search party found you unconscious, bleeding by the roadside. Your life was saved. Why do you doubt me?"

Roy walked out without a goodbye. I learned that Roy's blackened thumb was a war wound.

Mom sounded like a wizard. Maybe I could dream of finding Dad.

Alan tapped my arm, returning me to Uncle Bill's wake, now crowded with well-wishers.

He began squeezing his crossed arms. I pulled him to Mom.

He asked, "Can I go to my room?"

"Of course. You've been brave," said Mom, patting his head.

The harsh February storm did not stop visitors from coming to pay respects to Uncle Bill.

Aunt Augusta sat in Dad's Queen Anne chair with a veil pulled over her face, accepting handshakes and hugs of condolence. I stood with my hand on the chair, unhappy that Aunt Augusta was in it.

As Jimmy dished out food, we heard cars beeping loudly outside as a motorcade pulled up.

Uncle Bill's fleet of 15 limousines lined our block. Each driver deposited exquisitely dressed gentlemen. One regal man wore a cape. All wore fedoras and black armbands.

As they ascended our 13 steps and arrived at our front door, each stomped their shoes on our mat, releasing snow clouds, momentarily making these mysterious visitors vanish. As they stepped in, I noticed their highly polished shoes. Uncle Bill's death announcement flashed through my mind, and so did the odor of shoe polish. I was too distracted by the exciting visitors to dwell on it.

Uncle Fred instructed Alice and Nancy to accept the hats and place them on Mom's bed. Nancy donned one of the hats, tilting the deep burgundy fedora over one eye. Alice snatched it, laughing, and placed it on the bed.

Uncle Fred was in charge and introduced each gentleman to Aunt Augusta, the widow, and Mom, the sister of the departed businessman, Bill Morse.

The gentlemen retrieved their hats and left as mysteriously as they had arrived.

Slicing a large piece of pound cake, Aunt Augusta whispered something to Mom that upset her. I watched Mom take away Augusta's plate and hold the stiff spring screen door open for her sister-in-law's exit as she followed her into the freezing, pitch-dark garden. I stood inside the screen door, listening.

Aunt Augusta confessed to nagging Uncle Bill. She said that Bill's shocking anger toward her in his final hours of life made her secret about Uncle John too much to bear alone. She asked Mom to promise this secret would be buried with them. Mom reneged.

Mom saw me illuminated inside our screen door, rushed up the back porch, squinted at me, and closed the heavy oak door, ending my eavesdropping. I huffed, promising myself to get to the bottom of that secret.

It was almost midnight when the last guest left. Roy, who came for the funeral, drove Alice back to Bellevue

24

Hospital on his way to LaGuardia Airport. Nancy was in her room. Alan never left his bedroom. Uncle Henry remained, as public buses had stopped running. Mom helped him make up the couch. I snuggled next to Mom in her bed and fell fast asleep.

Chapter 5

Angel Question

Three weeks later, I turned seven. Although it was cold, Mom, Alan, and I were in our garden. Alan and I wore our thick brown tweed homemade sweaters with their matching hats with ear flaps. Mom wore a lavender sweater, fully zipped. Her violet head scarf was tied under her chin and around her neck, complementing her silver-streaked auburn hair.

Mom sat in her aluminum lawn chair on the chunk of pebbled cement directly below Alice and Nancy's bedroom window. I sat on a pocket-sized stool in front of her, my hands stretched out, waiting for her to unwind a skein of soft wool ceremoniously. These silent conversations mesmerized me, but I had to interrupt this one.

I asked, "Mom, could I have an angel with me like in the Sunday School books?"

Unable to hide her surprise, she removed the wool from my hands and laid it on her lap, encouraging me to go on. Mom explained that angels appear to help us, and with Dad dying, maybe one visited me. I was getting

26

fidgety, so she asked me to let her know the next time my angel was near.

"Maybe," was my response, running to help Alan build a cardboard fort.

A curved earthen path led me through our grape arbor, whose thick, bare vines twisted in and out of its wooden frame. Alan had me calling him Alibaba from his latest book, *Aladdin and the Forty Thieves*. I ran zigzag around the garden shouting Alibaba, Alibaba. Then, I ran straight into his belly. Lying beside each other on the cozy plaid blanket beneath our pear tree, we laughed till it hurt.

Over the years, making Alan laugh became a preoccupation for me.

Chapter 6

Murderer Out to Get Me

My seventh summer on earth had me trying a new path to my dead Dad.

My cereal bowl, full of cold milk and Rice Krispies, wobbled in my hands as I maneuvered through our wacky screen door. The sun was peeking over our garden. I felt damp through my thin summer pajamas as I sat on the back porch. I waited for Mrs. Garibaldi, our Italian neighbor, whose garden bordered Dad's vegetable patch.

Another summer was in the making. Mom percolated coffee while Nancy ironed her full-skirted lemon-yellow dress as she began her second summer work program in Manhattan. Alan, eight, was trying on his new uniform as he had made the Pelham Bay Little League.

Splashing my half-eaten bowl of cereal on the step next to me, I ran through Dad's Holy Gate as Mrs. G. appeared in her garden.

"Hello, Mrs. Garibaldi," I greeted, avoiding Alan's nickname for her, Mrs. Baldy. Her chin possibly had more hair than her head.

"Mrs. G, I haven't heard from my Dad. Do Italians or Catholics have a connection with heaven, and can I use it?" I asked.

She stared down at me, rubbing her chin.

"You're like an old lady. Go play and forget this," said Mrs. G.

"I can't. Please let me borrow your way," I persisted.

Scrutinizing my face, Mrs. G continued, "Ya wanna know how to talk with your dead Dad. Why?"

"It's a secret," I said.

"Sei pazzo," said Mrs. Garibaldi.

Mrs. Garibaldi, grabbing her breasts, said that her dead husband, Louie, kissed her one night when she was barely asleep. This vision turned the Rice Krispies in my belly, but it was worth it if I could talk with my Dad.

"Ask your Mother if I can give you Holy Water. Go, ask," said Mrs. Garibaldi.

I gulped, watching her backside beneath her thin cotton dress as she bent to weed her zucchini patch. I charged home.

"Mom, is it okay for Mrs. G to give me Holy Water?" I implored. "Whatever for?" she asked.

"So, I can talk with Dad," I declared.

Mom turned from the kitchen sink, wiped her strong hands on her apron, and hugged me for, well, forever. Then, shaking her head in disbelief, she agreed, "Mrs. G can give you Holy Water, but it may not work."

"It will work, Mom," I yelled, returning to Mrs. G.

That evening, I donned my pajamas early to say my prayers. I closed the door the best I could with the spinning glass doorknob and faced Mom's small bedroom. The maple wood bed had a white chenille bedspread already folded over the footboard, exposing crisp white sheets. Mom's dresser had a mirrored tray. On it, a perfume bottle with two doves on the stopper, one gold tube of Revlon red lipstick, and my jar.

Staring at the precious water in my ex-peanut butter and the ex-firefly-catcher jar was intoxicating. I knelt beside the bed and patted the Holy Water on my chest, where I felt my heart beating. I began, "God, tell my Dad, Charles Hoffman, I have a tough question. Thank you. Now I lay me down to sleep, pray the Lord, my soul to keep. If I should die before I wake, I pray to God my soul to take." I stayed on my knees, squeezing my eyes shut until they hurt, believing this helped plant my prayer.

The following week, in a musty, dark auditorium, Alice, 22, graduated from Bellevue Nursing School. Mom beamed like Alice was the only one in this swarm of graduating nurses buzzing by us with well-scrubbed faces, crisp white uniforms, and flying navy-blue capes.

A month later, Alice took a Surgical Nurse position in California. Alice was gone. Mom was on the phone with Tana, weeping about how much she would miss Alice.

Nancy complained that she had to share the bedroom with a kid, me. Alan threw his copy of Alice's graduation photo in the trash can. I barely knew Alice, but I didn't like that she made Mom cry.

I saw steam rising from the asphalt, which let us know it was a scorching summer day. Alan and I strolled with Mom to our small grocery store in matching blue and white tops and shorts. I felt tired. I didn't say anything because I knew we would go to the bakery, where I would choose my favorite cookie with raspberry jam in the center covered with sugar crystals.

"Jimmy, why do your cherries look over-ripe?" complained Mom.

Jimmy shuffled over to my Mom while tying a fresh white apron around his Santa Claus belly.

"Florence, why do your cherries look just right?" he asked with a grin.

Then, he said firmly, "Half-price for you, but don't tell anybody," as he held my Mom's face in his stubby hands.

At 51 years old, Mom struck a statuesque figure. I watched the neighborhood men smile as she passed. The Mailman rang our bell to deliver the letters directly into her hands. The street cleaners whistled at her. I saw Mom's gait quicken with appreciation.

I stood on a wooden crate where Mom had placed the last product she had purchased on the clean white metal counter. Jimmy pulled a pencil from behind his ear, licked it, and added up our purchases. His hand ran down the ones column, halting briefly to move over to the tens column. He underlined the total twice. I thought he was brilliant.

I felt dizzy as I stepped from the crate.

We left the bakery, nibbling our delicate cookies. Suddenly, my knees buckled, and I fell to the sidewalk. I couldn't hear. Mom must have thought I had stumbled and tried to lift me, but my legs were like rubber.

Noticing this event from his store window, our Pharmacist, Doc Phil, swooped me up and took me into his apothecary. He rushed past the rows of Band-Aids and tubes of toothpaste and deposited me gently on the black leather couch in his office.

Alan entwined his pinky finger with mine, sitting cross-legged on the floor below me. My shallow breathing was painful.

Mom clutched the pharmacy phone with shaking hands and dialed an incorrect number twice. Doc Phil tried to take the receiver and dial for her, but Mom refused.

Mom whispered into the telephone, "Dr. Stein, thank God I reached you.

It's Marion.

She's collapsed on the sidewalk. No, she did not trip. Please meet us. The address is… Mayflower Avenue. We're heading there now."

Hearing this, a young mother in the pharmacy picked up her baby and pushed the pram to Mom—no words needed to be spoken. Mom curled me like a pretzel into the stroller and let Alan, streaming tears now, help maneuver it.

Mom placed me in my bed in Nancy's room. Nancy wrapped a scarf over her mouth and nose and gathered her hairbrush and nail paraphernalia from the night table. She would sleep in the front room daybed tonight in case my illness was contagious.

Then, turning to me, Nancy whispered, "You'll be okay. You have Drs. Stein and Phil, and Mom. I'll help, too."

"You mean I'm dying?" I mumbled.

"No, funny girl. I love you," Nancy muttered and rushed from the room.

The front door chimes rang on and off in the distance, with doctors and curious neighbors coming and going. I heard suggestions over my head to place cool washcloths on my neck or forehead, close the blinds, open the blinds, let Alan sit near her, or keep Alan out of her room.

We may have to take Marion to the hospital.

"Can you see?" one neighbor asked, wagging her finger in front of my eyes as Mom escorted her out. Others arrived unannounced through the back door with a bombardment of questions: Can you lift your head? Are you hurting? Do you want water?

Every breath was filled with pain.

Mom wrapped Alan's cowboy scarf around his nose and mouth to protect him in case I was contagious, as Alan insisted on being in my room. Curled in a fetal position on Nancy's bed, clutching the Chenille bedspread, he stared at me. The doorbell chimed. He sat up, rocking nervously as Doc Phil entered. Doc placed his arm around Alan, reassuring him I would be okay. Alan released the bedspread and sobbed. Mom entered and immediately took in the event.

"Alan, come help me bake cookies," whispered Mom.

Doc Phil knelt beside me, fluffing my sweat-drenched pillow.

"This little fellow wants to be your friend," murmured Doc Phil as he laid a teddy bear resembling *Winnie-the-Pooh* in my arm's crook. I cried. Dr. Phil wiped my tears, refolded the washcloth over my eyes, and departed. I closed my eyes and floated into space.

I didn't know if the fever or innocence made me realize my imaginary friend was an angel. I greeted him politely by his full name, Archangel Azrael. I whispered that I saw him in my dreams and wondered if he was taking me to Dad. Was Dad angry with me or missed me?

That summer, I contracted Polio at the ripe old age of seven. It was a grave time filled with bouts of high fever where I violently shook and disappeared into dreams of angels.

As the sun set on Day One of this frightening episode, my curious neighbors gathered beneath my window to discuss my fate.

Mom said Dr. Stein confirmed it was a mild case. Ignoring others' blood-thirsty diagnoses, Mom toned down their fears with facts about mild Polio. Symptoms such as fever, weakness, severe muscle pain, and neck and back stiffness without paralysis were possible.

There may be temporary problems with swallowing and breathing, but these usually disappear in weeks. By the loud vocalizing over Mom's declaration, no one cared to hear this, wondering if I would walk again.

I heard my neighbors allude to Mom's heroism. Recently, she jumped the fence into Tony's garden and released a pet snapping turtle's grip on their baby's finger. I trusted that I would be well again if my healing were up to Mom.

Whenever I opened my eyes, I saw Mom sitting across from me, knitting. I remembered my hands stretched out for her to unwind a skein of soft wool. My head resting on my bear, I drifted back to sleep.

On Day Two, Dr. Stein returned with a stack of hospital masks, placing one over his face and showing

Mom how to do the same. He sat on the edge of Nancy's bed, discussing my dire situation with Mom as though children couldn't hear. Then, he gave Mom a box of aspirin dust enveloped in what looked like gum wrappers to lower my temperature. Mom immediately opened one into a spoonful of water for me to drink, quickly washed down with sugar water, the reward. Trying to divert her fear for me, she explained how marvelous nature was as aspirin came from the bark of a willow tree.

Finally, Doc Stein blurted out, "No iron lungs are available in New York, Florence. But I believe that may be good as Marion will have to use her lungs, which will hurt, but it might keep them strong. As I said, this is a mild case, and Phil and I have devised a plan requiring round-the-clock care. Your daughter could pull through in a few weeks."

I asked, "What is an iron lung?"

"Shh, we will follow the doctor's plan to the T," responded Mom without her usual patience.

The plan was a 24-hour vigil involving maintaining a massive pot of water on the stove to soak towels. Then, these hot towels were wrapped around me, and plastic was to be enveloped on top to hold in the heat. My packaging was to be changed about every four hours around the clock.

My bedroom was off our home's back entrance with the rigid screen door. Mom mumbled that I would surely need relief and started moving things. She propped open the white oak back door with an old iron. The screen door created a cross-breeze with one of my three windows. Mom and Nancy transferred Nancy's bed to the front room and centered my bed under a window in direct line with the door. I immediately felt a breeze.

A couple of hours after the plan was hatched, thundering through the back door, Jimmy and his nephew, Louie, struggled to carry an enormous pot. Jimmy had kept this vessel from his days of cooking for 50 men in the Army. Seconds later, I saw them returning the pot to our garden. Jimmy used our garden hose to fill it.

My Italian neighbors surrounded the vessel.

"One, two, three," five voices counted off.

Five neighbors were wet, but the pot hadn't budged.

Alan knelt on my bed in his new hospital mask and relayed the fiasco. I started to laugh, only to gasp for air. He gasped in fear and gently poked my belly, saying, "I better let you sleep."

The vessel reached our stove, which took up all four burners. Mom would cook in Gina's kitchen next door. Every four hours, a member of my sweet army changed the towels and plastic. Their styles were unique.

At 17 years old, Nancy matched the towel length. I resembled a Mummy. I screamed to free my arms. Mom ran in, horrified, and unrolled me.

Wearing her beloved 18K gold cross around her neck, Gina used the lasagna method, wrapping my feet and working her way up. She always ended the wrap sessions by kneeling beside my bed to pray with her rosary beads.

Mom would gift wrap me and ask, "What color hair ribbon today?"

Laying the pink ribbon on the chair next to my head for me to focus, her strong hands were no contest for wringing heavy, wet towels. I remembered Mom's laundry routine, which gave her defined biceps that Bodybuilders would envy. She knelt beside our bathtub and rhythmically scrubbed our clothing and sheets against the washboard with a large bar of brown soap. After several rinses, she brought this heavy basket to our back porch and hung each item on our clothesline. I watched her stretch her back and rub her arms for relief.

Shoving a dry cloth under me and flipping me, she lied, "You look much better today," as she washed my face. I struggled to breathe.

"I need the toilet," I moaned.

Mom swept me into her arms and carried me to the potty in the room. I was not embarrassed, concluding I must be dying.

"I saw a butterfly on your windowsill," Mom said.

Mom sped up the wrapping process by gripping my feet and one-handedly encircling me with plastic.

I lost consciousness.

I dreamt I was a baby again as Mom used to lift my feet into the air and toss my wet diaper over the crib to the floor. She whipped the washcloth from here to there in two seconds flat. Still one-handed. Mom secured my dry diaper with the pastel-colored safety pins jutting from the crisp white lapel of her blue, flowered dress. Sticking a bottle of warm milk into my mouth, I drifted off with milk dripping down my cheek.

Suddenly awake, I was vomiting into the potty.

"You scared me," Mom said, gently wiping my mouth.

"I think Dad is trying to take me," I whispered.

My shocked Mom quickly tied the pink grosgrain ribbon above my crooked bangs and carried me to the screen door. The garden was in full bloom. I wept. Mom placed me in bed and abruptly left the room.

In the middle of that night, I awoke, pouring sweat and ripping at the plastic wrap.

Suddenly, I heard wings unfurl loudly beneath me. Then, I was lifted above the bed from a point in my lower back. I felt incredibly cool as I floated on these enormous wings that filled my small bedroom. Flat on my bed again, I knew it was Azrael, but why was I still on Earth?

On Day 14, a Sunday, Dr. Phil and Jimmy changed the towels to relieve the ladies. I was breathing with less pain, but couldn't sit up without support.

When Uncle Henry visited on weekends, he offered to take his turn, but Mom suggested he draw for me. Henry agreed without hesitation. He asked, "Marion, what can I draw for you this evening?"

I said, "Archangel Azrael, please."

I fell asleep while Uncle Henry's pencil flew around the large blank paper, sketching. When Dr. Phil took his turn to change my wrapping during the wee hours of the morning, he picked up Uncle Henry's pencil drawing left on the chair next to me. "What is it?" I asked.

"It is a drawing of a magnificent angel," whispered Dr. Phil.

"Show me," I said in earnest.

Archangel Azrael filled the entire piece of paper. It had an uncountable number of wings filled with thousands of feathers. He held a rolled scroll tucked under his left arm. My dear Uncle Henry heard me.

A clue that I was healing was that my Archangel didn't feel close. I'd grown tired of hearing Mom's new word, 'hallucinating,' when I mentioned Azrael. She seemed to have forgotten our angel discussion. So, I saved my angel questions for *Winnie-the-Pooh* as he was a good listener. I knew Uncle Henry's drawing confirmed the visions I had during my fever-filled sleep.

Our local Pastor stopped by. Mom had alerted him that I had mentioned Archangel Azrael. That afternoon was spent with the pastor struggling to explain Him to seven-year-old me. Azrael, the Angel of Death and Comfort, helped souls leave their bodies and enter heaven at God's command. This Archangel softened the heavy blows of death around the grieving loved ones as He held them in his wings and gave them healing energy. The pastor said Azrael stayed longer with the children and believed I was blessed.

After about a month, my breathing didn't hurt. Then, finally, the body casing stopped, and my head was on angled pillows. Alan played outside. The world was returning to normal.

Six weeks after being afflicted with Polio, I emerged skinny and weak. Mom led me to our bathroom and into the tub filled with bubbles. She splashed me and encouraged me to splash her back. I knew she was making me strengthen my body. So, I splashed directly at her, soaking her hair, chest, and dress. I suspected this would be the only opportunity I would be given without consequence, so I grabbed it.

Mom and I ventured out a few days later on a shopping trip for a new back-to-school outfit and a present for Alan's upcoming birthday.

Arriving home tired, I stretched out on the bench under the grape arbor, squinting one eye and then the other as I moved the sun from one leaf to another. I heard our screen door's spring stretch. Mom touched my forehead and sat across from me.

"How would you like to spend the weekend at Rockaway Beach with Geraldine Martin and her parents?" asked Mom.

Sitting straight up, I groaned, "I'd rather stay home."

"Geraldine isn't a close friend, but they have a summer cottage, and the ocean air would be good for you. It's only a couple of days," Mom pushed.

I frantically waved to Mom from the backseat of Martin's car and resigned myself to the trip.

Mr. and Mrs. Martin settled on a blanket on the beach. Mr. Martin began reading a book.

Mrs. M, in her floppy hot-pink straw hat and winged sunglasses, made peanut butter and jelly sandwiches.

"Stay in front of our blanket so I can see you, and don't go out too far," Mrs. M instructed.

Geraldine towered over me as she reached for my hand and said, "Let's go further out and scare my Mom into coming after us."

"I don't want to," I said.

Tugging my hand, Geraldine insisted.

Waves smashed against our bellies. As I dug my heels into the moving sand, I felt my feet slip. Then, Geraldine released my hand and ran away, laughing. My feet lost their grip. I was underwater, rolling over and over like a ball. I saw the sun, but when I tried to stand, I was not fast enough and hit my head into the sand below. My eyes were open as I saw the sand explode around me.

A pair of giant hands surrounded by enormous, wet, feathered wings wrenched me from the ocean. Everyone thanked the mighty Lifeguard who had saved me. I knew Azrael assisted him. Wrapped in the Lifeguard's red blanket, I heard Azrael speak for the first time. It was unlike a human voice. His words circled the air around me. It was similar to organ music filling a church or distant thunder, but not frightening. It was fleeting. I was confused. He called me Little One and said we would be friends for a while.

I mumbled, "You saved me again, Azrael."

The Lifeguard turned me on my side, patting my upper back, making me cough more.

The Lifeguard said his name was Bryan.

The next day, we were stuck in the cottage to punish Geraldine for nearly killing me. I helped Mr. Martin pack the car to hurry our exit while checking the kitchen clock, as I wanted to go home. On the road again, I curled into a ball and faked sleeping.

Finally, relieved to be home, squashed in Mom's arms, I asked, "Mom, is Dad trying to kill me?"

Chapter 7

Death By Departure

Days rolled in and out with constant upheaval in our home.

On August 28, Alan turned nine. He blew out eight candles and told me to blow out the last one for having made it through my bout with Polio. I turned to Mom and asked when her birthday was. She slowly answered September 21 as though she had forgotten. I couldn't recall celebrating her birthday or cards lining the coffin table like mine. I was determined to change that. I grew up that summer with Polio. My promise to Dad grew, too, as I understood the miracle of Mom.

My heart pounded in my ears, signaling I was departing for school. I didn't like school before this summer of Polio, but now I hated it and the School Nurse.

Alan and I went directly from school to Tana's house, down the street from our home, until Mom picked us up after work. I didn't know if Mom knew how mean Tana was to us, as Alan and I swore we would not complain. I don't know if Tana realized her cruelness.

Montana's pets consisted of an albino boxer, Whitey, and a wolf-like dog, Wolfy. Whitey was allowed to sit on me, drooling. If I gagged, Montana continued sewing, laughing her head off. Wolfy sat in front of Alan. If he arose without permission, Wolfy bared his teeth. This was also hilarious to Montana.

One particular day, Whitey had a tik under his skin. Montana invited us to watch her remove it. The dog whimpered, and Alan screamed, but I glared disgustedly at Montana.

"Don't look at me that way, Marion. I sew your Easter outfits and fix your dinners. "Your Mom and I were friends for years before you showed up," imparted Montana.

Maniac Montana continued, "I nearly had Flo to myself."

Then, shaking her head as though awakening from a dream, the evil witch finished, "You know, your Dad didn't like me, and look what happened to him!" she said while jabbing at the poor dog's wound.

These two widows on this block clung to each other. This was Mom's buddy, neighborhood fruitcake, and now, I believe, a person who wished me dead.

Mom didn't rush us out that evening. Instead, she asked Montana if she would care for us after school at our home, as it would be more stable. Tana hesitated but agreed.

Going directly to our home presented a new, troubling situation for Alan and me. Tana had cookies and milk or egg creams (a Bronx or Brooklyn concoction of flavored syrup, a quarter cup of milk, and seltzer to fill a tall glass.

The frothy head on the top resembled a meringue) waiting for our arrival. She settled in Mom's rocker, but Alan refused to enter until Mom arrived.

One day, I was cold, wrapped in my pretty but itchy Tana sweater.

"Let's go in, please," I whined.

Alan curled up on our back stoop, leaning against the Borden metal milk box.

"I'm going in," I said as he buried his head deeper into his knees.

I sat inside on the pantry step, about 10' from Alan. Then, as darkness descended, I huffed, dragging Mom's old coat from her closet and snuggled next to my Alan, wrapping us in its warmth.

Mom arrived and hurried us in simultaneously, hugging and scolding us. "Montana, why haven't you coaxed the children in?" she asked, irritated. Tana snorted while gathering her knitting and departed.

Our exhausted Mom said we must try harder. We tried, sort of. Before opening our back door, Alan told me he would see me after Mom arrived. He grabbed his snack and said hello to Tana over his shoulder, locking his tiny hook and eye latch on his bedroom door. A couple of months ago, he asked for this hook due to our useless spinning glass doorknobs. I did my homework or read in Dad's kitchen chair with my back to Tana. To my recollection, Tana never checked for cuts or bruises the way Mom did or asked how school was—total disinterest.

Arriving early from work one evening, Mom announced, "This is it! I have been accepted as a Foster

Mother. At least I will be home for the children and loving others."

"More kids, Flo, really!" bellowed Tana.

Mom squinted at Tana and escorted her out. Mom patted the couch so we could nestle with her.

Alan asked, "What's a foster mother, Ma?"

"First of all, I'm home for you always," Mom responded.

Mom added, looking at our tired faces, "Let's see, there are children like Little Orphan Annie who need loving homes. We can make our home one of them."

"Sound good, children?" Mom asked.

Alan and I looked at each other, digesting this new information. We ran to our talking spot under the pear tree. We agreed to share our bed, food, toys, and everything with our foster siblings.

The next afternoon, a Friday, I charged in from school to Mom in her rocker, speaking on the telephone. She shushed me. I curled up on the couch and listened.

"Yes, I believe I know I am a widow, dear," Mom curtly said. "Yes, I understand I am only allowed short-term fostering. I will see your social worker and my first foster children on Monday."

Gawking at Mom, I became frightened. It was happening. That weekend, our household was busy preparing for the arrival of the first two foster children. Two little made-up beds from our church auction and a crib borrowed from Gina were in the corner of our front room. Tony, our artistic neighbor, reattached a French door where Mom's room adjoined the front room. I understood

Mom would watch over our new siblings like the hen in a storybook.

Alan and I rushed out of school that life-changing Monday, anxious to meet our new family members. Then we slowed down, loading each other with questions about them. Would they be boys or girls, or one of each? Will they be older or younger than us? To be polite, we would let them use the bathroom first for bedtime. We froze in our gravel alleyway. We rehearsed our greetings. Alan shouted Geronimo, and we charged through the screen door.

We didn't want to scare them, so we tiptoed through the pantry, past the kitchen, ignoring our favorite peanut butter and jelly sandwich snacks. I saw two boys, holding hands, squashed together on our couch. Their hair was damp, their faces polished clean, and they wore new clothing. They were grinning, munching on their snacks. I knew Mom had welcomed them.

Alan and I smiled broadly and introduced ourselves. Mom came from the front room and introduced Kenneth and Tommy. They were brothers. Mom smiled at them and asked if they wanted to tell us their ages.

After a lengthy pause, Tommy proudly said, "My brother is seven, and I'm four. Anything else?"

We all laughed. Alan invited Kenneth to see his books on whales. I asked Tommy if he would like me to read to him. Kenneth said that they couldn't be in separate rooms. Alan, nine, started crying. I saw that Mom was temporarily confused. Then, she corralled the four of us to the front room. Our Persian rug had been moved there to make it cozy. Stretched on the carpet, books piled high. I connected with my new brothers. Mom cooked dinner.

Halloween arrived. Alan refused to have a new outfit, so his cowboy chaps received an additional row of fringe. Fluffing my Forest Fairy skirt, I plunked myself in Dad's Queen Anne chair and watched our new brothers of three weeks fit into their costumes.

Mom cautioned, "Ken and Tommy are your foster brothers, but they may not stay long."

"Why? I like having them here. They seem to like it too," I insisted.

Tommy jumped into my lap. And Kenneth turned red and looked down.

Seeing the beautiful children's painful reaction, Mom exclaimed, "Tonight is Halloween. Let's talk about it another day."

I was left with a million questions. Where are these brothers' parents? Why do Ken and Tommy flinch while playing hide-and-seek with Alan and me, or when Mom rustles their hair with approval? Most of all, why does Mom think I am too stupid to hear these answers?

Mom guided us out the screen door into the autumn night and handed us cardboard boxes with the word UNICEF. I held Tommy's hand. Alan and Ken led.

Mom paused at the top of our back porch, gazing down at us, "You are a sight for sore eyes!"

What a night! We were content getting to know our new brothers, and Mom was home.

Alan could come in from the rain.

Christmas arrived. Nancy opened the coffin table, adding two leaves for our Christmas Lunch. Nancy's boyfriend, Cornelius, a skinny guy with curly dark brown hair, acne scars, and intensely blue eyes, was joining us. He wore a motorcycle jacket and barely grunted hello to Mom as he rushed Nancy to his black Packard car on Saturday nights. Mom was not wild about him. Roy, his wife, Dottie, and their 10-month-old baby, Susan, were on their way from Queens. Alice was flying back to us from California for a visit.

Alice arrived first. After significant chatter with Mom in the kitchen, Nancy pulled Alice into her bedroom for sisterly gossip. Mom chased the girls into the living room to open presents. The Hoffman house ritual was to have the youngest open first. Tommy opened his present, kissed Mom, and ran, placing his new stuffed bear on his bed. Kenneth changed into his new fringed cowboy shirt. Mom wiped Kenneth's tears.

Roy told Alice that California suited her. Mom frowned at him. I did think Alice was extra beautiful in her red Asian-inspired sheath dress.

My cuddly stuffed toy was a monkey like in *The Jungle Book*. Mom rushed me to our couch and cradled baby Susan into my lap next to my new stuffed monkey. Snap, snap. The flash blinded me. I wondered if I was the only one to notice the resemblance between baby Susan and the monkey as Mom's wicked sense of humor struck.

Our grand five-course Christmas lunch was filled with the clatter of passing plates and shrills of laughter. Alan and I decided to sit on either side of Kenneth and Tommy to make them feel comfortable. Dessert was served as the clock struck four. With bellies full, we waved goodbye to Roy and his family. Alice was staying until after New Year's Eve.

We watched *A Christmas Carol* on our first television set, which was Roy's present.

On New Year's Eve, Mom placed a silver tray of teacups holding twelve tiny grapes on the coffin table. She adopted this Italian tradition from our neighbors. We munched one grape for each minute Guy Lombardo, Bandleader, counted to midnight on this, his first traditional television broadcast. My brothers and I, in our pajamas, were allowed to stay up to midnight.

The phone rang. Mom handed the phone to Alice. Flustered, Alice had a short telephone conversation. Alice nervously looked up at Mom and whispered, "Bill proposed to me. I said yes. I know it means I'll be in California longer than we expected. But, Mom, I'd like to be married here in April."

Mom's hopes for Alice's return to New York were crushed.

I turned eight in March. Spring was budding in New York. Nowhere was it more evident than in Mom's garden.

Alice was a stunning bride in her tea-length gown. Bill Pack was a debonair groom.

Debonair was a new word Alice taught me that week. Mom was striking in her new violet dress.

Alice's wedding ceremony was at our Presbyterian Church, and the reception was in the attached church hall. My commitment to Dad's dying wish for me to be

Mom's warrior remained strong. I hugged her as I charged around with my brothers. I wondered if that was enough to satisfy Dad.

The Pack family, including the new Mrs. Alice Pack, departed two days later.

Over the telephone, Mom said, "At least Alice and Bill live in California. Bill's Mother, the pain in the ass, lives in Idaho. I waited on her hand and foot. Okay, Tana, goodnight."

Our eight-month-long brotherhood with Ken and Tommy was at an end. Mom returned to the living room, having tucked them in for the last time in our home.

Mom said, "Marion, go and kiss them good night."

"You mean goodbye," I muttered.

I knocked on Alan's bedroom door so we could say goodbye together.

Mom sternly said, "Alan, I know it's hard, but you'll regret it if you don't say good night."

Alan marched to Ken and Tommy and started crying. Mom encircled the three boys in a united hug.

Alan said, "I've packed the cowboy hat and feather for you. Bye," and ran to his room.

Mom left the room. I crawled into bed with my brothers because that was precisely who they were to me. I lay still with tears running into my ears.

"Ken, I'm sorry that I lied about putting Tommy on the back of my bicycle."

"It's okay, sis. I would have done the same thing," he whispered, squeezing my hand. Tommy was asleep. "Gee, it must be good to be so young," I said.

"Yeah, he can sleep through anything. I hear they won't let us write to each other, but I'll think of you, promise," imparted Ken.

"Me too, always. I llllove you," I sputtered, springing out of bed.

I snuck out to the back porch, pretending I ran away. I was too afraid to do that, but being outside the house in the dark made me feel disobedient, and that felt good.

The front doorbell rang two days later, making me cut off my paper doll's head.

"I thought it best not to tell you that we have a new foster child arriving today," Mom chirped as she opened the seldom-used front door.

Janet, the skinny, tight-bunned, four-eyed social worker assigned to our home, looked like a replica of the one in my *Little Orphan Annie* book. She sashayed in with a parcel slung against her chest. Alan solemnly went to his room. I heard the hook slide into place, locking his door.

Mom received the bundle.

Removing her coat, Janet said, "I'm afraid this one is a dilly, Mrs. Hoffman. At only two weeks old, Freddy suffers from his Mother's heroin addiction and is going through cold turkey. Florence, we understand that he could die on you."

I gasped. Mom patted my head with her free hand, reassuring me that all would be fine.

I witnessed Mom pacing the front room with Freddy firmly in her arms. She made fennel tea to soothe his stomach. His screams barely stopped day and night for several weeks.

One morning, I woke up to silence except for a bird chirping. I raced to the kitchen and saw Mom cooing at Freddy's yellowish face. Love for Freddy entered my heart without permission.

Chapter 8

Parting is Not Sweet Sorrow

At ten years old, I was happy that summer vacation was approaching. I was filled with fear every second at school. Stuttering limited my ability to make friends and answer questions in class.

Equally frustrating was that I had funny things to say that I swallowed instead. The lessons were boring or seemed so to me. There were no distractions to help me forget where Mom was and the promise to Dad. I charged out of school, cut across the cement yard, pushed the gate open, and breathed freedom. Alan was waiting for me. He excelled in all subjects and enjoyed school. He maintained his goal of being an Oceanographer and said that if his vessel allowed girls, I could be a shipmate. I didn't want to spoil his vision, but there was never a moment when I would ride the waves. All I wanted to do was dance.

"How did your history test go?" he asked.

"Teach gave me 90 for knowledge and 50 for my almost illegible handwriting," I said without fear, and we laughed.

"Let's have Mom make us egg creams," Alan said on our walk home.

Alan was much taller than I now and skinnier than ever. He strained to hold our screen door open for me.

"Ma, can we have chocolate?" I asked.

Stopping dead, I saw two tiny figures sitting at our kitchen table.

"Say hello to Debbie and Carol, your new sis, friends," Mom said.

"Are Debbie and Carol sisters?" I asked.

Mom said no and explained that Debbie had a twin brother living with adoptive parents in New Jersey. Mom told us that Carol came from a different family and was Jewish. She had a good mother who was gravely ill, but no father. We must root for her Mom to heal.

"Wait, where's F-freddie," I stuttered as I ran to the front room.

I walked to the crib. There was Freddie. I held his hand until my heart stopped jumping. Back in the kitchen, unable to drink my egg cream, I examined the two urchins.

Four-year-old Debbie wiped her tears, leaving dirty streaks down her cheeks. Her eyes seemed unusually large for her gaunt face. Her filthy blonde hair was only visible in patches on her head. Her too-big t-shirt hung off one arm, exposing her emaciated collarbone. Debbie's hands resembled one of our ancient neighbors' thin, wrinkled hands with nails chewed down to the quick.

Two-year-old Carol was healthy-looking, almost chubby, and had a full head of hair. She wore a pink blouse with a white Peter Pan collar. She hid her face in her folded arms.

54

Alan knelt to introduce himself to the wee ones. We loved our foster brothers and sisters as much as we loved each other.

Mom periodically said, "I just don't want you hurt."

Alan whispered, "It's too late."

That summer, Alan showed Debbie and Carol how to swing on the monkey bar with their hands. I watched from beneath our grape arbor. I remembered the first time I hung upside down from my knees and how it led me to discover another universe under the rose bush filled with spiders and insects. While Debbie got the hang of swinging on the bar, Carol never tried again.

Freddie was moved on to a long-term foster home. But I gave him 50 kisses before he was taken, expecting each kiss to lessen the tightness in my heart and stomach. They did not.

In Mom's words, Debbie was a rip. When Carol was using the potty, Debbie would lift Carol's chubby bum off the potty and pee in it. Then, after replacing Carol on the potty, she'd call, "Mrs. Mom, Carol's done," because Debbie was impatient to play.

As Mom fixed dinner one evening, Nancy walked in, sweating from the subway ride. She poked her head into the kitchen and said hi. Huffing, Nancy headed for her bedroom, her high heels clicking. Moments later, a screech that could open the doors of hell (we'd heard such an expression from our pastor) came from her bedroom.

Alan and I followed Mom as she rushed to Nancy's room, only to be whacked by the bedroom door as Nancy exited, dragging hysterical Debbie and Carol by the arms.

She handed them to Mom, "Do something with these brats!"

Mom picked up Debbie while Alan cradled Carol.

"What could a couple of toddlers do to infuriate you?" asked Mom.

Sitting at the kitchen table, we looked at the urchins' faces. Their faces had orange lipstick on their cheeks, black mascara brushed through their blonde hair, and tampons tied around Carol's waist like a belt. Debbie had just learned to tie her shoelaces, and we deduced she was practicing. Mom's eyebrows went up as she controlled her laughter.

Laughing freely, I whisked them to the kitchen sink so Nancy could use the bathroom.

On a hot August night, one week later, Nancy returned from a date with Cornelius. She thrust a diamond on her left-hand ring finger under Mom's sleepy face and announced, "I'm getting married."

Mom picked up the telephone and complained, "Hello, Montana. Can you believe Nancy just told me she is marrying Cornelius next month? I knew she wanted to escape the foster children. Yes, only 18 months after Alice. Well, good night, talk tomorrow," Mom muttered.

Two days before her wedding, Nancy permed my hair as I was one of her Bridesmaids, reminding me that Dad had adored her curly locks. On the wedding day, I put violet bows in Debbie and Carol's pigtails to match Mom's second wearing of the violet dress while Nancy was squeezed into her corset and gown.

Alan and I took our foster sisters outside to wait for the limousine. My gentle brother, now 12, was handsome in his tuxedo. At ten, I didn't know if I would miss Nancy.

The bridal party descended our 13 front steps. Nancy appeared almost angelic in Alice's borrowed wedding dress and halo-like veil.

In the limousine, Nancy snarled, "Marion, move over," as she pushed me against the far end of the limo's back seat.

"Ah, now I recognize you," I whispered.

Roy proudly walked Nancy down the church's aisle while Mom hummed to the organ music. The party was held at the local Knights of Columbus reception hall. I danced like a fool, frequently pulling Mom to join me.

Debbie and Carol were fast asleep in Mom's arms, heading home in the limousine. Alan sat in the front seat next to the driver, acting grown-up. I wondered how I would feel this first night alone in my bedroom.

Standing in my bedroom doorway, the room looked pinker than I remembered. The walls were papered in broad pink and white vertical stripes, the blinds were pink with white specks, and Mom surprised me with a new pink Chenille bedspread. I guessed Mom thought the pinker, the less lonely. I snuck into the girls' room and fell asleep with them.

September also brought my first knowledge of the Jewish holiday season. Since Carol was Jewish, Mom asked Janet, the social worker, if Carol's mother wanted us to take her to a synagogue. Her Mom was delighted.

The Rabbi greeted the five of us, Mom, Debbie, Carol, Alan, and me, by bowing to each of us with the palms of his hands together.

Standing behind the amud pillar, the young Rabbi began speaking in Hebrew. Then, the Cantor led the congregation in song. Almost instantly, Carol started to hum along. I watched Mom fold her hands in her lap and smile broadly.

The Rabbi addressed his congregation in English and instructed them to welcome us.

There was a lot of buzzing and clapping.

"Mrs. Hoffman, please stand," said the Rabbi.

Flustered, Mom stood and sat almost immediately.

The Rabbi said, "This woman, Florence Hoffman, has brought us a child, Carol, whose Mother belongs to this synagogue. When Florence phoned, she explained she was raised Catholic and baptized her children Episcopalian, but attended a Presbyterian Church. She hoped she could bring her family to this Shabbat. Today, her family consists of her son and daughter, Alan and Marion, and her foster children, Debbie and Carol."

That day, I learned Mom didn't care what house of worship she attended.

"Mrs. Hoffman is an extraordinary person who loves without question. In her modest home, children of all races are learning love. To bring Carol to us today, Mrs. Hoffman had to ask permission from the children's service. Then, she and these four children took a two-hour journey by bus and subway from the Bronx to Brooklyn. She wanted them to experience our synagogue," proclaimed the Rabbi.

I was bursting with pride, looking up at Mom. Her face was red. I realized this experience of receiving a well-deserved compliment was foreign to Mom. I never heard my older siblings praise Mom for her heroic efforts to save our home or for her generosity as she handed them each money as a wedding gift, depleting her tiny savings account.

I remember Mom saying she was healthy and young enough to build her savings again when the Manager at Westchester Square Bank suggested she give less. Mom's worn red shoes clicked against the polished black and white diamond-shaped tiles as we exited the bank. I wore new shoes.

Then, Cantor's lyrical voice filled the synagogue. Carol hummed louder and louder. Upon our departure, I whispered, "Mom, wait a minute," as I ran to the Rabbi.

"Rabbi, my Dad died when I was six. I'm ten now. I think the Archangel Azrael has been with me since then. Anyway, I'm trying to find a way to talk to Dad. I tried the Presbyterian and Catholic ways, but no luck. Can you loan me your way?" I asked.

The stunned Rabbi was tongue-tied.

"This is a serious request. I must discuss it with my elders," replied the Rabbi.

Mom gave the Rabbi our telephone number without blinking an eye.

On the subway ride, Mom said she liked the Rabbi and was glad we experienced a Jewish church. Our trip home from Brooklyn seemed shorter.

I had given up on a Jewish pathway to my Dad by Christmas when the Rabbi's call came through. Cradling the heavy telephone receiver in both hands, I held my breath to listen deeply. I hung up, ran to my bedroom, knelt beside my bed, and prayed. Then, I returned to the living room and shared the Rabbi's words with Mom. He said I was lucky to have Archangel Azrael with me, and I was to continue my prayers. He and his elders would pray, too.

Alan, Debbie, Carol, and I cuddled with Mom into a new nucleus family for almost two years.

When Mom announced Debbie's adoption had become final, the pain ticked in my ears like a time bomb in the days leading to her departure. I refused to eat with my family and ate afterward, if at all. Anger toward my Dad for leaving fueled my desire to find him in heaven or hell. If it wasn't for his death, we may never have had to create a foster home.

My new routine was to arrive home from school, take Debbie and Carol into my bedroom to play, and pretend not to hear Mom's requests to come to dinner. Then, when she fetched the girls, I went outside and sprinted the block to St. Raymond's Cemetery. I ran like a wild animal in and out of the gravestones, screaming like a banshee because no one could hear me. Alan avoided the upcoming pain by playing on the sidewalk with the neighborhood boys until the night's darkness forced him home. Mom never retaliated with lectures.

The night before her departure, I brushed Debbie's shiny blonde hair. I headed to the basement to alert Alan of my scheme to follow Debbie to her adoptive home in New Jersey.

Alan, at 13, lifted weights to put muscle around his visible ribs. He had been accepted for the Fall Semester into the all-boys high school, DeWitt Clinton, and would participate on the track and field team as their star shot-putter. When he practiced tossing the shotput across our garden to Tony's, I fetched it for him. Did that make me a shot-putter, too?

Alan threw the weight onto the supporting bar faster than I had ever seen. "Are you crazy?" he asked.

I considered that word. Folks seemed to call others crazy when they did not understand their actions or wanted to discourage them. Maybe following Debbie to her new home was bold and understandable from a different angle.

"I don't know," I replied and waltzed upstairs to the kitchen, where I found Mom writing. Mom did not look but said, "I'm writing a letter to Debbie's new family."

I scoffed, showing disinterest. Then, once Mom was asleep, I snuck to the kitchen, unfolded her letter, and read it, hysterically sobbing. Its contents unleashed a conviction that my following Debbie was sane.

Mom's letter:

All about Debbie,

Deb does not like to get her hair washed but loves to take baths, go to the beach, and play in the water. When Debbie is sick, which is very seldom, talk to her about the injection to make her well. And Debbie takes her vitamins and medicine without trouble. I keep her in pants, polo shirts, and a little sweater so she stays warm in winter. She loves snow and rain and loves sleigh riding. She loves to dress up when we go anyplace but is satisfied with wearing pants and a polo. She will scribble on paper, and

*I always let her sit at the kitchen table with paper &
pencil or crayons. And when she is finished, I tell her I
will put crayons and pencils away until she wants them
again. Then, she will ask you for them.*

She is clean, but you will have to wipe her.

Likes church and likes you to say prayers with her.

*She does not like carrots in stew, but I tell her they will
make her eyes glow, and her hair grow. All in all, she will
listen to you. Otherwise, she will eat anything but loves
small portions. She can't have puddings or ice cream unless
she eats her supper. I give her nothing between meals, only
an apple or banana and a glass of milk. Be sure she goes
to the bathroom before bed, and praise her. Debbie does
not get car sick.*

*Debbie does not catch a cold unless she gets it from
someone. So, give her tender, loving care and rock her for
a while if you have a rocker. She loves to dance, and look
at her face when she does. You will really have to laugh.
I think you will love Debbie as much as I do. God bless
you and Debbie.*

Mrs. Florence Hoffman

I quickly dressed when I awoke from sleeping with
Debbie and Carol in my bed.

"Mom, I'm going in early. See ya," I tossed the words
over my shoulder as I rushed out.

I found the stop for New Jersey Bus #2 in Port
Authority with over an hour to spare before Debbie arrived
with her social worker. I was physically shivering from the

weird people staring at me. Plunking myself on a filthy curb, I grabbed my notebook and scribbled a poem.

Miles

When all the love we cannot find
and all that mends we leave behind.
When we hit bus depots instead of airports for adventure.

"Hello, honey," said a familiar voice.
"You can't stop me," I protested, closing my notebook. Mom whispered, "I must."
I shouted, "I'm not stopping her from being adopted. I want to visit her. Why is that so bad?"
"It is not bad. It is illegal. Honey, I recently read an article stating that foster children are lonely. The agencies tell them not to bond with their foster families because they won't know how long they will stay with each parent. The maximum they generally stay with each family is 18 months. We know they fall in love with us as we do with them," said Mom.
Mom said, "You agree it's important for Debbie to be with her brother and never have to leave the adoptive family, right? You don't want to spoil that for her."
"No, no. The laws are wrong, then," I screamed.
Mom whispered, "Yes, the laws are wrong."
Mom said seeing how these departures hurt Alan and me was almost unbearable, but being home for us was her balance. Bawling uncontrollably, we departed the noisy, smelly Port Authority building. Mom reminded me that

Macy's wasn't far away. Maybe we could buy something silly to cheer us up. We didn't buy a thing.

I slept with Carol that night, not knowing if comfort would come.

Carol's removal two weeks later was agony for me. I felt my head exploding as I repeated the word no. Then my chest tossed my heart into my throat. I lost my voice.

I was supposed to be happy, Carol's Mother was healthy and capable of caring for her again. Instead, I was angry and retreated from happiness. My stomach tightened as the front door closed behind a chubby, happy little girl in her Mother's arms. I ran to the toilet, dry gagging until I realized it wasn't helping. Lying on my bed in mid-afternoon, I squeezed my threadbare *Winnie-the-Pooh* until my fingertips turned blue.

Archangel Azrael hadn't performed his direct hits of the inevitable death of one of my loved ones for several years. But the disappearance of my foster siblings was as though they had died. I believed Azrael understood this as he pressed against my back. I dozed, embracing the reprieve.

Chapter 9

Michael Crawley

I understood some humans have Guardian Angels on their shoulders, guiding them along in this earthbound tumult. As I saw it, most seemed to have an Angel on one shoulder and the Devil on the other, tormenting each over every decision. I was uncertain on which shoulder these conflicting entities resided. I suspected the Devil flitted and chased the Angel back and forth.

I was jealous of these folks as Guardian Angels sounded easygoing and fun. I didn't understand the enormity of being blessed by Archangel Azrael. All I knew was that death followed me around like a lost puppy. Was I to thank someone for this?

I entered my sixth-grade class at 11, younger than my 12-year-old classmates, which increased my insecurity. Nasty Mrs. Dunne, from the third grade, was my teacher again. Adding to this repeat performance by Mrs. Dunne was Michael Crawley, a student whom I had not seen in school since we attended our third-grade Dunne class. Where had he been? Michael had not laughed at my stammer and tried to help during my left-hand correction. These awful third-grade memories flooded my mind.

"Stand up and state your full name when I call you," asserted our third-grade teacher, Mrs. Dunne. I arose from the wooden chair attached to the desk, stepping on my dress tie, which tore itself from the waist. The roomful of giggles made my heart pound.

Holding the torn sash with my right hand, I whispered, "M-m-m. Marion."

The giggling turned into bursts of loud laughter.

"She doesn't know her name," distant voices echoed.

Glaring at her, I stood and gushed, "Marion Hofffffman."

Mrs. Dunne smirked and did not correct the classroom of mean-spirited children. To add to this disastrous third grade, Mrs. Dunne had beautiful penmanship, demonstrated by her chalkboard writing. According to Mrs. Dunne, clever people were right-handed. I am left-handed.

"Marion, you will write with your right hand," demanded Mrs. Dunne.

"My left hand writes okay. Come look," I suggested.

Grabbing my book, visibly repulsed, Mrs. Dunne stated, "This is scribble."

"I t-try with my right hand, but somehow, the pen jumps back into my left hand like magic," I said.

Looming over me was a shadow. First, the shadow raised its arm. Then I saw Michael stretch his hand to take the ruler's blow. I covered my left hand with my right. Then, smack, a wooden ruler hit my hand directly across the knuckles.

"Aaaaaah, you hit me, you b-b-bad person," I screamed, running around the classroom.

"Calm down, don't you call me names," screeched Mrs. Dunne.

Crying with all my might, I headed for the Nurses' Office. I screeched to a halt, recalling my stretch with Polio. The recess bell rang. I ran home and showed Mom my now pitch-black, swollen knuckles. Mom pulverized ice in the ice bag with several hatchet chops and wrapped a scarf around the ice bag. Minutes later, Mom emerged from her bedroom wearing her red shoes. We marched to school and into the Principal's Office, whizzing past the secretary's desk.

Ever so gently, Mom unwrapped my hand. "If this ever happens again, Mrs. Dunne will regret it. My daughter writes with her left hand. Understand?" Mom stated through clenched teeth.

The surprised principal never had a chance to stand up or introduce herself.

"I am taking my daughter home today." Mom concluded.

Mrs. Dunne never apologized, but I wrote freely with my left hand. I thanked Michael and was glad our desks were next to each other. I was also allowed to play my violin left-handed. I still wasn't sure a violin was for me, but maybe Dad would hear this music above my prayers.

Dunne of the sixth grade interrupted my memories and instructed, "Marion, sit in front of me."

I moped to my seat, resigned to the probable torture ahead of me. But, sadly, this school term presented itself with a more substantial problem: Michael Crawley.

Michael was assigned the desk to my left. While Michael glanced at my right hand's ring finger's flat knuckle, I noticed his hands were filthy, and his nails were bitten to their base. His sad, blue eyes were rimmed with heavy black lashes. His mop of black hair was lush, but crusty dirt was visible on his neck. His shirt was thread-worn. I struggled to recall his physical condition in third grade, but could not.

I nodded hello to Michael every day. He scoffed at my cordial attempts.

One afternoon, rushing out of school into the crisp autumn air, I opened the school gate and spotted my friend, Richard. Michael was nearby, glaring at me as though angry.

Richard offered to walk me home. I had forgotten my homework, and Richard ran to fetch it. Michael started poking my shoulder. I pulled my arm away. Richard returned.

With a strange look of anger and sadness, Michael pushed me with a great force beyond his frail body's ability and ran away. My head hit the curb as I fell. Richard picked me up and, at my request, did not chase Michael. Guilt flooded my thoughts. Should I have invited Michael to join us? I wished it was easier for me to speak without a stammer.

As I grappled with our screen door, Mom turned from the refrigerator. Then, seeing blood on my sweater's shoulder, she ushered me to our bathroom and opened her well-stocked medicine cabinet. As Mom's strong hands scrubbed my wound, she said, "Out with it. How did you get hurt?"

I surrendered, and the incident gushed out, along with my fears for Michael and how he reminded me of Kenneth, our first foster child. Mom and I were back in the principal's office. It took three years for this return, so I thought I was doing well.

Principal Cardinal looked exasperated, greeting us, "Mrs. Hoffman, it has been a long time since I had the pleasure of a visit."

"Pleasure, really," answered Mom sarcastically. "We must sort out a delicate matter.

Marion noticed that Michael Crawley was not pulled together and looked sad. Have you noticed Michael's sadness as the observant woman you are?" asked Mom.

Mom continued without giving Principal Cardinal a chance to respond.

"Michael and Marion had an incident yesterday, and I want them to shake hands and start fresh," said Mom.

Rushing to the file cabinets, Principal Cardinal pulled out Michael's file. "I see no teachers' statements about his appearance. He is failing, and his attendance is poor," revealed Principal C.

"Does that not raise a red flag for you?" asked Mom.

"Are you telling me how to do my job, Mrs. Hoffman?" asked Principal C.

Uh-oh, Mom's stare is cutting through Principal C.

"I suggest we bring Michael here," said Mom.

"What a good idea," said Principal C, buzzing her secretary to fetch Michael.

Michael timidly entered, spotted me, and started wringing his hands. Mom greeted him, patting the seat beside her. Michael didn't move. I wanted to hurry this process, so I stepped toward Michael and offered my hand. He grasped it in his sweaty palm and dropped it equally fast. Principal C. excused him. Michael ran out.

"I have no further time for this," said Principal C.

In the school hall, Mom said, "We'll try to help Michael. See you at home."

I forgot to ask Principal C not to contact his parents, as I worried this incident might cause trouble at home for Michael.

From then on, I greeted Michael with an almost audible hello. His response was either sticking his tongue at me or a slight nod of acceptance. His appearance did not improve. That could mean the school did not contact his parents, which would be good.

Michael and I did not join the break-time activities. Instead, we sat about 10' apart along the schoolyard wall, watching classmates play. I didn't like games, especially chasing ones, and Michael usually napped.

The Parents' Teachers' Meeting was the Friday night before Thanksgiving. I guessed school authorities didn't want us to have too much fun during school break, so they tattled on us to our parents. Would Michael's Mom attend?

Lying in bed later, I thought about Michael. When I closed my eyes, I saw the fear in his.

Did his parents hit him? I was upset with myself for telling Mom. Maybe I'll follow Michael home. Maybe Azrael can send one of his angel brothers to watch over him. I heard wings flutter. Panic washed over me. I said a second prayer for Michael.

Chapter 10

The Hunting Trip

The next day, the Saturday before Thanksgiving, Alan and I sat on our cold back stoop. It was 5:30 AM. We were waiting for Roy as he was taking Alan on his first deer hunting trip.

My Alan wrote poetry. His kindness was well-known on our block and probably further than that. He returned baby birds to their nests and stopped conflicts, quoting Mahatma Gandhi. Tana's dogs loved Alan. Tana was unhappy about that.

A few weeks ago, I overheard Alan on the telephone with Roy, explaining that hunting was not his thing. Alan admitted he had accidentally killed an insect with his magnifying glass when he was little and still felt awful.

When Alan failed to cancel the hunting trip, I heard Mom explain the recent weeks' situation to Roy. Alan hid in our basement 24/7 for almost one week. I made up a cot for him and ate meals with him in the cellar. Alan thought the Mafia was after him. He would describe the gangsters in detail, their clothing, their scars. I sketched these images, only for Alan to tear up my drawings, calling me crazy. Mom appeared calm because she knew where he was.

Dr. Balducci, Mom's wunderkind, said Alan would grow out of this fantasy phase and become a man.

Roy's response was to bark something about Alan, now 13, becoming a man. Roy, the man of the house, won. So, how could I lessen Alan's pain from this inevitable hunting horror? I suggested he shoot at tree leaves and turn away when these fools for men shot at deer. Maybe sneeze or stomp as they squeezed their gun triggers.

We heard Roy's footsteps in the alleyway.

"For Christ's sake, why are you crying, Marion?" demanded Roy. "I'll miss Alan," I exclaimed.

Roy stepped over us and followed the fragrance of rhubarb and strawberry pie in the kitchen. Munching a chunk of pie, Roy led Alan to his car.

Four days later, the day before Thanksgiving, Mom was bustling in the kitchen. I had no interest until Alan arrived home. Roy's car pulled up with a deer strapped to the roof. Before the car stopped entirely, Alan ran from the back seat. Standing on our front landing, I shouted, "Up here!"

"I didn't shoot anything," sputtered a shaky Alan.

He ran to his room, screaming, "They made me help carry the warm body of that beautiful animal. They're assholes."

I ran after him.

Mom stopped me, "Give him space."

Almost bedtime, Alan emerged and said he was starving. From the edge of the couch, I watched Alan's tall, lean body gracefully lope across the living room, lifting Mom from her rocker. He draped his arm around her shoulders as they walked to the kitchen.

Mom's full figure was illuminated by the stove's gas light under her black cast iron pan. She heated mashed potatoes and tossed in two scrambled eggs. They were chatting and laughing. It sounded good. I joined Alan for apple pie. He apologized for arriving upset. I told him he was my hero for surviving so much time with Roy. I was honored to wash his dishes, allowing him to join Mom in watching *Sea Hunt*. I polished our silverware for tomorrow's feast, laying it on the coffin table as Alan yawned good to be home.

I was startled awake by a thud! The glowing hands on the kitchen clock showed 3 AM as I ran to Mom's bedroom.

"Wait, Mom, let me check," I whispered, pushing her back into bed.

Alan's room loomed in front of me. I opened his bedroom door slowly, not wanting to wake him. An unrecognizable odor smothered my face. I turned away and gasped for air. Then, I saw Alan face down on the floor with the distant street light flickering through his window.

Paralyzed, I hesitated to turn on the lamp. Mom's hand slammed on the light switch behind me. Instantly, our eyes took in crimson globules dripping down the side of his bed, splattered across the room on his model ships.

I whispered, "It's blood."

Blood oozed from Alan's right side, staining the tan area rug filled with pictures of whales and octopi. In a metered, low-octave voice, Mom told me to call the number taped to the side of our telephone, our police precinct. Emergency Medical Technicians (EMTs) whisked Alan out of our front door into the ambulance. I saw Mom holding his hand as the ambulance doors closed.

I sat in Dad's Queen Anne chair, curling my legs up and tightly wrapping my flannel nightgown under my feet. I sobbed to the darkness, "Dad, where are you? Why aren't you helping Alan? He has your gentle way, unlike Roy. He is brighter than all of us, but not boastful like Nancy. Unlike Alice, who chases her adventures, he cares for Mom and me. I think Alan would be your favorite. I'm just a kid and need your help."

Sleep did not come. But I realized Azrael wasn't near, giving me hope Alan would make it. Dawn arrived. Somewhere in my head, I was thankful we were between fostering.

I remembered there was an enormous raw turkey in the refrigerator. I robotically opened Mom's *Betty Crocker* cookbook with its famous red and white checkered cover and eventually stuck the turkey into our oven.

Around 10 AM, Mom and a gray-faced Alan returned home from the hospital with his freshly bandaged forearms. I stared at the snow-white bandage. I was making Alan uncomfortable. The purity of the gauze almost made his bloody room an illusion.

"He won't do this again. He's promised," Mom lamented, offering Alan orange juice at our kitchen table.

I met his eyes with a nervous smile and said, "Glad you're okay."

Of course, I was glad. But what kind of a stupid remark was that? Why was I not holding him? Last night's terror was somehow preventing me. I was afraid to touch my favorite person in the world, Alan.

Mom whispered, asking me if I had cleaned his room. I couldn't recall and shrugged my shoulders. She returned from his room, nodded affirmatively, and said, "Thank you."

I examined her face, searching for answers. Is that all you have to say?

Thanksgiving Day was spent with Mom escorting the visiting siblings and their spouses to our garden, explaining Alan's incident in between courses. Alan, pale and sad, kept mumbling his apologies. Had I failed Alan? I swear I didn't notice strange behavior when he said goodnight last night. But, as tightness gripped my gut, I recognized that guilt had an extraordinary power over reason.

Roy and Dottie were the first to return to the Thanksgiving table from the garden talk.

Dottie patted Alan's shoulder and offered him piles of mashed potatoes. Alan and I exchanged a split-second grin. Then, Roy asked him to step outside. I followed them as far as the screen door. I couldn't hear Roy's words as he faced away from me, but I saw him poking Alan's chest over and over again. I ran to them. I wanted Azrael to smack Roy to the ground with his thousand wings. Instead, I took Alan's hand without looking up at Roy and walked back into our home.

Nancy and Cornelius returned from Mom's garden explanation to excuse themselves as Corny wasn't feeling well.

Neighbors gossiped. Only our young Italian neighbors, Gina and Tony, stood with us, striking down rumors.

Therapy sessions began in earnest with thrice-weekly appointments for Alan at Jacobi Hospital's Psychiatric Department. On these occasions, Mom chose to march out our front door, head held high, smiling at her tall, healthy-looking son. Tana arrived via our back door almost simultaneously to sit with me. She did not believe in psychiatrists, so she avoided Mom to retain their friendship.

Mom left a growing pile of papers from Jacobi in the silver tray on our coffin table. I worked hard to comprehend those notes. Alan's suicide attempt was met with an inconclusive diagnosis, but I saw Schizophrenia mentioned. The hunting trip might have triggered Alan, and hormones might have been involved. They would do further tests. I learned to spell Schizophrenia, but had no idea what that label meant. I suspected, like my Polio, it could be cured. Mom never explained why Alan tried to kill himself. Although, to be fair, Mom probably didn't know herself.

I overheard pieces of Mom's whispered conversation with Montana over the phone. I caught that the Emergency Room doctors couldn't tell if Alan cut his arm more than nine times, as some slashes were incised into the open wounds. But, of course, one doesn't slice one's arm nine times or more and not want to die, do they? So there, I said it out loud inside my head.

The few weeks leading up to the long mid-winter school break sped by. Mom baked her annual batches of holiday cookies while Alan and I shoveled snow for neighbors. That year, we wanted to buy gifts for our nieces and nephews with our own money.

Roy called and declined Mom's invitation on Christmas Eve. I saw sadness in Mom's eyes. Christmas cooking and present-giving were among her greatest joys of the year.

Nancy and Cornelius joined us for Christmas Day follies. As they drove off, Mom called Montana. "Cornelius barely works, so they are not saving."

Having heard this tale, I wandered to lie under the Christmas tree.

February was blizzard-heavy. Alan and I cleared snow drifts from our home's steps between snowball fights with Dennis across the street.

Mom interrupted us with, "We have shopping to do."

We entered Robert Hall's Men's & Boys Store in the Castle Hill section of the Bronx.

Alan rushed to the school uniform department to pick up his DeWitt Clinton track and field jacket. Mom agreed I could buy Michael a tie. Boys had to wear ties to attend our auditorium's weekly concerts. Michael was handed a stained, wrinkled tie from the school's lost and found box.

I placed the gift for Michael, bundled in blue tissue paper, in my school bag.

Chapter 11

Death Returns

Michael and I continued our non-verbal way of acknowledging each other. His new tie remained in my bag for a couple of months. One day in March, after my 12th birthday, I was filled with guilt that I had not given Michael his present, which forced me to be brave. I laid his gift on the schoolyard bench and walked away, hoping he would take it. I kept my back to Michael to avoid embarrassment, but Richard peeked.

Richard whispered, "Michael opened your present. He's trying it on. But wait, he's walking to the trash can. Huh? Michael threw the tie out."

I muttered, "I thought it would be nice for graduation. I'm off to saw on my violin. See you later."

I understood Michael's actions as I had witnessed odd behavior with foster siblings when Mom handed them new clothing. One would smile and pet the clothing. Another would bawl, refusing to wear the new outfit. Instead, wrapped in a blanket and freshly washed briefs, he waited until his old garments came off Mom's clothesline.

One little girl donned her new yellow cotton dress and twirled in it, bouncing excitedly when Mom said she looked beautiful. When I fetched her later for dinner, she frantically asked me to remove it as she did not want to spoil her only dress. Calm in her green corduroy overalls, she placed her dress into the shopping bag she had arrived with and stored it under her bed. We giggled and skipped off to dinner. As a little girl, I could not explain these actions, but my stomach understood.

June arrived, and Mr. Jacobs, our Music Teacher, kept us after school to rehearse for the upcoming graduation ceremony. I excelled in this atmosphere filled with a jovial teacher and musical notes that I read naturally, allowing me to communicate without words. While I was a mediocre violinist, my feet tapped circles around my chair as I played. I wanted to dance.

On stage, the day of our graduation, I searched for Michael in the audience. I wanted to hand him my address in case he needed me, as I was to be transferred to a Middle School in September.

Our graduation ceremony wound to a close. Fellow orchestra players rushed off to their families in the audience. As I loosened my bow, a powdery puff of rosin leaped off the bow's horsehair. The woody scent of frankincense jumped from it. Then, a string snapped on my violin. Panic filled me. I quickly closed my instrument case. Azrael pushed against the small of my back, forcing me to inhale the calming fragrance. I surrendered and closed my eyes. I momentarily danced along the Milky Way. My chair trembled. I opened my eyes. Azrael's massive being blocked the auditorium. Shaking my head and peeking with one eye, I glimpsed Azrael's figure with his thousand ocean-blue feathers. I ran off the stage and crossed the schoolyard to meet Mom and Alan.

As I ran past Richard, I asked, "You see Michael?"

"Nah, I'll look around and meet you by the gate," answered Richard.

That potentially happy June day was disrupted.

Seeing Mom and Alan waiting for me under a full-petaled Magnolia tree outside the school grounds centered me. As I arrived, I winked at Alan to look at Mom. Her hair-sprayed coif made the pink petals stick, forming what appeared to be a hat.

I saw Richard running across the schoolyard. He looked frantic.

"Michael is dead," said Richard, panting, bending over to catch his breath.

I stared at Richard as the pink petals drifted onto his new navy-blue graduation suit. My ears pulsed like they did at Dad's funeral. I slammed my hands against my dress to strike the words down. My cotton dress offered no relief.

Richard hysterically explained that he had overheard Mrs. Dunne telling Mr. Jacobs that Michael had jumped off the Westchester Square Creek overpass into traffic the previous night. He heard Mrs. Dunne say Michael was better off.

I turned to Alan, frightened that this would remind him of his suicide attempt or encourage him to try this new way to harm himself. He recognized my fear, frowned, and tousled my hair.

"Don't worry, Toughie," he whispered.

My schoolmate, Michael Crawley, age 12, died with no announcement or prayer service.

"Night, Ma. Yeah, I know you say I couldn't do more for Michael," I mumbled.

I sat on my bed with its pink chenille bedspread, wondering what Michael had slept on. My hands curled into fists, digging my nails into my palms as I contemplated Michael's demise. Was Michael really dead? Did he jump to his death? What final element was involved in convincing him to leap? I would almost feel better if a stranger had thrown him. On the other hand, could one of his parents have pushed him? Please, not that.

No one knew I had Archangel Azrael nearby. I had stopped sharing my angel experiences with Mom to avoid her concern. I was afraid to speak of Azrael to Alan as the word hallucinations poked through his hospital paperwork. So, I talked to my *Winnie-the-Pooh*.

For weeks after Michael's death, as daylight became twilight, I walked to the Westchester Creek overpass instead of jumping rope with the girls on my block or drawing for Uncle Henry to critique on weekends. I stood rigidly, pretending I had stopped Michael from jumping to his death. I grasped his dirty hand, feeling its stickiness. No matter how much he wriggled, I held Michael tightly, pulling him back. Over and over in my mind, I saved him. Michael was living safely in my Mom's home.

One night, I opened the pink blinds on my windows, inviting the moonlight in to keep me company. Collapsing onto my bed, I sobbed until I could barely breathe, and my swollen, tear-soaked eyes could no longer stay open. I never stopped wanting to save Michael.

Chapter 12

Writing on the Wall

I watched Mom, pressed against one end of our couch, reading the letter from her younger, 54-year-old brother John, who had remained locked away since he was 17 in Harlem Valley State Hospital. Mom passed John's letter to me for the first time.

I turned 13 that year. Was this a rite of passage?

I'd heard Mom called many things, but Strong Heart was new. The communiqué reads as it was written, including grammatical errors:

Friday, June 18,

Darling Sister Florence,

Thanks a lot for past visits. How's everything at home, sweet home? Please send a carton of cooling menthol cigarettes. **BLACKED-OUT BY INSTITUTION** *Our television is perfect. I hope is ideal too. How are your Irish-American foster children? How's your home* *protector, Molly? I hope you are all able-bodied. Please secure for me a canister of mentholatum ointment as my ear is all clogged up. Thanks a million. I shall always believe in you, my darling sister, Florence. This letter is intended for all my folks at home. God bless them. Your loving brother, John Arthur Morse.*

Can't wait to see you. You say you are bringing your daughter, Marion, this visit. Are you sure this is wise? **BLACKED-OUT BY INSTITUTION** *If you are sure, then with your excellent care package, please bring sharp pencils and paper so I can draw for her.*

Thanks a lot. Pet your foster children for me. Believer in my sister, I am improving day by day. So long, Strong Heart, with lots of love from your darling brother, John Arthur Morse. I hope and pray that, at your convenience, I may have blessed you in the new _____.
Thanks a lot. With kisses to all your loving brood, John.

As I re-folded this fragile dispatch, written in pencil, into a worn cigar box stuffed with similar past notes, I felt tenderness for my Uncle John and a new respect for Mom. But why was Uncle John questioning my joining Mom on her upcoming visit? Mom had waxed soulfully about John's gentleness, wishing he could come home with her. If he were as mild-mannered as Uncle Henry, I would help. However, Uncle Henry had never been confined to an institution for mental illness.

Mom's alarm clock screeched at us for the second time that Saturday, and it was only 6 AM. The brass clock's two wildly vibrating bells signaled our early departure that summer day. We rushed to catch the bus on East Tremont Avenue, which would take us to the subway directly to the Port Authority Bus Terminal in Manhattan, my crime scene from two years ago. There was a special bus for visitors to Harlem Valley State Hospital, and we planned to be on it.

Most of our fellow passengers carried brown paper parcels similar to ours. I noticed everyone smiling and nodding to one another. This cheerfulness made me want to announce, "You know, we are going to a psychiatric facility where our loved ones are incarcerated, and not a picnic?"

"Is this your little girl?' asked a woman about Mom's age.

"Yes. Marion, this is Maggie," Mom introduced us.

"Is this your first visit, Marion?" inquired Maggie.

"Yes, I'm looking forward to meeting my Uncle."

"Aren't you brave? Well, don't let the screaming bother you too much. You get used to it," Maggie drawled as she boarded the bus before me.

I squinted at Mom over my shoulder as I climbed the bus steps. Then, I moved to the middle of the bus and sat in a window seat. Smiling broadly with pride, Mom snuggled next to me.

Long bus rides nauseated me. I used the time to mentally journal the tenderness of fostering fragile lives in our home. It helped me repress Alan's brush with death and the slice in my heart carved by Michael Crawley's mysterious death.

After Debbie and Carol's removal two years ago, I tried the head-over-heart theory with the following foster brothers, Robert and Samuel.

Robert, 8, showed fierce determination to hold his 5-year-old brother Samuel's hand. Robert volunteered to brush Samuel's teeth and dress him. Even when Mom bathed Samuel, Robert stood beside Mom, clasping his brother's hand. Mom never told him to let go. I was glad.

Robert and Samuel were taken from our home while I was in school. I cannot remember how long they were with us. I wrote letters for weeks and threw them into the trash. I loved them as though I had known them for a million years.

Two weeks later, I had the opportunity to test my head-over-heart theory again with the arrival of Jessica, a Japanese four-year-old, and Jesus, a malnourished Latino colic-suffering 18-month-old.

Some nights, awakened by Jesus's pain-driven screams, I would rush to pace with him in my arms. I told myself it was strictly to help Mom. One night, after placing Jesus in his crib, I heard, "Psst, psst," from Jessica, standing up in her junior bed. "I sweated the bed," was Jessica's worrying statement.

She was soaked in urine. Grinning, I changed her into dry pajamas. She wrapped her chubby arms around my neck. Love for Jessica and Jesus filled me to the brim.

Jessica's aunt agreed to take her when the court papers were approved. Jessica left our home after six weeks. As Jessica and her kind aunt exited through our front door, the aunt told Jessie to thank Mrs. Hoffman. Jessica clasped her hands before her chubby belly and bowed.

Giggling, Jessica said, "Thank you, Mrs. Hoffman. You kind."

As tears welled up, I stepped away not to destroy her joy. Instead, I drifted to our garden, through the rusty, now-squeaky Holy Gate into our vegetable patch. I lay on the earth where Mom and I had recently planted lettuce seeds to search the clouds for Dad. It had been a long time. I knew Mom peeked through the screen door, but let me be.

The agency moved Jesus to a long-term home with a Latin family. I kissed Jesus's face and hands a hundred times hours before he was removed. I didn't stop when Mom said to.

I was interrupted by, "Marion, we'll be at the hospital in a few minutes."

Stretching, I was glad Mom had witnessed my agonizing reaction to Jesus's departure. She fought for and won an overdue raise and one long-term foster child, four-year-old Marcie, who weighed only 16 pounds and suffered brain damage from loss of oxygen during childbirth. She had scars from her father's cigarette burns on a significant portion of her body. Her Mom died during childbirth, and the brutish Dad blamed this innocent baby.

My initial vision of Harlem Valley State Hospital was of a manicured lawn and a long winding path leading to a dark brick building in a U shape, with small windows barely discernible behind thick iron bars.

"Do I look all right?" Mom asked.

"You look great, Mom. Let's do this," I said.

Florence Lilian Morse Hoffman held my hand for the first time in years as we marched along the path.

Then, I heard faint human voices from the building. Suddenly, these voices shrieked, "Visit me. I'm Bob."

"No, visit me. I'm Adam." I searched the brick walls and spotted men screaming for attention with their faces pressed against the bars and arms flailing.

New to this perplexing environment, I waved and shouted, "Hello, Bob, hello, Adam."

A fellow visitor rushed to me, "Shh, they will be disappointed later if you don't visit them."

Mom squeezed my hand. I swung my arm down and continued walking without lifting my head again. I felt guilty for feigning not to hear them, and that I would not visit them. The individual shouting changed to a united, terrorizing uproar.

Mom pressed the tarnished brass buzzer as fellow visitors stacked up behind us, now silent with tension. Two enormous guards pulled open the rusting, wrought-iron double doors. A cold gust rolled over me. Had ghosts just escaped the asylum? Good for them.

I stood in the dimly lit lobby encircled by 12' high light green walls and well-scrubbed marble floors. I imagined patients being released from their rooms to clean. Large oil portraits of, I presumed, doctors or donors and light sconces disappeared as quickly as I spotted them. The weight of the moment was crushing my memory. I turned to Mom, retrieving her parcels from a guard and wiping them off, complaining how roughly he had handled them. Gently securing the treasures from Mom, we sat on the uncomfortable wooden benches lining the lobby.

Before this visit, I researched psychiatric hospitals from the 1920s to the 1960s. By the turn of the 20th century, asylums became prisons where people could be warehoused out of sight and mind. Uncle John was admitted in 1925, a year after this asylum opened.

The 1920s through the 1930s presented severe overcrowding and poor sanitation in asylums. The use of brutal tactics such as ice-water baths and restraint as treatments for mental illness was due to the practice of treating mental illness with physical methods. Hydrotherapy, metrazol convulsion, and insulin shock therapy were popular in the 1930s. My Uncle John had probably endured these tortures. From that reading forward, I hated bathtubs and metal beds.

These methods gave way to psychotherapy in the 1940s. The encyclopedias made me believe that the 1950s barreled through with consistent improvements for these innocent victims.

"What do I s-say to him?" I asked, starting to panic.

"Just a friendly hello," Mom trailed off as a guard interrupted, "John is ready for you."

I wondered what ready for us meant. Did a staff member threaten him to behave? Was he heavily sedated?

We followed a sad-looking man, shoulders bent, in a tan uniform, along a corridor. The hallway seemed to narrow as we advanced. Then, I stopped, pretending to tie my shoelaces, to look into a room. The white metal beds were squeezed closely, with gray blankets tightly tucked around thin mattresses. The guard coughed to interrupt my spying. The corridor stretched as we turned right, then left, making me feel I would never find my way out of this labyrinth. Finally, the guard pressed a buzzer next to a thick metal door with a small window crisscrossed with wire. Another guard looked through the wired window from inside.

Jumping back, I clutched John's package and heard a crack. Rolling her eyes, Mom took the box from me. The guard opened the heavy door while inspecting over his shoulder. "All clear," he said.

As we were whisked in, Mom pulled me to the right side of the door as it closed. The inside guard tapped the door, alerting the outside guard that all was okay.

We were inside a large community room with many small, square, bare tables and wooden, slat-backed chairs. No paintings or plants to decorate the stark space. Tall windows with daylight streaming through the heavy iron bars offered some relief. Next time, I'll bring massive bouquets from our garden and lay them on the tables.

"Hi, Mrs. H. How have you been?" the guard said, smiling, causing my breath to release.

"Okay, Harry. How's John?" asked Mom.

"He's good today, extremely excited about your visit. I'll bring him to your table," said Harry.

Mom stood by a table and looked past me, arms wide open, welcoming her brother. I saw a skinny figure limping toward us. His baggy jeans were bunched up in his right hand, and his wrinkled, short-sleeved shirt displayed stick-like arms.

They hugged. His pants nearly fell off. They sat. Mom brushed John's gray hair off his forehead. I saw a wretched, worn face. His right temple was dented, and his thin lips were parched. I recognized the strong Morse jawline.

"Look who I brought with me, your niece, Marion," said Mom, wiping her tears.

"Hi, Uncle John," I whispered.

John looked deep into my eyes and wept.

"You called me Uncle. I am, aren't I?" he asked.

I was stunned. Mom pressed my shoulder to sit.

"Did you bring the cigarettes, Sis?" asked John, helping Mom tear open the package as cartons tumbled.

Puffing rapidly on an unfiltered menthol cigarette, John explained, "I read the Daily News today and saw President Kennedy is trying to get the youth more involved. What do you think, Sis?"

"It's a good thing, John. New energy," Mom brightly responded.

Uncle John picked up the family-size Hershey chocolate bar and devoured it while still smoking. This vision made me relax a bit. No matter what I feared, John, at this moment, was enjoying life to the hilt.

"My Niece Marion, has anyone told you about your Mom when she was young?" inquired a fast-talking John.

"She was a wild thing with a full Alto voice. When your Mom sang, a hush would sweep the room," he said.

I added, "Mom still has a great voice."

John tapped Mom's hand apprehensively and asked, "Is it okay, my telling Marion?"

Mom said, "Of course, John, say anything you want."

While I admired Mom's courage, I felt unprotected by her, yet wildly curious.

Uncle John began his story with abandonment: "Brother Fred bragged about driving gangsters to Harlem bars where liquor flowed and impromptu singers auditioned. This was two years short of Prohibition and speakeasies. Instead of these gangster tales terrifying your Mom, they intrigued her. One night, naughty Cousin Rose, I think she was 15, pulled down the fire escape ladder in our alleyway for your mom, 14, to sneak out. Their friend, Augusta, who was also 15, volunteered to cover for them and sit with me, 11 at the time. I loved Augusta. We brothers didn't tell Pops. I think your Mom belted out *Let's Mess Around*. Rose noticed two young men enter the darkly lit room. As the Hat Check Girl took Dutch Schultz's coat, Rose ran to your Mom to tell her they had to leave as Dutch had arrived. Your Mom grabbed Rose's hand, rushed them to Dutch, and introduced herself. Dutch was only two years older than your Mom, but his reputation as an up-and-coming gangster was common knowledge. Dutch invited them to join him."

Uncle John stopped to gulp his coffee.

Chuckling, Uncle John shouted, "Florence and Rose sat down at Dutch Schultz's table! In walked our brothers Bill and Fred. Fred approached the table. He explained that these girls were his sister and cousin and would be obliged if he could take them home."

John laughed so hard he gasped for breath and concluded, "The story goes that Dutch agreed, ending your Mom's adventurous night. Once on the sidewalk, Bill peed himself, and the girls laughed more."

Arm around Mom, John sat back, reminiscing.

Mom slipped cash into the guard's hand, "Please get us two more coffees and a cola. Get yourself something."

John was fidgeting.

"Flo, where is Augusta? I see her here sometimes. Is that true?" asked John with childlike innocence.

"Yes, Augusta visits you. She loves you too, John. Draw for Marion," said Mom, unwrapping pencils and paper, disregarding my raised eyebrows and open mouth.

Uncle John feverishly began drawing. I watched a forest emerge with a bird at the forefront of the once-blank paper. I asked him to sketch Archangel Azrael. Mom coughed, but I ignored her. Then, Uncle John filled a quarter of the page with a partial drawing of the same image as Uncle Henry had sketched six years ago. Uncle John's hand was cramping, and Mom took it between hers, stretched his fingers, and stroked his forearms. It was difficult for me to look at her pained face. I wanted to ask my uncle if he had ever seen Archangel Azrael, but I didn't. He was too fragile. I failed to go to the library a year ago, maybe hiding from more knowledge. Now, I must.

Pulled out of my head by John's words, "We have a farm. We are allowed to plant vegetables and, sometimes, even flowers."

Suddenly, Uncle John's mood changed. He started packing up his parcel, carefully folding every corner. He handed me the pencils, asking me to sharpen them for my next visit. I agreed and said I would bring my drawings next time, indebting myself. He jumped from his seat, with Mom rising slowly. They held hands.

"Keep writing to me, dear sister. I get to keep your letters now," John said while gently wiping Mom's tears.

Harlem Valley State Hospital patients, no, inmates, were allowed to keep treasured letters from the outside world to reread if they behaved.

Harry stood by, ready to return Uncle John to his room.

Uncle John abruptly cuddled the package to his chest, turned to Harry, and nodded.

John might be prepared to leave, but I was not. Watching him walk away, I noticed his severe limp again, rendering him unable to place his right heel down. I was totally at a loss.

What was happening? Mom sat down, putting the empty cups together and stuffing them with our mess.

"Mom, what happened to Uncle John's leg?" I asked.

"Let's go outside," Mom said, placing her hand on mine.

Chapter 13

A Morse Code

We walked silently until we settled on a bench at the end of the hospital property. Mom looked exhausted.

She began the story of gentle John. When John turned 14, madness entered him. From 14-17 years of age, John wavered in and out of psychosis, attempting to kill himself. First, he tried the meat cleaver on his forearms. Grandpa saved him. Then, months later, John offered to help shovel snow during a blizzard. Grandma let him go as his brothers, Fred and Henry, were already outside. But John went up the apartment building's stairs to the roof and removed all his clothes. Huddled in a corner, he hoped he'd freeze to death. John constantly apologized for the burden of his mind. When John sat in an unresponsive state for months with Grandma feeding him, the household was oddly peaceful.

I translated unresponsive to the psychological term, catatonic, a word any 13-year-old would know, right? Alan's paperwork from Jacobi Hospital started mixing with John's account.

John struggled with voices in his head, and one night, his last night at home, he crushed a lightbulb and ate most of it. Uncle Bill found him and fetched their beat cop. Grandma wiped Johnny's mouth, picked out fine glass pieces, cleaned the blood, and wrapped him in his coat.

Officer Jim said John was a good kid as he led him out. Mom doesn't know how they removed the swallowed broken glass.

Mom wiped more tears and blew her nose, determined to bring me up to speed.

There was no medicine to calm Schizophrenia in those days, and John was sent to this awful place. Mom, as a young girl, visited with Grandma.

Was I to consider myself privileged to travel this heartbreaking family journey?

Sniffling, Mom hurried to finish. John was physically healthy and allowed to participate in the gardening program. After John had tried to run away a couple of times from the fields, they butchered his calf muscle. The administration said it was an accident, but Uncle John repeated the exact gruesome details at different times. He was taken to an operating room and strapped down. The inhumane doctor sliced his calf muscle. John didn't know if they had sedated him or not.

I trusted Uncle John's explanation, seeing how lucid he was about the news and his spot-on recollection of his youth.

I asked if Uncle John was Aunt Augusta's love. Mom stared at me and nodded yes.

"Let's walk. The bus won't be here for another hour," I suggested.

Meandering along the hospital's perimeter path, I asked, almost whispered, "Don't be upset with me, but is Schizophrenia catching?"

"No," Mom swiftly answered.

I asked a more difficult question, "Do you think Alan is well? I know he lifts weights with his friend and is an A+ student, but..."

Mom cut me off mid-sentence. "I don't know, Marion. I pray nightly."

I crawled out of a fog I preferred staying in and vowed never to surrender to a similar outcome for my Alan. There was medicine and real board-certified psychiatrists.

Mom and I finally ate our too-warm, squashed sandwiches. Grapes from our arbor saved us.

To lighten the atmosphere, I teased, "Any juicy tales about my other uncles?"

Mom turned to me. "Well, yes."

I pictured myself stepping back and swallowing my words like in a film.

"Am I old enough to hear them?" I asked in a high-pitched voice.

Clearing her throat, Mom declared, "Let's sit where we can see the bus pull in. You are an old soul. You can handle this."

Was I? Could I?

Sitting down and wiping her brow with her delicate hanky, Mom began, "Your Grandpa taught his boys how to drive cars when they weren't tall enough to peer over the steering wheel and knelt on the driver's seat to see. It paid off."

It was as though Mom had waited a lifetime to reveal this secret. And I was the lucky recipient. Mom began, "As you heard from John, your Uncle Fred drove for the mob. He made them laugh, and in return, they tipped him heavily. He married Aggie far too young. He still had wild oats to sow."

I placed my hand on Mom's shoulder and said, "Wait, I never met an Aunt Aggie."

"I'm coming to that," Mom zealously continued. I saw that sharing this account lightened the moment, and I was all for that.

Mom explained that Aggie was a petite thing with a terrible temper. One day, 7 AM rolled around, and Fred had not returned home from work at his usual 5 AM after dropping said gangsters at their homes in Staten Island or Westchester. So, Aggie decided to teach Fred a lesson. Standing tippy-toe on a chair in the middle of their living room, she tied one end of her blue satin bathrobe sash to the sturdy chandelier and the other knotted loosely around her neck. We never learned how long this determined sprite remained in that fatiguing position. When Fred walked in, she threatened to hang herself. To her surprise, Fred kicked the chair from under her and stormed out.

Mom stopped and sipped water.

"Thankfully, Aggie slipped from the robe's satin sash and fell to the floor. Gramps suggested Fred join the Merchant Marines. They would look after Aggie. When Grandpa spoke, we listened," said Mom, coughing.

"You can stop," I said, worried.

Mom, determined to conclude this family scoop, continued. Aggie was several months pregnant before anyone knew. Her apartment was near them, and Grandma Apolonia visited with food and gossip. Aggie gave birth to a baby boy. To spite Fred, she named the baby Billy.

Grandma loaned her a baby carriage and beautiful hand-stitched baby outfits. As months passed, it was feared that Aggie was not caring for Billy. Grandma arrived at Aggie's one spring day, insisting they take Billy out for some sunshine. Still in her infamous ice blue satin robe, Aggie filed her nails while unfortunate Billy whimpered in his cradle. At 14 months old, he was unable to stand. Grandma changed the soaking wet diaper, placed him in the carriage, and left the apartment. That was the last time Aggie saw her son without his protective grandparents.

"Mom, that baby is my cousin, Billy, right?" I asked. Yes, was Mom's reply.

Billy's hunchback took on a whole new meaning for me. I wondered if others noticed the strange family that was ours. And that was only the Morse side!

"Mom, what about the Hoffmans?" I asked, terrified.

Mom smiled as she said, "The Hoffman family supposedly arrived in America in 1664 and became dairy farmers in upstate New York. They probably fought in the American Revolution. I never heard of any oddities in their family."

I exhaled.

Our bus pulled in. Visitors solemnly boarded, including a woman hysterically sobbing. I clutched Mom's arm and hurried us onto the bus. These quarterly outings with Mom became an ordinary part of my life, and I treasured them. Was I a weird kid? Maybe, but who was looking? All that mattered to my older siblings was that it wasn't them.

Chapter 14

Sweetish Sixteen

As I turned 16, I decided to grow my Archangel team. I chose to invite Archangel Raphael, the protector of nurses, physicians, and medical workers, as I was heading to a hospital's Candy Striper summer volunteer program. Was this teenage foolishness?

Sometimes, Azrael sparked my sense of humor as he leaned on me while I brushed my teeth, smearing toothpaste across my face. The most challenging episodes were his appearances in my dreams: I strolled a path lined with large, multi-colored flowers only to feel a gush of wind as Azrael flew overhead, making me run to exhaustion. I would wake without refreshment. Yet, I had a renewed drive to face life's problems.

Archangel Azrael influenced my choice of study, directing me to Mathematics. Alan said numbers would help him unlock mysteries in the ocean. I wondered if death had a number and could reveal a path to my Dad.

On the last day of my Junior year, I stayed after class as Mrs. Linda, my history teacher, instructed. This class bored me. I feared the worst. Mrs. Linda signaled me to approach her large, pinewood, ink-stained desk. She handed me a tiny pink box, coaxing me to open it. Inside was a silver brooch with my three initials, MRH, swirled in a delicate pattern, the "M" blazingly prominent. "Marion is a good name," she declared, dismissing me with a knowing smile.

Stunned, I thanked her and placed her gift into my Army & Navy surplus tan backpack.

What just happened? I had never discussed my struggle to accept being named after my peculiar Godmother, Marion Montana. Could Mrs. Linda be an angel? How else could she know?

I hurried along to retrieve my Algebra Regents' score. I had noticed my Mathematics teacher connected my stuttering with my intelligence, so I asked Doc Nathan, my Chemistry Instructor, to tutor me in math. His thick white mustache and round belly comforted me.

Dr. Nathan handed me my Algebra Regents Exam with a 98 in the upper right-hand corner, saying he was proud of me.

"I'd like to tell you something, but you may think I'm bananas," I said.

"I'm the one who eats chalk, Marion. Rest assured, it will not go beyond this conversation," replied Doc Nathan. He referred to the time he bit on a stick of chalk to get his class's attention, saying it was just calcium.

I spilled the beans: My Dad died when I was six. My Uncle Bill died the following February, a month before I turned seven. That summer, I contracted Polio and nearly drowned. That autumn, foster children began entering and exiting our home over the next nine years. I loved each one of them as my brother or sister. They might as well have succumbed since they disappeared from my life without an opportunity to say goodbye or stay in touch. When I was 11, my brother Alan attempted suicide. As I turned 12, a troubled schoolmate supposedly committed suicide.

Doc Nathan nodded his head without flinching, encouraging me to go on.

Inhaling with all my might, I exclaimed, "I believe Archangel Azrael, the Angel of Death, is my best friend."

Covering my mouth, I gasped as I spoke those long-overdue words.

I squinted, waiting for Doc Nathan to tell me I was crazy.

He took my hands from my mouth and folded his arms across his belly. I sensed he was dusting cobwebs off his angel knowledge.

He said, to the best of his knowledge, almost quoting from books, that Azrael was the Islamic counterpart of the Judeo-Christian angel of death. He was counted as one of the four archangels: Archangel Michael, Archangel Gabriel, Archangel Raphael, and Archangel Azrael. Nonetheless, through centuries of cultural exchange, Azrael had since percolated into Christianity and European cultural consciousness, where he was often equated with the otherwise unnamed angel of death mentioned in parts of the scriptures. In Islamic tradition, the Angel of Death is named Azrael. The Quran uses the term Malak al Maut, which means Angel of Death.

Jewish Kabbalistic tradition uses the names Azriel and Malakh ha-Mavet, which also means Angel of Death.

101

I believe that before the creation of man, Azrael proved to be the only angel brave enough to go down to Earth and face the hordes of Iblis, the devil, in order to bring God the materials needed to make man. For this service, he was made the angel of death and given a register of all mankind.

It was written that he had one foot in the seventh heaven, the other on the bridge that divides paradise and hell.

I had read about the seventh heaven, but not how it was divided.

"Marion, death is part of life, and, yes, it might have its own number, but my advice is to pursue life. You may be lucky to have Azrael as your friend. More than this, I don't know," counseled Doc Nathan as he stood. I enthusiastically shook his hand with thanks.

His words echoed the Clergymen. Unknown to each other, three scholarly men confirmed that having Azrael as my friend might be a blessing. Crazy or not, I felt better.

Were my teachers revealing themselves as angels? Laughing and leaving my high school for the summer was momentarily tranquil.

Out loud, I asked, "Are they angels, Az?"

Jessica, my nemesis, and her gang were a few steps ahead of me.

"You speaking to m-me?" joked Jessica, the boy pleaser. "No, not you," I whispered.

"Weirdo," Jessica said, entertaining her entourage.

I walked on, shaking my head in agreement as my peculiar plate was full of stammering, a thorny family tree, and my shoulder jockey.

Later that night, I reached out to Azrael, asking for a sign about my invitation to his brother, Archangel Raphael, to join us.

The following Monday, I sang along with the Rolling Stones' "Time Is on My Side," ironing my pink and white Candy Striper Uniform. Mom was pleased I was giving nursing a chance while I daydreamed about attending the Martha Graham Dance Studio.

As I hopped into Darren's (my sort-of boyfriend) jalopy for a lift to the hospital, I had to crush his fantasy with, "No, the title is Striper, not stripper."

Darren had joined the Army to avoid being drafted and used every opportunity to extract my sympathy. Our neighborhood was abuzz with the Vietnam fiasco. My only interest was how Azrael instructed his angels to peacefully lift the souls from the fields of war.

I tied my pink and white smock over my white blouse and stuck the cap on my head in the nurses' locker room with my long, dark hair in two neat braids.

Nurse Nice assigned me to the men's ward. She led me to an ice cabinet and fountain in the supply room, glumly stating, "You are to fill the pitchers found on the patient's nightstand with ice and water. Be sure to greet the patients cheerfully."

Saluting her, I headed to the far end of the hallway to begin my day.

"Hello, Mr.," while grabbing a chart from the end of the bed to discover a name. "Mr. Jones. How are you feeling today?" I chirped.

"Like shit, what do you think," replied dear Mr. Jones.

I returned with his pitcher and a fresh glass. I continued to the following rooms, realizing I did not like working in a hospital. The smells, the sickness, and the uniforms did not interest me.

I heard a scream from down the hall. I ran and slid into Mr. Amen's room. Leering at me, the young, handsome Mr. Amen appeared fine.

"I'm hot. Please turn my pillow over," he requested.

"Sure thing," I spunkily said.

Lifting his head and shoulders gently, I took his pillow. I felt his hand on my butt. I stood back, fluffing his pillow.

"Sit up, please," I asked.

"I have a hernia and can't," Mr. Amen responded.

I fluffed the pillow beneath his head as he wrapped his arm around my waist.

"Whoever gave you the hernia, kudos to her," I declared, stomping out with his empty water pitcher.

As my 4-hour shift wound down, I untied my uniform and rolled it into a ball in my bag, assuring myself that nursing was not for me.

I heard Mr. Amen screaming again as I waited for the elevator. Nurse Nice arrived as the elevator door opened, sputtering, "You filled Mr. Amen's urinal with ice water. I can't imagine you did this on purpose."

The door squeezed shut. "Of course not," I responded.

Then, rolling my eyes to the elevator's ceiling, I said, "I know, Archangel Raphael. I'm sticking with Azrael."

Two days later, I hung up the telephone and exclaimed, "Mom, I have a guaranteed spot in September at Martha

Graham's! I'll figure out how to pay for the classes. No worries."

"Jimmy is looking for a helper," said Mom.

Cutting her off mid-sentence. "I'll run over there now."

Mom and I headed to Macy's Herald Square on Tuesday to purchase pretty things for Alice. We ascended the subway on 34th Street, between Broadway and Seventh Avenue. I spotted the green-eyed iron owl monument. Mom inferred that the owl had something to do with a secret society, but that discussion was left for another time.

After we shopped, we found our way to Macy's café. Smothering my hotdog with mustard and tons of sauerkraut. I took a bite.

Mom asked, "Marion, would you like to spend the summer with Alice in Pocatello?"

I chewed my hot dog slowly as I considered this outrageous request. Then, taking another bite, I looked at Mom. She was getting little joy from her hamburger.

I asked why. Alice had been diagnosed with Multiple Sclerosis when she was in Bellevue Nursing School. She was told the disease could remain in remission for years if she took excellent care of herself. This included not having children, as the trauma of birth would overtax her body.

I bombarded poor Mom with an annoyed, obvious question: Why couldn't Roy or Nancy go? They know her. I understood why Alan could not go.

Mom said she had asked them. They declined.

I pushed against this request, reminding Mom I had secured a job at Jimmy's grocery store. She offered to pay for the dance lessons even though we both knew it would painfully tighten her budget. Mom whispered to forget about it for now. Our lunch ended.

Going to bed had become more about contemplation than sleep. I would never disappoint Mom or Dad, still.

I accepted Roy's invitation to fly in a 4-seater plane to save Alan from going alone. Flight day arrived, and the skies were exasperatingly clear. I waited for Alan in the kitchen.

The multiple pills Alan took for his mental health with breakfast made him initially lethargic. He also had to cope with a dry mouth, so he carried wet handkerchiefs to pat. I never heard my brother complain throughout the years about his various medicinal cocktails. Some caused his hands to shake, and one caused seizures.

I watched Mom pack Alice's bundles bulging with fragrant lotions, dressing gowns, and a hand-crocheted throw. A handwritten letter, at least one recipe, and the latest Bellevue Nursing School news edition were included.

"Alice's Multiple Sclerosis will get worse, Marion. I have been struggling with her moron of a husband, Bill, to have Alice back in New York for better care. I have spoken with Mary Manning Walsh's facility. She should never have married that bum," Mom fervently declared, punctuating bum.

"Is that why Alice's old beau, George, visited us last week?" I asked, grinning.

"Yes, he never got over your sister and will help," Mom smugly said.

Standing in the small airport hangar in Westchester County, Alan and I eyed each other. The engineer checking the plane said I was the spitting image of Roy. I took it as a compliment and would ensure it was only in looks.

Roy, the pilot, hummed, "Up, Up and Away," while buckling in Alan and me.

I grabbed Alan's hand and said, "I've never liked amusement rides, riding my bike fast, or tag. How do you think this is going to end?"

Roy shouted, "You don't appreciate all I do for you."

The co-pilot intervened, "Don't worry, you'll enjoy the flight."

Initially, I was exhilarated as the tiny plane spirited down the runway, nose pointing up. As we soared above the clouds, I searched for, as Mrs. Garibaldi said, un segno di Dio that Dad was around.

"Alan, you okay?" I asked.

Nodding his head, yes, unable to speak, he alerted me to grab the barf bag. Pilot Roy and co-pilot Nameless laughed and took us higher.

"That's high enough. I'm okay, and Alan, for sure," I said.

"No sissys on this plane. Hold on," Pilot Roy boomed.

We were going sideways, perhaps to turn back.

"Ah…Aaiiee," I screamed at the top of my lungs. Roy ignored my shrieks.

The funny pilot flipped the plane upside down. Alan quietly vomited on the ceiling of the plane. I followed suit as a sister must. Roy flipped the plane upright, and the vomit dripped down on us, including bits of the Carvel ice cream cone we had before boarding.

Settled at home, cleaned up, and in pajamas, I had Mom and Alan laughing about the incident.

"If I didn't know better, I'd think you planned this flying fiasco," Mom suggested, squinting at us.

"Nah, angels to our rescue," I offered.

Then, I said, "I accept the Pocatello challenge."

Chapter 15

Next Stop Pocatello

I strutted across the airport in white knee-high boots, a royal-blue mini skirt, an ivory sleeveless turtleneck, and a tan maxi trench coat. Mom had gifted me this fun traveling outfit. I was escorted onto the plane, hoping I would not have a seat companion. The flight attendant sat me next to a fresh-faced, uniformed Army Private.

"Are you a princess?" inquired the adorable soldier. Giggling nervously, I responded, "No, why?"

"The attendant is falling all over herself to make you comfy," he drawled.

"Oh, that. No, my brother is a Pan Am Pilot, and this must be the f-family care routine," I said, feeling a stuttering attack coming on.

"I'm Wyatt. What's your name?"

"My name is M-Marion. Aha, Wyatt, like Wyatt Earp," I quipped, trying to relax. "Marion as in Lady Marion of Robin Hood tales," Wyatt said.

Afraid of stuttering, I smiled, glad the announcement began as we taxied onto the runway. I pretended to nap for the remainder of that lengthy first leg of my journey.

I was grateful my magnificent, winged friend furled his glorious feathers inside the plane to comfort me as I headed to a strange place where sickness reigned.

I was relieved that my thoughtless request to Archangel Raphael had failed. The insolence thinking I needed more than Azrael.

At one point, Wyatt gently laid my head on his shoulder and tucked the airline blanket over me. I wished I could talk.

As I ran across the Chicago Airport Terminal, Wyatt caught up and pulled my ivory Samsonite makeup case from my hand.

"Idaho bound?" he asked. "You too?"

"Yeah."

"I am glad you are with me," I said with conviction, noting that conversing flowed more easily when walking.

My second leg of the trip was fun. I learned the rancher's kid was heading to Vietnam in two weeks. We exchanged addresses and a kiss before landing.

I readied myself for the onslaught of the Pack family, which consisted of my brother-in-law, Bill, a Pharmacist demoted from Surgeon, four-year-old Chuck, two-year-old Billy, and my sister, Alice, whom I last saw when I was eight.

I was in dusty Pocatello for one week and wanted to go home. The miles of flat, treeless landscape stretched as far as the eye could see from these suburban row houses. The distant foothills and white-capped mountains gave hope.

Although they had lived there for almost a year, my sister's home was dismal with its lack of artwork, cozy area rugs, sparse furnishings, and bare windows. I asked Alice if we could head to a curtain store to find a red pair for her bedroom, like her gorgeous red Asian dress I had admired when I was eight. I was prepared to hang them. I had already written Mom a letter asking for photo frames, as the photos of her beautiful children lying haphazardly on her dresser deserved to stand up and greet Alice daily. The rocking chair Mom sent was a shining beacon. Thankfully, I slept on a cot in the boys' room, not the living room's sleeper couch.

I accepted that Alice either didn't believe in discipline or was too ill to notice. My nephews, Chuck and Billy, charged around like banshees. They relaxed during baths and bedtime, so I allotted as many hours as possible to those sweeter moments. Billy tried to snuggle in Alice and Bill's bed, but was always returned. Those nights, Billy crawled in with me. I squeezed him tightly, trying to wring out his sadness. His childhood, paralleling mine, was fraught with pain.

I felt Azrael close by in this bleak house.

My arrogant, unfriendly brother-in-law, Bill, rarely spoke to me. However, his comment, "Doesn't she use deodorant?" to my sister, denigrated me and brought on my stutter with a vengeance. He scrutinized my nonexistent skills, such as ironing, coffee making, and how to lift Alice out of the tub. His excruciating, detailed narration knotted my stomach. He made me feel inconsequential, so I tried to avoid him.

"He doesn't mean it," was Alice's explanation.

I found her excuse for Bill unsatisfactory. Her love for Bill overshadowed her wisdom.

For instance, Bill wanted a family. So, Alice went against the MS Medical specialist's advice and gave birth twice. The strain traumatized her body, sending her Multiple Sclerosis from an isolated syndrome to Relapsing-Remitting MS.

I heard the boys call their mother by her name, Alice. She told me she preferred it. I found this wrong, but I was 16, so what did I know?

My days began with the boys. I gave Bill and Alice privacy until he left for work.

Then, the boys would charge in and jump on Alice's bed. I watched Chuck swing her legs to the side of the bed to help her sit up as Billy pushed slippers on her feet. I felt Azrael's manifestation there was the strongest. I admired my sister's courage as she joked when her shaking hands spilled the black coffee when she first sipped. I cut the boys' soda straws and inserted them into her coffee. I pretended not to see her tears.

My sister's Relapsing-remitting MS (RRMS) stage follows a predictable pattern, with periods in which symptoms worsen and then improve. Eventually, it may progress to secondary-progressive MS.

When I tried to lift her spirits with my funny Candy Striper story of Mr. Amen, she looked through me and asked if Bill had mentioned what he wanted for dinner when he left for work that morning. My attempts to impart funny moments about Mom were curtailed with requests to add to her grocery list. As a sister far away and a nurse, I thought she would want details about Alan's illness and offer advice or concern. As for Roy and Nancy, with whom she grew up, she showed no interest in their growing families. Instead, I learned that Multiple Sclerosis was destroying her world, inflicting on her another disease, resentment.

I learned that Alice enjoyed sitting in a lounge chair to bake in the sun. So, cane in one hand, leaning on my arm with the other, she joked about her wobbly gait as we walked to her sunspot.

Our 17-year age gap created an undeniable strain. I worried about my zero cooking skills heading out to this foreign land. But as fate dictated, this lack of talent or interest in cooking was a plus.

Most days, around 4 PM, Alice and I congregated in the kitchen. Her California specialist advised her that one glass of wine might steady her hands at this time of day. So, Alice sipped wine through a straw and led me through recipes from Mom's gift, the familiar red and white checkered Betty Crocker cookbook. These afternoon hours bonded us with barrels of laughter as our main course.

I watched Alice lovingly cut her boys' food without tremors as tears rose in her eyes.

Alice was an enigma to me as she did not express affection toward her boys if Bill was around. Then there was their pet mammoth, the untrained Weimaraner named Mack-the-Truck.

This massive dog charged around, knocking down the boys and anything in its path.

I browsed the set of Britannica Encyclopedias that Mom had spent years purchasing over time and gifted to Alice upon graduating from nursing school. I aimed to learn about this dog breed: Originally bred as a gundog to handle big game, the Weimaraner, or "Silver Ghost," was highly sought-after in their native Germany. These demanding dogs can make fine family friends if they get enough exercise. My obvious solution was to exercise the heck out of Mack-the-Truck.

While Mack gobbled an enormous plate of food, I placed the unused black collar around his neck. Then, feeling confident, I hooked the heavy metal leash onto the collar and picked up my laundry basket of wet clothes. Mack took the lead before the door closed behind us.

"Heel, stop, sttttop," I shouted in vain.

The laundry basket was down, leaving a trail of clothes behind me. I hung on to the leash, swaying my body toward the distant drying pole to wrap his chain around it. It worked, but I failed to step away quickly, jamming my ankle into the chain. Blood poured from my leg as I used my brute strength to undo the leash from the handle. Pressing one of Bill's white shirts to my bleeding ankle, I squatted on the ground, watching the Silver Ghost run from one yard to the next. Mack had such a good time that he decided to love me. My face became raw from his licks.

On Sunday, at the start of the third week, Alice ordered me to bring the boys to the family next door. Bill wanted time alone with her. I saluted her and blew a Bronx cheer behind Bill's back.

The neighbor, Janine, greeted the boys warmly. Her dried-up looks, stained blouse, and worn jeans made her look older than her 31 years. Her husband, Austin, was missing one of his top front teeth, but that did not stop him from grinning. Matthew, their 14-year-old son, saw too many James Dean movies. I bit my lip to halt a chuckle at his attempt at a swagger in his tight jeans and cowboy boots. Austin and Matthew were taking me out for the afternoon.

I spent the 45-minute bumpy drive squashed between two country boys. I was not frightened to be alone in the pickup cab as they had a gentlemanly innocence. Matthew reminded me of Wyatt. They talked up a storm, supposing my life in New York City was mighty dangerous. They were going to help.

I was about to ask how when we entered the Rocky Mountain foothills along the Oregon Trail. Austin slowed down the truck as a holy moment flashed through the cab. My eyes climbed the mountainside. I never saw rocks change color from slate gray to marbled beige as they rose to meet the dripping lavender snow. I had to squint to see the mountain peak's pure white snow, throwing off a dusting into the sun. I experienced something I'd heard about: peace.

Austin parked the truck in a splendid pine tree grove, explaining that the trees were the finest Ponderosa Pines. My relating this to the TV show, Bonanza, annoyed these proud Idaho folks.

"City girl," mumbled Austin.

I hopped out of the truck and felt the first cool breeze since arriving in Pocatello.

115

Stretching my arms and opening my chest, I took a deep breath. Matthew shoved an Army surplus canteen into my ribs. I coughed and took a swig. I felt the cold water trickle down my throat. Our hike commenced. I touched trees with gratitude as we stepped on soft fallen pine needles between the slippery rocks.

"This is a good spot," announced Austin, with Matthew humming in agreement. "For what?" I asked.

"Teach you how to shoot a gun," Austin said.

My head rushed to find excuses not to touch the gun. Could I say I was allergic to metal?

Matthew's two open hands held a sparkling silver handgun before me like a sacred offering.

"I'm allergic to gunpowder," I whimpered. "This ain't no cannon," said Austin.

Matthew continued holding the gun.

"No, thank you," I said.

Austin took the gun and spat on the ground after his coaxing failed. He flipped the weapon from his left to his right hand, terrifying me. Finally, he laid the gun back in its carved leather case.

Matthew lined up cans on top of a boulder, and they practiced shooting. Then, again, Austin tried to hand me the gun. I declined. After calling me a sissy-girl for, I don't know how long, Matthew finally gave me a strip of beef jerky as we returned to the truck. I chewed on it and kept my being a vegetarian a top secret. It was a silent ride back, letting me know I had disappointed them.

Pulling up at Austin's house, I tried to rush away. Regrettably, the macho men invited me to see their cross-country freight truck parked on their lawn, as their driveway was crowded with used car parts. I climbed into the driver's seat and learned to shift 15 gears, the best part of that day's adventure, besides touching the trees.

My departure day finally arrived. I hugged Alice and the boys. I felt my month-long attempt to love them missed their hearts. This made me angry. I was only 16. How was I supposed to know the nuances of this situation?

Alice's departing words were, "Sometimes sisters can get MS."

I stared at her in disbelief. Her anger with her disease caused her to almost curse me. I was practically dismissed as she told me not to keep Bill waiting. The boys scattered into their old banshee ways. Mack laid his head on my suitcase. He was going to miss me.

Bill drove me to the airport. I recalled getting in the passenger seat, but my memory did not retain that ghastly ride.

I lost the sixteenth summer of my life in Pocatello, but found that my love for Azrael grew more worthwhile than human love. Humans seemed to love pieces of each other, not the whole. Was there a complete human being for each of us to love, or are we on earth simply practicing?

Chapter 16

Alan Is Missing

Waking up the first morning back home was temporarily comforting. The heat felt like New York in August, but the calendar read September.

I told Mom about the good times. How Alice and I used her cookbook, sharing the boys' bubble baths, and how Alice soaked in the sun.

As we sat at our kitchen table, I unloaded the bad things about Bill, the sparsely furnished dwelling, and the undisciplined nephews. Finally, I ended my report by showing her the blueish scar around my ankle. I needed to release some pain. Guilt muddied this for me as I saw the hurt in Mom's eyes. I felt ashamed. I whispered that I was sorry if I had upset her, adding that I was glad to be home. I didn't share Alice's disinterest in her family back here. I didn't reveal how Alice fell on top of Chuck once, bending down to kiss him goodnight, how often she spilled hot coffee on herself, or her inability to brush her teeth alone.

Mom took my hand and led us to the garden. We sat on the pale blue metal glider, sliding back and forth, watching the fireflies and slapping our arms to chase the mosquitoes. We were going to be okay.

Mom reminded me there was a parcel from Wyatt on my bed. His sweet words and the copper brooch shaped like an artist's palette were a distraction from family problems, allowing sleep to capture me. Early the following morning, still in my yellow pajamas, armed with a writing pad, I sat beneath the grape arbor, heavy with globe grapes. Mom and I would soon pick the swollen sweet ones for her winter jams. Knowing Wyatt was already in Vietnam, I wrote as funny a letter as I could create and mailed it to the lengthy overseas address.

Unfortunately, Wyatt never read my letter. The day after mailing it, I received a note from Wyatt's distraught mother, explaining his death three days after he arrived in Vietnam, two weeks after I met him. She expressed her unending sorrow. No, not Wyatt, the innocent country boy one could hardly call a man. I had imagined showing him my New York City on his way home from Vietnam and buying a silly Statue of Liberty souvenir for his mom.

Scrunching his mother's letter, I rushed to St. Raymond's Cemetery. No one questioned tears there. Staring at a white stone angel, I fought the pain by saying I scarcely knew Wyatt and that being sad about a future event was ridiculous. Thankfully, I saw Alan leaning against the 20-foot-high iron gate of St. Raymond's Cemetery entrance, waiting for me.

"We lost friends in Vietnam, Marion," said Alan, his jaw twitching with anger as we walked home. I tried to change the subject by apologizing for being stuck in Idaho

119

and missing his 18th birthday. But he said my card made him laugh, especially my note about Austin and his son.

Alan lost his best buddy, Dennis, in Vietnam. The kid who helped him through our Dad's death ten years ago. Dennis, the friend who played stickball until his arms ached, to ease Alan's pain from the departure of our foster siblings. Alan spoke of joining the Vietnam conflict to honor their friendship. I touched his back, but his rigid stance would not be relieved that day. On the contrary, I feared that Wyatt's death fueled Alan's resolve to join the armed forces.

Back home, again, under our grape arbor, I began writing Wyatt's mother as dusk settled.

I told her how Wyatt accepted my stammer and made me laugh, and I'd keep in touch if she would like.

I knelt beside my bed that second night home, adding Wyatt and his Mom to my prayers.

"Azrael, you traveled to and fro Pocatello with me. You left my sister standing. Yet, death smacked me anyway. Please, what am I to learn about you and death? No matter, I love you."

The next day, leaving my first dance class at Martha Graham's Studio on East 64th Street in Manhattan, I realized that the three hours of focused dance instruction created a secret world where no one asked me questions about my family or knew I stuttered. As I perspired, pain oozed from my pores. By the second hour, I was in a dance frenzy, and nothing else existed.

Hallelujah.

Autumn graced our garden. Leaves began their journey to death by creating an abundance of rich colors so we don't forget them—and we don't. As Mom and I scratched our rakes into the ground, I remembered Dad whistling as he raked. He would create a pile of leaves beneath our pear tree, whose thick, gnarly branches reached beyond the holy gate into our play area. Alan and I would dive into the pile over and over. The sound of our collapsing into the leaves became crisper as the days passed. Then, there was silence as the leaves softened into the soil. Their death smelled good. I relished their decay as they nourished new life.

Never invite death. But, during our body's autumn, let's dress in our finest, be extra kind, and laugh more. Then, as the brown leaves succumb to Earth's invitation, we may peacefully accept death's arrival. Who knows what wondrous life lies beyond?

"Mom, I'm afraid if the Army accepts Alan," I said.

"Alan's chances of being accepted by the Army are slim to none due to Schizophrenia, a blessing in disguise," imparted Mom.

Then, we heard Alan's familiar footsteps in the alleyway. We stopped, anxious to listen to the local Army Recruitment Office results.

"Hi, Alan. You're just in time to take over my rake," I cheerfully said. Ignoring me, Alan angrily said, "I've been classified 4-F. Happy, Mom?"

"You have much to give your country by furthering your education, don't you think?" asked Mom.

"I don't know, I'm disappointed," Alan glumly stated.

My brother, Alan, was a New York State Shot Put Champion at DeWitt Clinton High School. He received a New York University scholarship to pursue his dream career to become an Oceanographer, but the U.S. Armed Forces found him an unacceptable specimen.

Mom and I hovered over Alan, aware that this classification was his fresh, open wound of humiliation. My sleep pattern became a series of one-eye-open-at-a-time naps. My heartbeat quickened at cars backfiring, distant doors banging, or even laughter on the street. Occasionally, Azrael wrapped his feathered wings around me, plummeting me into a deep sleep.

A week later, as Mom arrived home from her weekly shopping jaunt with Montana, I grabbed the brown paper bags from her arms, impatient to share my earlier telephone conversation.

"Mom, listen, Alan's Psychiatrist called. Alan missed his last two appointments. I counted Alan's pills. He skipped his last five doses," I spat out.

"Put the groceries away. There's ice cream in that bag. I'll call for his advice," Mom said.

Mom returned to the kitchen and shared, "Dr. Greenberg said to be honest and let Alan know he called us."

"I'm not looking forward to this confrontation," I mumbled.

Mom shrugged in agreement.

"It's 3 o'clock. Alan will be home any minute," hurried Mom.

"Marcie, grab your sweater. Marion will take you to Montana for dinner. I need to have a boring big-person talk with Alan," said Mom.

I liked that Mom explained things to her children of all ages. I knew I'd do the same.

Seven-year-old Marcie was flourishing. She attended a special education class. Mom patiently re-read Marcie's favorite story, *Sleeping Beauty*, nightly. Her scars from the cigarette burns had almost disappeared due to Mom's application of her concoction of oils, and her long, thick, coarse hair was neatly braided. Marcie had a dazzling gift to love.

"Montana, let Marcie have dinner with you, as I need to talk with Alan. Tell you later. Give her only vanilla egg cream," said Mom, remaining in her rocking chair as I left.

It was 5:30 PM, and Alan was two hours late. The phone rang. Mom grabbed it.

"Nancy, it's good to hear your voice," said Mom. "Listen, Alan is hours late coming home and has missed a couple of his psychiatric appointments. We are worried."

"You're sure he'll be fine. You didn't call to hear our troubles," whispered Mom, her jaw grinding from side to side.

"What?" Mom asked.

"No, Marion has a part-time job and is not available to babysit this weekend," Mom injected.

"Nancy, I must keep the phone clear. Kiss Donna goodnight for me," said a disappointed Mom, hanging up.

I gathered Marcie from Montana around 9 PM. We walked along as she yawned and whispered, "The dogs slept on top of me. They were heavy."

"Were you brave and ask Tana to remove them?" I asked.

"Oh, no, n-n-never," an upset Marcie shouted.

I stopped, bent down, and piggybacked her home.

Around 11 PM, I heard our squeaky screen door open and someone knocking on our locked back door.

Rushing past Mom, now in her nightgown and robe, I turned the lock on the back door, plastered on a huge grin, expecting to see my Alan. But instead, Detective Lieutenant John Russo from our local precinct stood before me. His broken nose, scar across his eyebrow, and somber nature did not detract from his handsome Roman face, with his dark hair graying at the temples. I had seen him often in the neighborhood. His tall frame was enhanced with custom-made suits and pointy, light brown soft leather shoes. Only his brown fedora looked worn.

"Your Mom called," said Russo.

Walking past me, Lieutenant Russo said, "I just finished my shift and thought I'd check in, Mrs. H."

Our clock struck midnight. Mom walked Russo to our front door, armed with caffeine from Mom's espresso, his notes, and Alan's graduation photo.

"Mrs. H, I'll drop this at our precinct and put out a citywide bulletin," said a sincere Lieutenant.

"Please, John, make sure they know Alan is no danger to anyone and just turned 18," Mom begged and broke down. John held Mom until her sobbing stopped.

"Marion, tuck your Mom in. We will do our best to bring Alan home safely," whispered Russo.

I slipped into my bed. Eyes closed, I felt Azrael's essence forming near me. A loud whoosh blasted his enormous being across my room.

"Tell me where I may find Alan. Anything," I whispered.

A frantic, on-and-off night of sleep tossed me around like when my head repeatedly hit the sand, and I almost drowned. All that came out of the intermittent dreams were crashing bright-orange ocean waves. I dismissed this as old drowning fears.

Eleven agonizing days passed without a word about Alan's whereabouts.

"Mom, we're home," I shouted, entering our kitchen. I had brought Marcie to my part-time job. She had no interest in Jimmy's math skills but did a great job lining up the assorted fruit. Mom greeted us from our basement laundry room.

"Hi, girls," and continued, "Marion, look at this scrap of paper I found in Alan's pants pocket."

Handing me a wet, almost unreadable square inch of cloth, I discerned the letter 'e' followed by the word 'Krishna.'

"Mom, I don't know what this means. But let me run it to our precinct," I said without removing my jacket.

Luckily, Russo was on duty. He took me upstairs to the Detective Division.

Detective One looked at the scrap and, without hesitation, said, "Yeah, these words are Hare Krishna. These followers started showing up on Manhattan streets, especially in central travel hubs like Grand Central, Times Square, and Penn Station. Their orange robes and shaved heads remind us of Buddhist monks, but they are not Buddhist. The religious order began in India, but the groups in New York City came down from Canada."

Russo asked, "Is it a cult?"

Detective Two said, "We don't know yet, but they are growing fast as they take in the homeless, especially young ones from the street. They are on our Watch List."

Russo thanked him for the possible lead. Outside the precinct, Russo offered advice, "This isn't enough for my men to chase. But, since I know you will go to Manhattan the minute I turn my back, I'll notify the three precincts to respond if you call them. Promise me that if you luck out and find your brother, you will call one of these precincts before attempting to bring your brother home."

"I will, scouts' honor," I responded, walking away.

Russo's massive hand was on my shoulder as he said, "I think you're missing something, scout," handing me the three scribbled telephone numbers.

"Marion, one of the detectives feels you should start at Times Square. Good luck. Alan is a fine young man, like I told your Mother," added Russo.

Back home, my dried-out but warm dinner was in the oven. Mom turned on the TV as the Flintstones started, and Marcie adored them.

"Mom, Hare Krishna is a religious group or a cult that may induct street people. But here's the thing. About two weeks ago, I dreamt of orange waves. That's the color of their robes. What do you think? Can I go?"

"Tonight, are you crazy!" shouted Mom.

"I don't think so," I said without conviction.

Without waiting for a response, I continued, "Mom, we have a target now, and Russo gave me the telephone numbers of three downtown precincts. Here, write them down. He told me to start at Times Square."

"You cannot go alone if I have to tie you to the chair," shouted Mom.

With that, the phone rang.

"Finish your dinner," Mom said sternly.

On the phone, Mom exclaimed, "Detective Russo, I cannot let Marion go alone to Times Square. She's only 16."

"Oh, okay, she'll be ready in five minutes. Thank you." Mom suddenly whispered.

Mom rushed into the kitchen and said, "One of the detectives you spoke with is going off duty and is willing to join you. He'll be pulling up any minute."

I brushed my teeth to steady my nerves. Then, I ran down our home's 13 steps. Then I ran back up and grabbed clothes for Alan, with hope in my heart.

The detective turned out to be Detective Two, a young man with a bodybuilder's physique, a cherub face, and reddish blonde hair. He signaled me to jump into the front passenger seat. I had barely sat down when I felt the car accelerate from zero to 50 mph in seconds.

Our police car slowed as we approached 49th Street and 7th Avenue, heading southbound.

We inconspicuously slid into the heavy traffic. Before the sights, the stench of ripe trash and stale sewage invaded my nostrils.

"Roll up your window. If you see your brother, I will pull over. We go together, got that?" instructed Detective Two.

I refused to take my eyes off the sidewalks but answered, "Yes, sure."

"I'm Matt," he added, reaching and locking my door. Does he think that will stop me? "I'm Marion," I mumbled.

Pouring sweat in minutes, Matt allowed us to crack open our windows.

The flashing neon signs of porn shops distorted my vision. People rushed along, bumping into others and shouting to be heard above the traffic noise. Did I have a chance to spot Alan?

Then, a fistfight broke out on the sidewalk from a filthy bar. People surrounded the already bloodied pair.

"Matt, stop it, please," I begged.

He pulled up and stopped the brawl.

Matt slid back into the car, cleared his throat, and said, "We can't stop like this again. I'm off duty, and this is not my precinct."

I took a moment to thank Matt, who became a bit of a hero.

One Times Square's flashing signage disappeared from my view as Matt turned the car west on 45th Street as Broadway and 7th Avenue intersected. I was thankful as this darker, seedy street had a slower vibe. Every doorway had a barely clothed prostitute leaning in it. I was grateful I could not see their faces. Finally, at 45th and Eighth Avenue, I spotted a group clad in orange robes with shaved heads.

Matt pulled over. We approached them with my photo of Alan. They cautiously looked at the picture with blank faces. By 1 AM, we had pulled over to four Hare Krishna groups of at least 20 members each. I struggled to note their facial features above the swirling orange robes. Matt explained that the tufts of hair at the napes of their necks distinguished them from Buddhists who had fully shaven heads.

Matt and I returned to the car from this fifth group of almost 30 members spilling around the corner of 43rd

Street and Seventh Avenue. Matt turned around, facing the group we had just spoken with, and noticed one of them running.

Matt tossed the keys and shouted, "I had a hunch. Wait for me in the car and lock it."

Then, he took off after the orange-clad figure.

"Keep your keys," I shouted back, struggling to keep pace with him. Suddenly, a whoosh of wind sped me along faster.

"Thanks, Azrael," I whispered.

We arrived at 43rd and 11th Avenue as our orange-robed runner jumped over a wrought iron gate into the building's outside, dark trash area.

"Give me a couple of minutes. Don't come down. I mean it this time," ordered Matt. "Over here, Mister, I think this is her brother," a breathless voice said.

As the sweaty runner charged up the stairs, his flowing robe momentarily wrapped around my face. My hands tore at it. Then, face freed, he had disappeared like an illusion.

"Marion, I'm bringing Alan. I want you to sit on the steps with him while I bring the car," whispered Matt.

"Oh, God, Matt, has he been beaten? What?" I begged.

No answer.

What if Alan was visibly injured? I had nothing but a crumbling tissue for first aid. I wasn't ready for this new agony. Matt half-carried and half-dragged Alan, placing him gently on the stoop. I was shocked to see my brother's shaved head, but no visible bruises.

"Alan, Alibaba, it's me, your sister, Marion. You know, Toughie Maroono. Alan, can you hear me?" I whispered.

I cradled his head to my chest and rocked him. Sweet Azrael bundled us in one of his soft, multi-toned blue wings on those filthy steps in Hell's Kitchen.

As I cuddled Alan's rigid body in the police car's backseat, I began struggling to breathe. Then, I realized I was staring at myself from the vehicle's ceiling, the not-quite-sad Marion, not-quite-strong Marion, not quite Marion. I shook my head, and the image disappeared. Was insanity pulling me in, too? I yelled my out-of-body experience to Matt. He said I was in shock and to hang on. He had similar moments during his early detective days at gruesome crime scenes.

Matt told Russo over the car's radio, "I'm taking Alan to the hospital. There is no doubt it's Alan. So, yeah, call Mrs. Hoffman. Tell her Marion is safe with me."

I figured Matt was taking us to Bellevue Hospital. Instead, we arrived at an apartment building on East 76 Street. Matt jumped out. My antenna went straight to fear and mistrust. The car door opened on Alan's side. I held Alan harder and looked up with renewed fierceness. Matt and a male nurse with a name tag I couldn't make out reached for Alan. I screamed like never before and held on tighter. The nurse stepped back. Matt sat on the car door's floor edge. He explained that this was Gracie Square Hospital and that they would treat Alan better than Bellevue. They owed him a favor. We could bring him in together. Matt uncurled my hands from Alan, who was not reacting at all. I climbed over Alan, exiting the car on his side to ensure I was blocking him from everyone.

Gracie Square Hospital's admissions office didn't smell antiseptic. The lighting was not institutionally bright. I held Alan's hand with my right and scribbled the necessary information with my trusty left. A nurse steadied the forms. It was about 4 AM. I looked at Alan's face. Tears rolled down his gaunt cheeks. I believed he felt safe. I released him. Alan stood up and nodded to the male nurse. I beat down how Alan's nod reminded me of Uncle John. I kissed Alan's cheek, holding back the hysteria in my chest. Matt handed in the bag of clothing I left in the police car. I'm sure Matt drove me home and explained everything to Mom, but I can't remember. Nope, I cannot recall.

Alan's recognized journey into Paranoid Schizophrenia spiraled me into roles beyond sisterhood. I was his guardian while trying to be a kid. I was his close friend. Yet, I was a stranger during his bouts of abnormal behavior. I argued with ignorant neighbors who spoke against Alan while wanting to be peaceful. My stutter angered me as neighbors smirked at my attempts to defend and separate Alan from his disease. I reeled against Nancy and Roy for their cowardice. My sweet brother's disease left me no choice but to step out of my safety zone, my childhood.

Alan spent two healing months at Gracie Square Hospital. The hospital's hand-picked staff followed the Founding Family's (Zirinsky) core concept of focusing on each individual's needs. Every staff conference, every menu prepared, and every discussion was directed to one goal— the patient's peace of mind and recovery in the shortest time.

Their interdisciplinary team of psychiatrists, psychologists, nurses, social workers, nurse practitioners, internists, rehabilitation therapists, pastoral care workers, and volunteers flowed together like a gentle ripple on a lake.

I never found out what they owed Matt, but from then on, I owed Matt.

Mom brought Alan home on Christmas Eve. I sat silently with Alan on the edge of his new bed, my hand on his. Then, as though we were kids again, I dragged him to our Christmas tree and handed him the star. He stood on a chair and placed this symbol of new beginnings on our 7-foot Douglas Pine. Mom plugged in the tree's rows of blue lights. Then, in her pajamas, Marcie wandered out and reached for Alan's hand, making his months away disappear.

I grabbed my coat and sat on our back porch when everyone was in bed. I needed the wintry cold biting at my face to contemplate my future. Then, too tired, I rushed back in, telling myself I had time.

Alan thanked the police force by registering his name as a notable blood donor of his rare blood type. I thought that he had either AB-negative or AB-positive. I wondered if his blood type had a significant connection with Schizophrenia.

The following summer of 1964, the Harlem race riots, a six-day period of rioting that started on July 18, 1964, left one dead, 118 injured, and 465 arrested. At least, those were the statistics released.

During that week, our front doorbell rang before our alarm clocks. Alan was whisked from our home in a police car to Metropolitan Hospital in Harlem to donate his rare blood to a police officer with the same rare blood who had been stabbed multiple times. Mom slipped on a dress, grabbed her broom, and brushed our sidewalk slowly to proudly tell passing neighbors on their way to work about Alan's heroic act. I poured cereal for Marcie, explaining that Alan was our hero today. She was going to make a card for him. All I did was wait for his return.

Chapter 17

The Gynecologist and the Maiden

Traveling on a public bus with my Mom was tricky at best. She coaxed me into the window side of a two-seater. Even though the surrounding seats held the butts of fellow passengers, Mom acted as though we were in a private taxi. That bus ride had the potential to surpass all other embarrassing experiences in my brief history on earth because we were going to my first gynecological examination. I was 19 years old.

Hormones had been cutting a new facet into my body. I grasped dating boys and friendships with young men, but the concept of falling in love deluded me. Was I holding back love from boyfriends to avoid its painful side?

Roy had five children by then, but love did not live in his perfectly appointed home.

Cupid might have hung out at Nancy and Corny's upstate trailer, precariously hooked up next to the frequently flooded foundation of the dream home they had not completed. But I wasn't sure.

Sometimes, I tagged along with Alan, especially if he seemed despondent, to his appointments with Dr. Greenberg. I would chat with the doctor after Alan's sessions ended. His words thumped my chest but did not penetrate. He told me that loving was a brave act and warned me that pain was part of the process. He dared me to be fearless. He was becoming my father figure. I wanted to please him.

Mom interrupted my thoughts as her interrogation began.

"Marion, have you let a boy touch you there?" Mom asked.

My face, ears, and neck turned crimson. Spinning wildly through my brain was the debate of truth or consequence.

"No, Mom," I whispered.

That began a string of lies about my sex life to Mom. I was saving her worry and God knows what catastrophic caterwauling I was protecting myself from hearing for hours, days.

Mom babbled, "Dr. Pisano will know anyway, so no mind."

Whimpering, I nodded in agreement.

Then Mom continued, "Our parents didn't take us to a gynecologist. We didn't even know what that was. We just carried on. You're lucky."

The young man departing the bus was staring at me, chuckling. Oh, yeah, that was my lucky day.

We arrived at Dr. Pisano's office. He opened a glass-paneled door, loped toward us, and reached for Mom's hand. He held her hand between his two manly hands while kissing her cheek. On top of everything else, he was handsome enough to make me blush. Doc was making Mom giggle like a schoolgirl as they kibitzed at length.

"Hello, Marion. I'm Paul. Your Mom speaks proudly of you," he smoothly offered. "I b-b-b-b-b-bet," I responded in a whisper, pressing my arms to my sides to avoid shaking his hand with my profusely sweating hand.

Dr. Pisano noticed my nerves, placed his hand into the pocket of his white coat, and ushered me through the glass door. Pointing to the stirrups on the sides of the red pseudo-leather examining table, Dr. Pisano instructed me to hang my clothing on the back of the door and put on the gown. Once comfortable on the table, I was to relax and place my knees into the stirrups.

That was an oxymoron if I ever heard one. As Dr. P turned his back on me, I charged the table and missed it, landing on the floor. Dr. P scraped me off the floor and left the examination room.

I collapsed on the table in the paper gown. With each breath, the gown crackled loudly. I peeked at my shaking feet in the stirrups. A nurse took a couple of vials of blood without a word and walked out.

"Marion, are you okay?" asked Dr. Pisano, knocking on the door.

"Ye-e-e-s," I stammered.

Dr. P. rolled up to my bottom, snapping on rubber gloves. I was suddenly aware of his Old Spice cologne, adding to my embarrassment.

"I will ask you a few questions," said Dr. Pisano.

"Let's wait until the examination is over, and I'm sit-t-t-ting up," I pleaded.

"Sorry, no," Dr. P. firmly stated.

Beginning his inspection, he confirmed, "Your labia are nice and pink, healthy."

I was going to throw up.

"I have an important question before we begin the internal exam. Have you had intercourse?" queried Dr. Pisano, his arms crossed over his chest.

Here it was. The words bounced off the examination room: bounce, bounce, bounce.

"No, Dr. Pisano, I have not had sex yet," I uttered the most precise, concise sentence since 6 AM that morning.

Dr. P. arose and stared directly into my eyes. I stared back and refused to blink. The contest was over, and I won.

He conceded, "Then I can't examine you today."

I promptly sat up and swiftly raised my feet from the torture rack.

"One minute, Marion. You are in a hurry," he snorted. "Let's examine your breasts," Dr. P continued.

I laid back down, but at least my knees were locked together. I opened the stark white gown and closed my eyes.

Rubbing his hands together, he grumbled, "I'm warming my hands."

I winced. My breasts were small, so the exam should go quickly. Dr. P pushed hard in a circular motion and did not miss an inch. "I swim a lot," I prattled.

"Yes, I can see that," responded Dr. P.

Oh, no, why did I say that? Why did he respond?

Dr. Pisano jumped back as I gripped his coat. I've frightened the Gynecologist. Still clutching Doc's jacket, head bent, I tried to catch my breath.

Dr. Paul Pisano said, "Good thing I don't have this effect on all my patients."

He pried my fingers open and released his coat. Then, brushing himself off and walking away, he mumbled, "You are free to get dressed. I'll see you in my office."

Mom was elated in shoe stores, and her belief in my virginity had her spirits soaring. She caressed a white straw flat with a low-cut vamp. I picked out a pink flat. Mom added a pair of sneakers. Later, stretched out on my bed, pink flats on, I giggled without guilt that my lies had saved the day.

The following Sunday morning was overcast. I awoke to the familiar whiff of pancakes.

"Morning, Mom," I cheerfully said, kissing the back of her shoulder.

"Morning, you missed church. What time did you get in?" Mom asked.

Grabbing Mom, I responded, "Around 2," and danced with her in the kitchen.

"I danced. It was fun. We need more of that around here. Come on, I'll teach you the Hustle," I giggled and gently pulled her into the living room.

Mom was graceful on her feet. I danced her back to the stack of pancakes and coffee percolating. Then, the phone rang. I ran for it and momentarily stumbled as Azrael's earthy fragrance misted over me. I was hesitant to pick it up.

Mom shouted from the kitchen, "Answer it."

"Is Alan home?" I asked.

"Yes, he's exercising in the basement," said Mom. I answered the phone, "Hello, Hoffman House."

"I know who Dr. Pisano is, but why are you calling us on a Sunday?" I inquired.

I panicked that Dr. P had discovered something wrong with my bloodwork.

I said, "One minute, I'll get her."

Leaping back into the kitchen, I signaled Mom to pick up the phone, "It's Dr. Pisano's office."

Mom slumped into the kitchen chair about ten minutes later, staring at the table.

"Paul, my friend, confidant, and doctor of over 20 years, shot himself. They found him dead in his office," Mom said, and headed for our garden. I followed.

"Why are men so stupid?" Mom shouted as she snipped dead flowers.

Not responding to this rhetorical remark, I said, "Feels creepy that he committed suicide less than a week after seeing me."

Leaving Mom tending her flowerbeds, I tied my bathrobe tighter and wandered past the Holy Gate to our vegetable patch. I pulled weeds, squeezed off peppermint leaves, and tore mature Swiss chard leaves, not noticing my growing resemblance to my Mom's coping skills. Squinting at a passing cloud in the blue sky, I beckoned my best friend as Paul Pisano's death dug into my gut.

I whispered, "Azrael, when do you take a rest? Do you have a quota with God like traffic police with their Sergeants?"

I let this question ride and thanked the universe for my night of dancing.

Chapter 18

Pocatello Rides Again

I had just turned 20, and four years had passed since I spent time with my sister, Alice, in Pocatello. Her Multiple Sclerosis (MS) reached the Secondary progressive MS (SPMS) stage. At 37, Alice could no longer walk, her tremors were almost constant, and her ability to swallow had become difficult.

Eight months ago, Alice agreed to be a guinea pig for a brain operation called Thalamotomy. The surgeon drilled a hole through her skull, and a probe guided itself toward the thalamus. Once there, the surgeon injected liquid nitrogen, a freezing substance that destroys the targeted brain tissues. Alice awoke from the surgery legally blind and had no improvement in balance or tremors.

Mom's letters to Alice were returned unopened three months after the operation. I leaned my ear flush to the receiver as she called Alice's home telephone.

"Bill, where's my daughter? What have you done with her?" my mom asked without even a hello.

"I placed Alice in a nursing home. It became too much for me," a weeping Bill explained. "You asshole. Why didn't you call me? Our facilities here are far better than in Pocatello.

I could have helped pay for a private nurse to be with her. But you know that you scum," said Mom.

"And my grandchildren?" continued Mom. "They are with me," whimpered Bill.

"Give me the name and telephone number of the nursing home. Now," demanded Mom.

The next day, I called Roy and Nancy and said this trip with Mom was their turn. I reminded Roy that he and Alice had grown up together and that this might be his last chance to see her alive. I added that Mom needed his strength to try to reach his ego. Roy replied that he would pay the 10% tax so Mom and I could fly free, as he couldn't bear seeing Alice like that. I had misread his machismo for strength.

Nancy's excuse was her husband's diabetes. I pushed, saying this was an emergency.

Cornelius is not working, so he and Donna could stay with his Mom. Nancy refused.

My skull burst with anger toward my older, cowardly siblings. They never visited Alice.

They never saw her alive again. They didn't seem to care.

At 22 years old, Alan was an almost cheerful young man. He took his medicinal cocktail daily, kept his weekly appointments with Dr. Greenberg, and worked as an accountant. He immediately volunteered to care for our home.

I helped 12-year-old Marcie pack to stay with Montana.

"I don't mind Tana's 'cause she's teaching me how to knit," said lovable Marcie.

"I never learned, and my left-handed approach infuriated Tana," I laughingly shared. "You mean I can do something you can't?" Marcie asked with unabashed pride.

"Yep," I said, tickling her.

I assured Marcie she could call us day and night as I placed the hotel and nursing home telephone numbers in her suitcase. We would call her daily to say goodnight. Alan agreed to take Marcie for regular walks and dine with her at Tana's place.

It was an unusually chilly April day as we headed to the airport. We stopped at St. Barnabas Hospital in the Bronx to wish Uncle Henry good luck for volunteering for an experimental brain surgery method* for his early-onset Parkinson's Disease. Dr. Irving Cooper would use cryothalamectomy as a surgical technique to control tremors in patients with Parkinson's disease. Alice and Uncle Henry suffered from tremors and balance issues, so I wondered if Parkinson's disease had some correlation with Multiple Sclerosis.

What is it with this family and their unwavering belief in medical experiments? Too many Frankenstein movies or not enough?

"Henry, we'll be back the day before your surgery," said Mom as she kissed his forehead.

---

* Irving S. Cooper (1922–1985) pioneered functional neurosurgery. While at New York University, Cooper developed a chemopallidectomy. Later, at St. Barnabas Hospital in the Bronx (1954–1977), he used cryothalamectomy as a surgical technique to control tremors in patients with Parkinson's disease primarily.

On our way to the airport, Mom dove into the lighter side of how her brothers kept partially blind Uncle Henry employed in Uncle Bill's limousine service with a legitimate Chauffeur's License. When the driver's road test began in 1925, one of my uncles supposedly took the road test under Henry's name. I believe he surrendered his license in the 50s and started working at St. Barnabus Hospital as an orderly. It was not a story of heroism, although the way Mom spun it, it had that lilt.

The jet plane could not fly fast enough for Mom. Huddled in the window seat next to her on this flight to trouble, I feared Mom's anger and frustration would not end well in Pocatello. I stared at the clouds beside our plane, thinking of Dad. It had been fourteen years since his death. Only Azrael knew I held hope for a sign from Dad. I had learned his cancer was Colorectal, and the cut on his chin did not cause his death, but my heart wanted more.

Settling into our red rental car, I inquired, "Where to first, Ma?"

"Alice," said Mom.

Mom appeared fragile. This was new emotional territory for me. My joking would not work here. We sped down the highway directly to the Pocatello Nursing Home. We pulled into the dirt patch next to a one-story, flat-roofed, putty-colored building. The sand hadn't settled before we alighted from the car. We wiped each other off.

Mom asked, "How do I look?"

There was that nerve-wracking phrase Mom had uttered outside Harlem Valley State Hospital when I first

143

visited Uncle John. It meant I was to ensure this visit was accomplished according to Mom's dearest wishes.

"Beautiful and strong, of course," I lied.

As I held one of the smudged double glass doors open for Mom, I noted no antiseptic smell. We arrived at the Nurses' Station without a nurse. Mom grabbed the opportunity to peek at the room register. The blue cover had sticky fingerprints. The hand-written entries were sloppily input with various colors of pen and some even pencil. A nurse appeared. She pointed down the hall and informed us that Mr. Pack had deposited his seven-year-old son, Billy, to take his turn with Alice.

Stopping short in the doorway of Alice's dimly lit room, I saw tubes in my sister's arm.

Next, I saw Billy sitting in a metal chair beside her with a cigarette in his mouth. He struck a match, lit the cigarette, and brought it to Alice's mouth. He did not acknowledge us.

Then, the sweet smell of fresh soil overcame the cigarette odor. Slowly, as though growing from a seed, Azrael's magnificent figure arose at the end of Alice's bed, his pale blue feathers hovering over Billy. I stared at my best friend, thankful for his compassion.

"Hello, Billy. I'm your grandmother," whispered Mom, her hands shaking as she touched her grandson for the first time. Alice had visited us in New York once when Chuck was a toddler, but her illness never allowed her to bring Billy.

"Aunt Marion will take you for a walk and a bite to eat," Mom continued.

While Billy sipped a cola, I inquired about school and if he had friendly teachers. He did not answer. When he finished his drink, he asked to return to his Alice. So, I piggybacked him to his Mother. His little body did not soften to mine.

We heard Alice laughing as Mom helped strip and bathe her daughter with two nurses she had ushered in. Mom was up to her old tricks.

"Marion, grab the red suitcase from the car," Mom instructed.

My sister was soon dressed in a flowing floral gown with a newly crocheted afghan lying across her legs. We sang Happy Birthday to Alice. I knew April was her month, but not the date. Finally, the nurses departed, kissing Mom for their New York souvenirs and envelopes that I suspected contained money. Worn out, we walked to the Nurses' Station.

"I expect my daughter to be bathed and changed daily," instructed Mom, handing an envelope to the Desk Nurse. Then, Mom tiredly inquired how her seven-year-old grandson could be alone here and lighting cigarettes. We were informed they were short-staffed and would try to do better for Alice.

"My grandson insists he wants to stay. But please confiscate the cigarettes," Mom bawled. I entwined my arm in hers and tucked her into the car.

Parked in a Dairy Queen Drive-through, "Where to now, oh wise one?" I asked, trying to lighten the stress.

"To that bastard's house. He thinks I don't know where he lives, but I do. Dr. Eisner had his lawyer search," said Mom.

"Let's call first," I timidly suggested.

"To hell with that. Let's look at the map," Mom insisted.

Staring at the map, turning it now and then, I admitted, "I have no idea where we are or where we are going, Mom."

We took off using the waitress's directions and eventually pulled into an unmarked driveway, assuming it was Bill's.

"Mom, slow down," I ventured uselessly as she rushed ahead.

Mom rang the doorbell. The partial face of a blonde woman peeked at us through a slit in the too-short beige curtain of the large window. Bill opened the door, surprised as hell. Pushing past him, Mom screamed, "You bastard!" He followed at her heels. So now I was frightened for Mom and followed him. Grabbing the rocking chair, Mom carried it out the door we entered, smashing it repeatedly on the ground until it resembled firewood.

"Feel better, Ma?" I asked.

Crying and laughing, we hit the road.

Over the following week, we spent every waking moment with Alice. My sick sister was wildly cheered by Mom's gossip, continuous feeding, and scolding her about smoking.

Bill had refused Mom's requests to take Chuck and Billy to dinner. I spoke to Bill and asked him not to punish Mom because of her warranted outburst. He denied this accusation and said our timing was off, as the boys were busy.

One morning, we finally met Chuck, almost nine, in Alice's room. I recognized his plaid shirt and corduroy jeans from Mom. He scrutinized us.

"Is what Dad says true that you want to take Alice away?" asked Chuck.

Mom explained that his mother would get better care in New York. When school ends in June, he could visit and stay with us. Chuck stood up and spat at Mom. Wiping her chest with her embroidered handkerchief, she softly said she was glad he loved Alice. I asked if he'd like to take a walk with me. He stormed out of the room. With tears running down her cheeks, Alice whispered that she would discuss the possibility of New York with Bill, as she agreed it would be superior care.

On our last evening, Mom surprised us by sharing a cigarette with Alice, making us laugh as she puffed and coughed. Alice barely acknowledged me. This hurt me, but its explanation could wait. Then, we three women cried together. Would this be the last time Mom saw her eldest daughter alive?

As we left Alice, a nurse stopped us.

"Flo, I want to show you something," said Nurse Number One.

Two more aides joined us as Nurse Two opened a door and flicked on the light.

"Look at this," squealed Nurse Two with laughter.

A human with an adult's head and a toddler's body was lying in a crib. Startled awake, his doe eyes blinked at us as he bellowed an odd screech.

"Stop. Why are you disturbing this poor man?" I implored.

Giggling, ignoring my plea, Nurse One pulled down his diaper to show his adult penis.

The women laughed loudly.

"Get out," seethed Mom.

Pulling up the cloth and stroking this human's face, "Shh, it's okay." Mom whispered as she shoved me out the door and turned off the light. Mom rushed to the nurses' station with me scurrying behind her in a mix of fear of her next move, sobbing for the human, and holding down my Dairy Queen chocolate shake. Changing direction, Mom and I exited the building. I held Mom's trembling shoulders and helped her into the car. Her L'Air du Temps perfume wafted up to me, out of sync with this horrifying moment. I ran to a hedge and barfed and sobbed. One of Azrael's firm wings pressed against my forehead.

I challenged him, "Here's your chance to take a pained soul. Come on."

Azrael spoke to me for only the second time since we met 14 years ago. Again, his words echoed through the sky, not as a single voice. He reminded me that God instructs him when to remove a soul.

"Maybe God makes mistakes," I whispered.

Azrael tapped my head and faded. Sliding into the driver's seat, I asked, "Mom, how fast have you ever been driven?"

"Sixty miles an hour, probably," answered Mom.

"Shall we floor it?" I ventured as I took the wheel.

"Yes," said Mom with the first sparkle in her eyes this trip. Then, pressing against the steering wheel to steady the rocking car, we hit 110 mph.

CHAPTER 18: POCATELLO RIDES AGAIN

We headed to the Sheriff's Office on our way to the airport the following day. This woman, whom I was honored to call Mom, showed her enormous capacity for love. I watched her report the agonizing man/boy incident at the Nursing Home. Unfortunately, the deputy's sneer gave us little hope that they would investigate.

Chapter 19

Circle of Death

We arrived home on a Wednesday. Sharing this painful passage with Mom and participating in saving Alan left me little time to discover myself. Articles in the magazine Cosmopolitan led me to believe that by 21, I should be exiting college and establishing a career of some sort.

The next day, I signed up with an agency offering temporary administrative jobs in the Manhattan Garment District. I believed being close to design might satisfy my love of the arts. I arrived on the fifth floor of a run-down building on 38th Street off Avenue of the Americas on Monday, 9 AM sharp. Azrael had decided to escort me.

"I'm Mrs. Goldberg. This is your desk," glumly stated a chubby woman with hair the color of a carrot. A loud belch flew out of Mrs. Goldberg without an apology.

"Here are your instructions. We'll review in a few minutes," Mrs. Goldberg mumbled. Upon returning, standing in front of my creaky desk, she asked, "So, any questions?"

"No, Mrs. G., I answer the phones with Goldberg's Dresses and write down their requests. All good," I responded.

The phone rang, and I grabbed it.

"Goldberg's Dresses, good day," I said, smiling at Ms. Carrot Top.

My friend, Azrael, flittered around the derelict room. Uh-oh was all I could think of before Mrs. Goldberg started shaking. Her eyes rolled into her head, and she collapsed on the floor, her body spinning.

"I need to hang up now, sir. No, I can't take your order right now. Please call back," I said into the telephone receiver.

Panicking, I pulled open the frosted glass office door and screamed down the hallway.

Then, leaving the door open, I was back on the phone, asking the operator for the new emergency number. Finally, the folks across the hall arrived, saying a rescue crew was coming. Once Mrs. Goldberg was removed, I grabbed my purse, locked the door, and dropped the keys through the door's mail slot.

I headed for the Fifth Avenue Library, a few blocks away. I remembered Mom holding Alan and my hands as we maneuvered up the library steps during a snowstorm. I had witnessed Alan's wild energy among the masses of books. He had pulled me to the Librarian, asking for books about the ocean. His excitement was a first.

I entered the majestic Main Reading Room with 52-foot-tall ceilings displaying murals of vibrant skies and billowing clouds. I was in awe and was sure this space would give me answers. Sitting at a long polished table with a scattering of literature, the librarian said, may contain information about Archangel Azrael. The 1903 Jewish Encyclopedia, articles about Kabbalistic and Quran literature. I learned that God once ordered the archangels to collect dust from Earth so that Adam could be created, and only Azrael was brave enough to do so. As a result, he was destined to become the angel of life and death. He held the book of all lives on Earth. I wasn't sure if that meant only human lives, as I had witnessed emotions and souls in the eyes of pets and wildlife. It continued with information that, although beautiful, I had already learned. I must return and dig deeper.

That night, I vowed to discover if my repeated proximity to death was my life's lesson. I cradled the brief, profound words of the Pastor, the Rabbi, and my high school Chemistry teacher. Three scholarly men who never met.

I heard Mom's cheerful announcement, "Up and at 'em, honey."

I was off to the Blumette Bra Company in Manhattan's Upper East Side. After three months of packing the Blumette bra and reassuring Mrs. T. of her beauty, I gained her trust to fetch her standard brown poodle, Blu, from the groomer. Blu bit my knees at every street crossing on our return to the office.

"Mrs. T, do you have a first aid kit because Blu used my knees as a chew toy?" I asked, showing my bleeding knees beneath my miniskirt.

"My baby didn't mean it," said Mrs. T., cuddling the dog.

"I'm sure you won't mind picking him up from now on," said Mrs. T.

On the next trip from the groomers, I wore Alan's knee braces from his track and field practice, which I rubbed with garlic. Blu whimpered. I gave him an extra treat at the office.

The Blumette design featured a pair of bra cups a woman could affix to her breasts with an adhesive that causes neither pain nor sticky residue when removed, so the package ad states. My phone answering time was spent 80% listening to women rant and cry about the rashes left behind when the Blumette was removed.

Of course, I tried it at home, and removing it was agony. Mom, laughing her head off, helped me swipe around the cup with witch hazel, nail polish remover, and olive oil.

Mrs. T left me in charge of the office for a two-week vacation. When she returned from her holiday in Florida, she announced she was moving to Miami. C'est la vie.

That August, five months after we visited Alice, death took my sister while the court battles raged between Bill Pack and Mom, delaying her return to New York.

I wept as Mom announced Alice's death. Was I faking my sorrow? After all, crying was how most humans reacted to sadness. I thought Alice was in a better place, maybe with Dad.

Then, relief of duty to one less family member sank into my heart. Was I wicked to feel this? I decided not to debate this and get on with prayers. I repressed worry about Alice's sons as the boys' father, Bill, and his mistress were with them. Again, extended prayers. Was this the easy way out?

Mom called Roy and Nancy with this news. The short telephone conversations let me know Mom didn't listen to their false words of sadness or attempts to console her. However, her discussion with Montana was sorrowfully long. I left the room.

Mom did not go to this faraway funeral. Instead, her goodbyes were said earlier, during telephone calls and nightly prayers.

But we attended Uncle Henry Morse's funeral ten days after Alice's death.

Henry, like Alice, was never the same after the experimental brain operation at St. Barnabas Hospital. His headaches were severe and relatively constant. However, the hospital allowed him to do light duty, as he liked being useful. His weekends in our home were the highlight of his life for many years, and they continued uninterrupted. No matter what tendencies he may or may not have had, my Uncle Henry remained an untarnished, gentle soul to me.

"Mom, you think Uncle Henry volunteered to make amends for his supposed tendencies?" I asked.

"How did you know?" asked Mom.

"Your million instructions to never sit on his lap," I said.

Mom sighed and kissed my cheek.

I asked Dr. Greenberg about Pedophilia as I felt it was a way to send Henry to rest in peace. There were misconceptions that pedophilia is the same as child molestation. One can live with pedophilia and not act on it. It is not that these individuals are "inactive" or "nonpracticing" pedophiles, but rather that pedophilia is a status and not an act. Research shows that about half of all child molesters are not sexually attracted to their victims. A second misconception is that pedophilia is a choice. Research, while often limited to sex offenders — because of the stigma of pedophilia — suggests that the disorder may have neurological origins.

"Possibly, Marion. I don't know anymore," answered a weary Mom.

On a sunny morning, two days later, Mom and I headed to the local funeral home to choose a casket for Uncle Henry. Mom, overwhelmed with the loss of Alice and her brother, sat motionless as the mortician babbled about the choice of caskets. I signaled the funeral director to show me the coffins. They say there is always a first time.

Azrael chose the casket. Yes, this is true. As I meandered from one coffin to another, noting a satin pillow here and a walnut finish there, I kept Uncle Henry's art background in mind. Suddenly, my shoulders lifted as I was planted before a shiny black lacquered coffin lined with ivory satin.

"Mom, this is it. Uncle Henry wants to be sent off remembering his good old days as a driver for the Mob in his black limousine," I declared.

Towards the end of Uncle Henry's funeral service, I removed my copper brooch, trusting Wyatt was in heaven and understood. Then, I stood over Uncle Henry's casket and pinned the brooch onto Henry's suit lapel, laying my dreams of becoming an artist with him.

Chapter 20

Suicide Attempt Score 2, Love's Detour Score 1

A year passed, and I was dating Joseph T. Bastone. We had met at a local party. Our attraction was undeniable. He drove me home, and we leaned in for a kiss. As I felt his breath, he turned away with a gentle smile. This intrigued me, and our dating began. Joey was a gentle gentleman. He opened doors for me, treated Mom respectfully, and was generous.

Last summer, he asked Mom for my hand in marriage, showing her a diamond engagement ring. Her reaction was lukewarm, tentative. I understood. At almost 21, I was uncomfortable speaking about my love for Joey with Mom and Alan, now 23. We three lived so intimately entwined that I believed I would betray this union. I wore the sweet engagement ring when I went out with Joey, and I removed it at home.

Thanksgiving was two days away, and I got that this holiday was marred early on by Mom's stories of what settlers did to their saviors, the Native Americans. Alan's first suicide attempt at thirteen years old was right up there in the Holy Shit; let's skip this holiday once and for all. But instead, Mom sang, "I am a cockeyed optimist…," as she wildly chopped celery for her delicate stuffing.

I darted out to spend the evening with Joey as we continued celebrating holidays separately to maintain peace within our family circles.

I pecked Mom's forehead, "Wake me at dawn for our Thanksgiving charge. Yeah, I noticed the ironed apron on my dresser," I giggled.

Mom reminded me, "Nancy and Corny are coming with the girls."

"Can't wait," I mumbled.

Interestingly, Nancy and Roy rarely visited, expressing fear of Alan. In other words, they were cowards. Oh, yes, that is the only answer I know to be true.

Arriving home around midnight, I pulled up my pink blinds and gazed at the night sky laden with stars. Then, sighing, my body sank into the soft bed.

I jumped from my bed and started running before my eyes opened as Mom's screams echoed, "Marion!"

The kitchen clock's luminous arrows showed 3 AM as I charged through it.

This time, I switched on the light in Alan's room. He was face down on the floor, apparently unconscious. Masses of blood were splattered on the blue walls. Mom knelt over Alan, and her turquoise nightgown began to turn red as it absorbed Alan's fresh blood.

In dazed horror, I called 911 and moved Mom to the living room. Then, as I heard Marcie stir, I swiftly wrapped Mom in a robe to hide the blood-stained gown.

"Marcie, Alan slipped, but he'll be okay. Go back to sleep. We have a busy day tomorrow," I reassured.

Rushing back to Alan, I noticed that blood was no longer streaming from his arms. I held my Alibaba, waiting for the ambulance, whispering nonsense, "I know Mom's cooking isn't the best, but really."

I looked around while rocking him, believing it would ground me. I noticed his sheets and blankets were untouched by his ferocious efforts. An indent remained on the edge of his bed from his probable upright body. Directly across was the darkest, hardened blood, sticking to his desktop. I imagined the gush from Alan's first slice into his arm. The oceanography books on his night table were dripping with the freshest flow of life. An empty glass lay on its side with bloodied fingerprints.

Maybe I was in a nightmare caused by Thanksgiving Eve jitters. No, my brother's cold, clammy body was bundled in my arms, and the weight of Azrael made me know this was my reality.

Mom dressed and hopped into the ambulance with Alan. Sadly, one of the EMS guys knew us.

Closing Alan's bedroom door, I collapsed on the couch. I envisioned cutting his room away like cancer. Alan's suicide attempts were killing me.

I forced happy images of Alan into my head: Alan and I watching American Bandstand on TV and practicing the Lindy and the Cha-cha, fetching his shotput, listening to the radio program, Inner Sanctum with the lights turned off and flashlights in our hands scaring each other; attending his Little League baseball games and screaming for him when at bat. Alan was a serious boy. But, on rare occasions, if he found something funny, his eyes shaped into crescent moons, tears rolled down his strong face, and his laugh was hearty.

A knock on the back door startled me. "Tana, who called you?" I said.

"Let's clean Alan's room," Tana said with enthusiasm.

"No," I said, stumbling back to the couch.

Tana grabbed a large white metal basin under our kitchen sink and headed for Alan's room. She left the bedroom door open so she could prattle.

Picking up blobs of coagulated blood, Tana said, "Look, it's like strawberry jam. Don't think of it as blood," going back and forth past me to the kitchen as the stench of the blood wafted up at me.

"He lined up 12 glasses of water. He meant it this time, Marion. I must get back to waking my boarder for work. Call me when you have news," said Tana nonchalantly.

I felt my nostrils flare like a bull's facing a matador. My breathing was significant, as though my lungs were about to crack open my chest. I rushed to our screen door to stop Tana in her deranged rush to ignite the neighborhood gossip trail.

I said, "Don't step foot in this house if I am in it. Do you want to know the truth about the beautiful clothing you sewed for me as a child? I used to look underneath for bugs or something that might hurt or kill me. You've hated me since before I was born."

Turning ashen white, Tana left.

Still shaking, I chose to sit in Dad's old Queen Anne chair. The sun's edge filtered through the dark as the living

159

room became soft gold. I would not cook. I refused to pretend the Hoffman home was okay.

What if I could trade places with my best friend, Azrael, even for a moment? I whispered my offer into the air, trying to summon him. I wanted to see the world through his unique eyes. I already thought he was misunderstood. Would this exchange damage the universe? What if we couldn't switch back? Of course, my insolence didn't work. Slapping the chair's arms, I stopped my twisted direction.

Marcie passed me on her sleepy way to the bathroom. Then she sat on my lap.

"Happy Thanksgiving," I whispered.

"We're going to have Chinese takeout for dinner with tons of fortune cookies," I added.

Marcie grabbed a throw from the couch and fell asleep on me.

We jumped awake around 9 AM as the phone rang. I stared at the green monster, the bearer of drama. I picked up, interrupted Mom with can't talk right now and hung up. I liked and loathed that I was making her worry about us.

"Marcie, turn on the television. The Thanksgiving Parade will be starting," I suggested.

I picked up the phone and called my absentee siblings. I robotically and curtly canceled Thanksgiving and said Mom would explain later.

The phone rang again. This time, I grabbed it.

"Marion, the doctors say Alan is stabilized. He can come home in a few days," declared Mom.

"Of course, we would have to take turns watching over him," whispered Mom.

"R-really. Let's install a glass door to his bedroom with a chair in the hallway," I stammered, pain and fury rising from my gut. I was fighting for my life for the first time. This battle was between me and the two people I loved the most. What would I gain? Stop. You would gain time. Time to dream about your future and take steps to attain your goals. Actions I hadn't contemplated. How could I fit them into this tightly wound nucleus?

Mom sheepishly continued pulling at my heartstrings, "The policeman with the same rare blood that Alan's transfusion saved five years ago arrived minutes after us. Remember him?"

I hesitated to respond. Finally, I whispered, "Yes, Mom. We'll have to thank him. So glad."

Now, Mom had me engaged. My heart sank. Desperately, I fought to regain the courage to save myself.

She resumed, "Alan was unconscious on one stretcher with the policeman on the stretcher next to him."

"Tell me when you get home, Ma," I whispered.

"No. Please let me finish. Roy showed up towards the end of the transfusion and punched our unconscious Alan. The guards grabbed Roy by the back of his collar and led him out of the hospital," Mom finished.

"I declined to press charges. But they told Roy to go home," offered Mom. "You and Tana are the only ones who listen," said Mom.

Struggling to avoid being categorized with Tana, I asked, "How many pints of blood was our savior, the policeman, able to donate?"

Mom said, "Almost two."

"Good, Ma," I whispered.

Silence ensued except for coins dropping into the telephone box.

"I can't handle this. Alan needs to stay in the hospital and heal. Please don't delude yourself. I called the hospital. I know he nearly died," I said through grit teeth as rage grew in my gut.

"I know we don't know what we are doing with him," I screamed, hands shaking.

Mom had hung up on me.

Around 4 PM, Mom arrived home and gave me a small brown paper bag. Feeling guilty about wanting Alan to stay in the hospital, I opened the gift. It was a little book titled *In This World Full of People... I'm Glad I Found You.* Inside its cover were Mom's handwritten words: "To My Marion, Always there in times of trouble. Love, Mother."

I placed fresh cups of coffee on the kitchen table and fired up the percolator. The coffee's caramel-like fragrance was soothing. I stared at Mom's face as she sipped her coffee. The last rays of sunlight streaked through the kitchen window, making her heavy-lidded hazel eyes Lioness gold. I've seen her large hands holding the delicate porcelain cup a million times, but I wanted to rub warm oil into their deep lines and brown spots today. She deserved that much. We hadn't shared a silent interlude like this since I was six and asked about angels.

I made Marcie a second helping of Chinese food and a pile of fortune cookies and brought them to her on the couch to watch TV.

Huddled at the kitchen table, the rooster's sconce cast a dim light on us. Over our warmed-up Chinese noodles, we discussed a plan of action and how we would divide visits to Alan. After the school bus picked up Marcie, Montana would drive Mom to visit him. I would see Alan on weekday evenings and weekends. Mom knew Saturday nights at psychiatric hospitals were short-staffed.

Our plan was temporarily blown apart when we were informed that visitors were prohibited for at least two weeks. Those two weeks were unbearable for us. I went to Jacobi Psychiatric Hospital several times, asking if I could glimpse my Alan. After all, our knowledge of Harlem Valley State Hospital did not give us hope for kind care. Words were barely spoken at home during that two-week interlude. We survived.

My maturity and the realization that we were alone without help from my older siblings strengthened our Mother-Daughter bond.

Alone in the dark of my bedroom most nights, exhausted from the nearness of death, I peeled my smile from my face and laid it in my dish, which had bluebirds painted on the four corners. I prayed to God and the Archangels to refresh my smile's burden.

Chapter 21

Survival

Mom put on a brave front, but I witnessed her crying during household chores. I became sensitive and stopped surprising her so she could wipe her tears before turning to greet me.

I continued my job as Mom's warrior by performing the best comic routines I could concoct. I was almost ready for my Saturday night date. "Mom, do you like this perfume?" I asked. "You smell like a French whore," teased Mom.

Then, I waltzed from our bathroom and glimpsed Mom in her rocking chair, sluggishly knitting. Spinning in my short, fuchsia mod dress, I asked, "Mom, what do you think?"

"Short," Mom answered, glancing over her eyeglasses. We laughed.

"What am I bringing Alan tonight?" I asked.

Mom's hands dropped into her lap. Silence choked our laughter. She was pulling herself together to speak without crying. I visualized vertical furrows down her cheeks like the narrow irrigation tunnels we dug along our vegetable garden each spring.

"The brown bag on the table. Careful, there's a cake in there and Alan's clothes," replied Mom.

Joey arrived at our back door. We snatched a kiss before leading him to Mom.

"Hi, Mrs. H. How are you tonight?" Joey cheerfully asked. "Okay, young man. How about you?" Mom replied.

"Let's set up the TV for you," he said, tweaking our old set.

As in the past two months, my Saturday night dates began with my visiting Alan in Jacobi Psychiatric Hospital. Joey patiently sat in his car without complaint.

Waiting for the familiar clang of the psychiatric ward's metal door, I recalled how my attempt to add cheer with my flower bouquets caused havoc at Harlem Valley State Hospital and caused Harry, the kind orderly, to be reprimanded. I thought the chaos was joyful as I saw patients wake up. Some inhaled the flower's scent; one counted the petals, and one put a rose into his shirt's buttonhole. Others petted them. A security guard roughly confiscated all when one ate a bright yellow daisy. The patient's distress tore me apart. I circled the tables, apologizing, but their angry faces shut me out.

I entered Jacobi's stale-smelling communal visitors' room, spotted my brother, and rushed to him.

"Hi, Alan," I said.

His lack of response was chilling. I repeated my greeting. I tilted his chin toward me and saw his distant gaze. Cupping his hand in mine, I felt his cold, clammy skin. I searched for an orderly.

"Where is the doctor?" I asked.

The bored orderly explained that Alan had been in this catatonic state all day, so he was cold.

"Thanks. The doctor, please," I repeated.

"Alan, you'll feel warmer in a few minutes," I hinted, pulling his thick, navy-blue sweater over his head. Feeding Alan chocolate cake made me feel better.

"I'm taking you home on Tuesday, only three days away. We'll see Dr. Greenberg in Brooklyn. He is our friend and the best at creating a custom-made medicinal cocktail for you." I reminded Alan.

Alan continued to stare. We held hands for another hour, and I mumbled news and an old episode of Sea Hunt. Brushing his short hair and kissing his cheek did not affect his stance, but his hands were warmer. The ward doctor never showed. I started to clean up the table, ready to leave.

Alan squeezed my hand, mumbling, "Sing with me."

Alan started singing *Knocking on Heaven's Door* by Bob Dylan.

I joined in, *"Mama, take this badge from me*
I can't use it anymore
It's getting dark; too dark to see
Feels like I'm knockin' on heaven's door
Knock-knock-knockin' on heaven's door.

Two other patients drummed their tables, staring at us. Alan released my hand.

"Remember Tuesday, not even th-th-ree days," I whispered.

That first step outside the hospital was traumatic for me. My desire to remain in the hospital and be with Alan never subsided. I exited by the side door, as the revolving one might allow me to steer back in. The first sniff of fresh air gave me guilt, not freedom. The fact that I did not possess the same blood type as Alan, rendering me unable to store transfusions for him, deepened my guilt. Walking was my savior. I chose to take long, determined steps. Joey's car was in the distance.

I whispered to Azrael, "Thank you for sparing Alan."

Joey jumped out of the car. "Princess, who were you talking to just now?"

"Myself. Let's go dancing," I coaxed.

I couldn't fault Joey for not understanding the intensity of my life. He was carefree. He worked in his father's small printing business. He had two younger brothers and neighborhood friends. Joey joined the Navy to avoid the draft. His high scores on naval tests and his vast knowledge of cameras that his sweet uncle imparted gave Joey the option of an intense photography course. He chose to squander this opportunity because he was homesick. I became argumentative with him.

One's first love needs to be encouraged. It was torn apart by families and our emotional inability to cope. I tested his love with arguments and flirtations, creating unceasing pain for us. We broke up. I returned the ring. Scheming how to get him back frequently skimmed my heart. Believing this act would be selfish, I shut it down. I suspected I would never forget his eyes, our caresses.

Alan's February homecoming was low-key. Dr. Greenberg said no fanfare was recommended. We were to resume life as usual. Alan awkwardly apologized for his behavior. Mom embraced him. I hugged him, but did not feel his body. I hugged him tighter. Nothing. I looked into his eyes. His sad eyes helped me connect. Our third hug was solid. I found no need to question this odd circumstance as I was learning to love my brother in a new way.

My 21st Birthday arrived. I dug into a Mom-made chocolate cake with Alan and Marcie. Marcie had been part of our family for eight years.

Opening a velvet jewelry box, I gasped, "This is incredible."

I slipped on a thick, gold bangle bracelet, aware of Mom's financial sacrifice.

Mom closed the clasp and murmured, "I've put a spell on it."

Chapter 22

Not My Mom

In late March, I found a job in the advertising department of a chemical company to release my creativity and get paid. I also attended jazz dance classes two nights a week. This combo was like living in a parallel universe to my home life.

Four months later, I sat across from Ed Reilly, Advertising Director, fiddling with Mom's gold bracelet. Ed harshly critiqued my illustration boards because he said I had talent. His phone rang.

"Hello, Mrs. Hoffman. Marion's right here," Ed gruffly offered.

A call from Mom at my job was rare.

"Hi, Mom," I chirped.

Mom whispered, "Marion, please come home."

"Is it Alan?" I asked.

"No, honey, I'm sick."

The sweltering subway ride home, with loud overhead fans blowing hot, filthy air, made the journey longer. I rushed through our new storm door at 3 PM. Mom replaced our wonky, warped screen door with a sturdy storm door. It had upper and lower glass windows, which Mom playfully slid open to expose the shiny screens. She hoped this new door would give fresher, happier memories to our home.

I found Alan pacing in the living room. Marcie was sitting on Mom's bed, squeezing her hand. Mom was pouring sweat and shaking.

Turning on the air conditioner in Mom's room, I instructed Marcie to get the thermometer from the medicine cabinet so we could take Mom's temperature, as she takes ours when we are ill.

Mom complained, "Turn that thing off. I can't stand the noise."

"I love it when you complain," I said, turning it off.

"Alan, grab the ice bag from the fridge and wrap it in a towel," I continued. Mom's temperature was 102. She accepted the ice pack.

"Marion, look at my toe," whispered Mom.

Gently pulling the blanket from her feet, I saw that her left big toe was red and swollen, the flesh wrapping the sides of the nail.

"Let's call Dr. B," I said.

Mom agreed.

An hour later, Dr. Balducci arrived and went directly into Mom's bedroom.

Alan took Marcie to our local pizza shop. I sat in Mom's rocker, staring at her knitting basket of fine, sand-colored wool in a pearl stitch. My world felt out of control as my body stiffened with fear. I was not as strong as I acted.

After 20 minutes, Dr. B hurriedly addressed me, "Help your Mom get dressed. I'm taking Flo with me to Westchester Square Hospital."

"Her toe is that serious?" I asked, jamming my nails into my palms.

Mom's demi-god, Dr. B, cleared his throat and stated, "I think your Mom has had a heart attack."

Kissing Mom, struggling not to cry, I placed her into the passenger's side of Doc's car. "I'll see you in the hospital later," I whispered.

All I wanted to do was go to the hospital, but instead, I grabbed that horrid green telephone and called Nancy and Roy. Nancy disgusted me, saying Mom was 65, and this sort of thing was expected. Roy coughed, hiding emotions, and mumbled that he would try to change his flight schedule. Then, I buckled down to phone Tana. We hadn't spoken since my outburst.

"Tana, Dr. B. has taken Mom to the hospital," I hesitated but knew she deserved to understand, "Mom might have had a heart attack."

Had the spoken words made it true?

"Tana, I know," I said. "Yes, we need your help."

"I want to keep Marcie in school and Alan maintaining his trice/week therapy sessions while I work," I continued in a business-like daze.

My demeanor softened. I was talking with the woman who had stood by Mom for over 30 years.

"Tana, I'm sorry. Here's Dr. B's telephone number. I'll call the hospital to ensure your name is on Mom's visitor list. What? Yeah, you old crank, I am growing up. Good night," I gently ended the conversation.

Montana, Alan, and I ran the situation beautifully for a week. Marcie wanted to visit Mom, but the hospital would not allow it because she was under 16. So, I took her notes to Mom and faithfully placed Mom's return messages next to Marcie's breakfast dish.

On day ten of Mom's stay in the hospital, I arrived determined to uncover details of Mom's condition.

"Hey, pinch any doctors today?" I cheerfully asked, placing flowers from her garden in a nearby vase.

"No, but I'd like to punch a couple of nurses," Mom responded.

"Stop fussing with the flowers and come talk," demanded Mom.

I pulled up a chair and grabbed her hand.

"Dish the dirt. Is Tana giving you a hard time? How is home? Molly out for walks?"

Mom shot questions as fast as bullets.

I answered, "I pick up dinners from Tana as I pet the dogs and rush out. Our home is still standing, Alan seems well, and Marcie is worried but helpful. Alan treasures Molly. My turn, Ma; your progress?"

Silence filled the room.

Mom reluctantly replied, "Apparently, I have latent Diabetes that had gone unchecked.

We are sorting it out. Don't run off and scream at Dr. B."

"Sure. Glad Doc saved your toe, although your foot looks gruesome," I ribbed as I peeked at her infected toe, now with a drain hanging out of it.

Chuckling and sparring, an hour passed.

"See you tonight," I said, dashing out.

A few floors down, I was directed to a large office with a massive, dark wood executive desk. Behind it, I saw Dr. B. in a black leather chair. The demigod remained head down, staring at his hospital notes.

"Why did you not evaluate my Mother for Diabetes even though she is overweight?" I asked the obvious, not expecting an answer but wanting him to know I knew.

"I have no time to discuss obscure medical facts with you. We are getting everything under control. Flo should be able to go home in a couple of weeks," the doctor said.

I was dismissed.

After visiting Mom twice daily and residing at our house for the next two months, not two weeks, Ed Reilly fired me. This bomb exploded my fragile, hidden self, the artist no one knew. I no longer had the office and dance class as my safety net.

As I left the hospital on a warm September Sunday, I decided to stop at our First Presbyterian Church to surprise Marcie. The pastor told me Marcie didn't show.

I hurried home. Alan was sitting in Dad's worn Queen Anne chair. I saw his hand, veins popping from gripping the chair's arms. I sat down on the couch near him.

"They took Marcie," said Alan.

I felt rage tearing through him, so I did not touch his hand.

Alan shared that a surly social worker arrived with paperwork to remove Marcie immediately due to Mom being hospitalized. I called the hospital to reach you, but Mom's room doesn't have a phone. The social worker packed Marcie's belongings. I wrapped my arm over Marcie's shoulders and felt her body trembling. I lied that this was temporary. As they left through the front door, I whispered and begged the unnamed social worker for a telephone number to reach Marcie. Just to let her know we were thinking of her. She snapped back that I knew better. Without a farewell, our now 13-year-old Marcie was gone.

I slipped Molly's leash on her red collar, grabbed Alan's hand, and headed to Pelham Bay Park. We walked silently for hours. Halfway through our walk, Molly lay down and looked up. Alan and I took turns carrying the tired dog.

We skipped dinner and went directly to our bedrooms. I knelt at my bedside and prayed for Marcie, crushing thoughts of how frightened she must be. Knowing sleep would not come, I tiptoed to Mom's garden and sat in her lawn chair. The fragrance of night blooms, a scattering of stars, and a stray cat curled up on a warm slate kept me company.

I had experienced 14 years of the arrival and departure of young and old souls encased in children's bodies. They filled our home with many cultures, skin colors, likes, and dislikes. Most were abused and/or neglected. The common denominator was their need and capacity for love.

Mom loved. Alan loved. I loved.

Why wasn't the foster care system aware of the harm inflicted on these innocents by prohibiting them from staying in touch with families they had bonded with?

The following day, I paced the hospital parking lot, struggling with how to explain the social worker's kidnapping of our Marcie. Do I gingerly state a positive outcome, such as Mom having more freedom? Do I whimper so we can share the pain? Do I spit it out and wait for her emotions to direct me? Was I capable of not becoming hysterical? This was Mom. The caregiver extraordinaire to any poor schlep arriving on our doorstep. Mom was strong in body and spirit, an opinionated, funny woman. But her heart took a beating for all this.

I entered the hospital, still confused. I went to Dr. B's office. He wasn't there. I explained the situation to the Head Nurse on Mom's floor. She alerted the doctor in charge.

At the entrance to Mom's hospital room, I decided not to put on a false smile. Mom was in her fluffy pink nightgown; her hands were folded behind her head, and her cheeks were shiny from a fresh wash. She smiled. I looked down.

"What's wrong, honey?" asked Mom.

I let her know Alan was good and the house was still standing. Then, staring at the floor, I shared the painful removal of Marcie. I don't know how long I stood there silently waiting for Mom's reaction. I didn't reach for her hand as that gesture seemed trivial for this scenario. I froze, feeling I was failing Mom at this crucial moment.

"It's for the best," lied Mom as she started coughing.

I fetched the doctor and excused myself by lying that I forgot to put the parking tag inside my car's windshield. Turning at the doorway, I looked back and saw Mom's head in her hands, sobbing. The doctor touched her shoulder. I remained outside her room to allow her to cry with this stranger. She could let down her guard with him. I returned with one of her favorite magazines, *True Romance*, telling her I would see her after dinner.

I revved my car in the hospital parking lot only to turn it off. I knew better than to drive as rage filled me with this new loss. Marcie didn't stand alone in my thoughts. Around 30 fostered ghost children came to mind. Their names and faces meshed over each other, but their eyes never left me. I pretended that they were returned to healthy parents or were adopted.

Home again at nightfall, Alan and I sat on our back stoop, silently contemplating the empty house. Molly's barks gave us momentary life. Alan walked Molly, and I collapsed on Marcie's bed, weeping. I wondered how much pain a human heart could handle. We casually recite the phrase, "My heart is breaking." Was it, or was mine disintegrating so I wouldn't suffer anymore?

As I passed Alan's room, I noticed his door was wide open with an antique iron as a doorstop. Thank you for giving me this peace, dear brother. He was asleep with Molly curled up on the new tan shag rug beside his bed.

I dozed off while kneeling in prayer.

I awoke to a phone ringing. Alan was holding the receiver.

"Mom had a second heart attack. It was mild," mumbled Alan.

I didn't feel Azrael on my shoulders, so I said, "This happens a lot to first heart attack patients. Not to worry."

Alan bravely joined me to visit Mom. The car ride from our home to the hospital was under 15 minutes. A tap on my shoulder startled me as Alan and I waited for the hospital security to ransack my bag. Roy and Nancy arrived. They were a day early for their monthly visit because of Mom's worsening health. I stared through them. Alan ground his jaw.

"Why is the guard frisking you?" Nancy repulsively asked. "None of your business, sister," I muttered.

Barry, the guard, turned to Nancy and said, "Your young sister snuck vitamins to her Mother. So, these inspections began when the substances appeared in Mrs. Hoffman's urine tests."

"You just can't leave things alone," snarled Nancy.

"F... you," I spat out, shocking myself.

Alan intervened by draping his arm over my shoulders and directing us to Mom's room. He kissed Mom's forehead and whispered something that made her laugh. Then he stood by the doorway, reminding me of his stance 19 years ago in our Dad's hospital room.

I strutted to Mom with a false sense of joy. I touched her cold hand and lost it, hiding my head on her shoulder. She stroked my hair. Ashamed of my outburst, I told her I would bring Alan home and return.

When I returned with Mom's mail, Roy and Nancy headed to the hospital's shop. Mom tore at her mail, giving her the appearance of control over her life.

"Marion, The Children's Service has invited me to a dinner honoring me with a medal for my 15 years of service," Mom dryly said.

"We will go. You can speak your mind without consequence," I encouraged.

Our visit wound down, and I alerted Mom, "I'm heading to the Anti-War Rally at Riverside Church, so I'll see you late tonight."

"Sure, keep your bra on," my tolerant Mom joked.

In the parking lot, I asked Nancy and Roy to follow me home to visit with Alan. They looked at the ground, fumbling for each of their car keys.

"We have families of our own," said Nancy.

This comment infuriated me. Wasn't Mom, who gave them life and funds for their dreams, part of their family? Wasn't Alan and I who babysat their children family?

"How could you not visit Alan all those months in the hospital? Come home and spend time with him now," I begged.

Nancy mumbled, "I have to get home to Cornelius."

While silent throughout this interchange, Roy revved his car and said, "I'll drop off the shutters for Mom's room later this week when you're home."

After three months, not three weeks, in the hospital, Mom was home happily complaining that the shade of yellow I painted her bedroom was too bright, and the maple wood shutters Roy bought made the room dark.

Hearing Mom's funny way of acknowledging our loving efforts let me know it was time to live a little.

I renewed my jazz dance classes. Working out at the barre with the aroma of rosin wafting up smelled like freedom. As I arrived home from a dance class, our telephone rang for the third time. I dove into it.

"Yes, sure, Monday," I said into the phone.

I told Mom that Reilly wanted me to return to work. The taste of freedom was sweetening.

Chapter 23

Tradition

In November of my 21st year, I began participating in the Morse/Hoffman clan's cemetery tradition to haunt a family member's grave, rotating visits to our increasing number of entombed relatives.

A sharp wind blew in the open field of white gravestones. The green grass was barely visible beneath the brown leaves. I hung back, enjoying the sound of the dried vegetation crackling beneath my feet. Alan had an appointment with Dr. Greenberg. I missed his company. I imagined he would say they didn't know where Uncle Bill's grave was located and didn't care. They had a grand time chatting about any gravestone they passed.

I watched my uncles take turns lugging the 6′ long spruce blanket, sometimes over their heads, then wrapped around their shoulders like a shawl, hurrying to keep up with Mom as she roamed from one area of the cemetery to another.

When we arrived at Bill's grave, they gently laid the blanket, shed tears, and an inappropriate song, *For He's a Jolly Good Fellow*, burst forth.

Afterward, we scuttled into a roadside diner, taking over one section. I chose to sit next to Uncle Fred, the storyteller.

Gently poking his rib, "What are you thinking about," I asked. "Your Uncle Bill, kid," said Uncle Fred.

Fred continued, "We hated watching Bill's embarrassment when Augusta pecked at him. I'd take him outside for a cigarette and ask who the hell wore the pants in his family. Bill would say that he wore them, but Augusta starched them. We'd have a good laugh."

I patted his hand and asked, "Is there any truth to the story about Uncle Bill's limousine service?"

Winking at me with mischief, he snapped into his storytelling mode.

"Shh, Uncle Fred has a story," I announced.

The flatware clattered to a halt as everyone quieted down.

"As a young hustler, my limo business thrived, hoisting big shots around New York's nightlife. Brother Bill was tucked away studying accounting. One night, I asked him to drive one of my customers home to Staten Island because I had a hot date," reminisced Uncle Fred.

Uncle Henry chuckled. Uncle Frank, the younger, serious brother at the farthest corner of our gathering, rolled his eyes.

Fred continued, "Uncle Bill was kindhearted and didn't hesitate to help me even though he did not know Staten Island's roads. I alerted my client, who liked that I kept it in the family."

Uncle Henry grinned and said, "You son-of-a-gun, I remember poor Bill."

"Uncle Bill got lost driving the gangster home," said Uncle Fred.

The word gangster made our two servers lean in. Fred welcomed them, and they scrunched into our booths. One waitress waved her hand to patrons sitting at the counter, and a crowd gathered around us.

Seeing these strangers gather above our heads, Mom added, "What the hell? Let's have it, Fred."

Uncle Fred eyeballed his audience and said, "After an hour of driving in circles, the gangster started cursing Bill. Then, he began punching the back of the driver's seat with his black leather-gloved fist. Finally, he asked Bill to pull over. It was pitch black amidst nothing but swamps. Bill reminded his passenger that he didn't know how to drive. The passenger punched the back of the driver's seat one more time. Bill thought that was it for him."

Service in the diner halted as the growing audience gasped.

Fred continued, "The client stepped out of the car, shot a couple of holes in the trunk, got back in, and asked Bill, 'You know where I live now?"

Choking with laughter, Uncle Fred said, "It worked like magic. Bill turned that car around, and they were at his passenger's front gate 15 minutes later."

Then, Uncle Henry said, "Before driving home, poor Bill had to grab a rag from the car's trunk and wipe the urine from his seat."

Now, the diner's customers were clapping and slapping Uncle Fred on his back. The diner's owner said the meal was on him.

Mom said, "And that, dear family, was the start of Bill's legitimate limousine business."

We left the diner laughing, and it felt good.

The Christmas season arrived, and the Hoffman house had Mom home to celebrate.

"Hop in, Ma," I commanded, squeezing Mom into the passenger seat of my dilapidated convertible Karmann Ghia to fetch our holiday tree.

We chose a seven-foot blue spruce. Unfortunately, it started snowing with a mighty force. My convertible car top did not respond to my attempts to yank it up. Our tree man laughed as he roped our gigantic tree between our seats.

"Mom, wriggle under the branches," I suggested, shifting into first gear.

I turned to Mom. Her knees were curled up to her chest, and her handmade multi-colored knit hat with ear flaps blew wildly. I turned the windshield wipers on, only to watch them drag against the glass. Our visibility was almost non-existent. Giggling like schoolgirls, we chugged along as the car filled with snow, etching a new Christmas memory.

Chapter 24

Ch-Ch-Changes

At 24, I experienced the chemical firm's annual New Year's Eve party in their offices. We, women, wore our jewel-colored cocktail dresses and velvet or satin high heels throughout the day, just waiting to slip off our sweaters. Cases of champagne and catered food were delivered to our conference room, awaiting our 1 PM closing. Each department had more goodies spread on the desks.

Whipping covers on typewriters and covering our drafting boards, we crowded into the conference room. Armed with a drink in one hand and hors d'oeuvres in the other, coworkers mingled. The party allowed office romances to bloom. Rumors about last year's love stories spread as thick as the cream cheese on toast triangles being passed. Radio stations were synced to a station playing dance music.

The two young lawyers from the legal department drifted into the advertising department, my domain. We connected with laughter, as always. The new Canadian internal auditor, Edmund, interrupted, and they, annoyed, walked away.

I kindly offered, "Inside joke. Are you heading home for the holiday break?"

Edmund looked surprised at my interest and changed from forthright to shy. He whispered, "No, traveling to western Canada in the winter is difficult. I'm going to complete the audit here."

His country-boy timidity intrigued me. Edmund's rugged good looks were hidden behind the latest fashionable sideburns and mustache. Heavy-rimmed glasses made his green eyes look small. His three-piece suit looked tailor-made to fit his healthy physique. He followed me from department to department, exchanging our backgrounds. He had a full scholarship to university due to his ice hockey skills. I didn't like sports, and my hit-and-miss night classes fell short of his education. Likewise, he met my love of dance and painting with disinterest. He shared that he had wanted to be introduced to me from day one. I barely looked up whenever he greeted me.

Yet, hours later, I surrendered to his kiss as our taxi rolled uptown along snowy Park Avenue.

Rodriquez Edmundus Koenig had entered my life.

Our dating rapidly deepened. His power of persuasion was compelling. I revealed my hesitation in this relationship with Mom. She said to slow it down. She believed Edmund did not understand trust, demonstrated by his frequent calls that felt like checking up on me.

I began to know Edmund, the 6'4", well-educated jock who could not bear to see scary movies or watch boxing. We shared this inability to witness violence. Edmund recounted that when he was eight, he teased his two older sisters enough to cause them to complain to their mother. She, his protector, locked him in the cellar overnight, with no dinner, warm clothes, or chance of getting out. Edmund said he felt ghosts swirling around him. His screams were met with silence until the following morning. I suspected there were further frightening episodes in his childhood.

Edmund finished the audit in February and returned to Saskatoon indefinitely. He said he would apply for a transfer to New York. I was thankful for the break.

Mom gussied up and accepted her new neighbors' invitation to join them for dinner.

They were her age and made her laugh. Alan was in control of his disease and had begun night classes at NYU. Their new adventures inspired me to accept a workmate's offer to join her on a weekend ski trip upstate. I realized my warrior mode, created by Dad's dying wish to care for Mom, stopped me from doing anything except school and work. I decided to see what I was missing.

I headed home from the ski weekend, wishing I'd never gone. My co-worker persuaded a guy back to our room. Half-asleep, blanket in hand, I wandered to the lobby couch, unknowingly leaving my precious gold bracelet on the night table. I wondered if the lost bracelet was my self-punishment for leaving Mom.

Back home, I took advantage of Mom's eternal silence dealing with her children's mishaps and pretended Mom didn't notice my missing bracelet. When we couldn't bear the silence anymore, we would blab. The gold bracelet held too heavy a value for me to admit losing. Mom and I were at a standoff.

Edmund's transfer to New York came through in June.

We learned that we temporarily escaped haunting fears through physical exercise. He was ecstatic while skating during his weekly amateur ice hockey games. I was blissful jazz dancing, lost in form and step.

In September, Edmund's marriage proposal to me every Saturday night added a new crinkle in our dating. I repeatedly declined. He stopped asking me after New Year's Eve. I missed his request. Did I pine for the flattery or the possibility? By my 27th birthday that March, I knew, fears and all, that I was in love with Edmund.

The only kinks in life were the missing bracelet and the burly Elm tree Roy had unwisely planted behind the Holy Gate. Its relentless roots were strangling Dad's fruit trees. Mom despised this tree, an oxymoron for her.

Chapter 25

I Do?

A month later, walking on a rainy April evening, Edmund nervously closed the umbrella, reached into his pocket, and slipped a large, green emerald-cut Tourmaline with two diamond baguettes on my finger. Soaking wet, we kissed. He whispered, "Thank you."

Poor Mom and I argued about my impending marriage. I agreed with Mom's doubts but chose to turn red flags pink. She felt it might be what she called "Foster Children Syndrome." Our witnessing and sharing love with so many broken children caused us to be attracted to those in pain.

Six weeks later, on May 31st, my wedding day, Mom and I wandered out our storm door, opened the rusty Holy Gate, and entered our thriving vegetable patch under a blue sky. Mom wore a pink silk shantung dress. I wore a slim-fitting East Indian silk ivory dress and a halo of flowers on my newly permed, frizzy hair. If I had studied this altered image of any other bride, I might have questioned their commitment to this imminent marriage. How did I miss this clue?

Mom stepped into the rhubarb patch, admiring the healthy red stalks. I admired Mom.

Her salon hairdo, freshly scrubbed face, and red lipstick hid years of pain. Her smile still lit up a room.

"Mom, wanna hear something extraordinary? I had this ridiculous perm because I thought if I had curly hair like Nancy, Dad might appear," I revealed.

"What!" exclaimed Mom.

Then, Mom opened her hand. My gold bracelet sparkled in her palm.

A young lady had returned the bracelet two days ago after repeatedly begging the ski lodge for our address. She told Mom she had had nothing but bad luck since wearing my gold bracelet.

I leaped over the rhubarb and kissed Mom's hands. Mom had put a spell on my exquisite bracelet. I hoped I could do the same for my daughter if I were lucky enough to have one.

"Time to go, Marion," whispered Mom. "No rush, Ma," I said.

I wondered what I would do if Joey or someone tried to whisk me away.

"I'm troubled that his sister, Rachel, and husband are staying in your apartment on your wedding night. The hair on my neck went up when she hugged me," said Mom.

"I agree. Glad only one night," I said.

Roy arrived, sporting two cameras dangling from his shoulders, which he had purchased during his recent trip to Japan, enjoying his status as a Pan Am pilot.

I smiled at him and asked, "Do you understand why I want Mom to walk me down the aisle?"

"No, but it's your choice," ranted Roy. "What are we waiting for?" he inquired.

"Don't know," I whimpered.

"Well, it's too late to back down now. So, let's move it," Roy commanded.

Unfortunately, my First Presbyterian Church, where I attended Sunday School, received Communion and sang in their choir, albeit poorly, turned us down due to Edmund's divorce. We were to be married in the nearby Methodist Church.

The simple brick structure of the Methodist Church didn't create the joyfulness I felt entering my familiar church with its towering steeple. I didn't feel angels smiling down. However, I felt my Archangel Azrael's feathers occasionally slapping my face, quite the comedian that day.

A Cellist began playing Mozart's *Ave Verum Corpus*. The music made my toes tingle. I squeezed Mom's hand as we glided down the aisle.

"I'll always be here for you, Marion," Mom tenderly whispered.

Crushing her hand, I mumbled, "I'm counting on that."

Standing at the altar, which appeared miles away, I gazed at Edmund. My heart quickened. We had decided to exchange the traditional wedding vows, and I believed we sincerely meant to uphold them:

"_____, *wilt thou have this woman/man to be thy wife/husband, and wilt thou pledge thy faith to him/ her, in all love and honor, in all duty and service, in all faith and tenderness, to live with her/him, and cherish her/him, according to the ordinance of God, in the holy bond of marriage?"*

"I, _____, take you, _____, to be my wedded wife/husband, and I do promise and covenant, before God and these witnesses, to be your loving and faithful husband/wife, in plenty and want, in joy and in sorrow, in sickness and in health, as long as we both shall live."

Our wedding reception was held at Lüchow's, 14th Street, near Irving Place in Manhattan. We chose it for the old-world ambiance.

Edmund's sister, Rachel, sat on his right. Mom sat on my left. Edmund grasped my hand and whisked me to dance. He whispered that his sister was talking about a witches' coven she had joined and was learning spells. I made light of Rachel's words, adding that she was due to have twins soon, and hormones might be at the core of her baiting.

Mom and I danced a few times until the Maître d stopped us.

Standing outside Lüchow's, hailing a yellow taxi, I said auf wiedersehen to Mom and Alan, trying to lighten the moment.

I said, "Alan, call me anytime. I mean it. Understand?" Alan's meager yes did not reassure me.

"I will give it the old one-two, Ma," I whispered and waved until the taxi was out of sight.

An hour later, Edmund inserted the key into the lock of a beautiful brownstone in the East 80s between Park and

Madison Avenues without the giddiness of a bridegroom. His free hand was shaking. I reached for Edmund's hand. Holding hands, we climbed the wide, winding, dark wood staircase with its well-polished carved banister to our second-floor apartment.

I smelled fresh earth. Azrael was sticking with me. Oh, Lord, why?

Edmund swept me into his arms and carried me over the threshold into our living room. I lifted my face to kiss him, but Rachel and her non-communicative husband interrupted me.

Smirking, Rachel said I was lucky I had angels around me. This did not phase me. Azrael and I were buddies. My eyes narrowed toward Rachel, a foolish woman unaware of the strength of love around me and within.

The velvet sofa bed Mom had gifted us under the Roche Bobois domed metal lamp welcomed us.

Edmund turned the sofa bed down for our guests. As I walked the hall to our bedroom, I glimpsed Rachel pulling strands of hair from my brush, shoving them into her robe's pocket. She swooshed by with no explanation, creating a chill.

Finally, Edmund closed our bedroom door and placed a chair under its knob. I was too tired to question him. As the moonlight streamed through tree branches into our west-facing window, I saw tears in Edmund's eyes.

"I know she took your hair," Edmund mumbled.

I assured him she had teased him at dinner, and they would be over 2, 000 miles away tomorrow. We will burn incense, say prayers, and consummate our marriage tomorrow night.

I didn't sleep. I would head to the library as soon as possible to research present-day witchcraft.

Living in Manhattan was delicious. I worked for a kind gentleman, Mr. Fontaine, lunched with girlfriends, and visited Mom and Alan most weekends. In addition, I began a class at The Art Students League and resumed jazz dance classes.

Edmund asked me to quit my evening classes to have more time with him. I reminded him that his auditing job had him away for at least two weeks a month. We let that dilemma be.

We fell asleep shortly after our passion was depleted on a hot August night. Awakened by our bed shaking uncontrollably, I saw Edmund sit up, staring at the floor between our footboard and the window. Then, he bellowed with fear. I had witnessed Edmund's strength during his ice hockey games, so I was reluctant to tap his shoulder.

"Medusa, go away," he pleaded.

Abruptly, Edmund turned to me, asking, "Did you see it?"

Still afraid to touch him, I cautiously whimpered, "I felt our bed shake." His body went limp, and he collapsed back as though plummeting to earth. "I love you, Marion," he drawled, falling asleep.

Over coffee that morning, I pried, "Don't you think we should talk about last night?"

"Relax, it was a nightmare," he responded, almost bubbly.

"Edmund, nightmares don't shake our bed," I said.

Then, with a kiss, he rushed off in his well-fitted navy suit. I felt my face flush with his nearness.

I was alone in our apartment a few weeks later as Edmund was on a business trip. Settling down to watch an episode of I Love Lucy after checking in with Mom, I sipped Chamomile tea. I cracked the bedroom window open to enjoy the fresh September air before snuggling into my side of the bed. Prayers uttered, I trusted my night to God.

Around midnight, I awoke, my hands frozen beside my hips, unable to lift them. The bed was shaking uncontrollably. The gyrating bed stopped as suddenly as it started. I jumped up, locked the window, grabbed my covers, and headed to our couch. Then, remembering Rachel, I returned to the bedroom and napped in a chair.

I headed to the 42nd Street Public Library the following Saturday. Last time, I researched Archangel Azrael. This time, I hoped he was with me.

Seated in the massive, formidable reading room, I devoured books about witchcraft, taking down stenographic notes until the Librarian whispered, "We are closing, Miss."

I grabbed a slice of Ray's pizza with my friend, Pat, sharing my discoveries about witchcraft. For example, one superstition stated that witches often used hair to cast spells. One of which might be to stop your hair from growing, but usually something much worse! The library closed before I found out how to prevent a spell.

"If Rachel is a witch, her stealing strands of your hair is not good," said Pat.

I rolled my eyes at her obvious observation. Pat offered to keep my notepad in her apartment.

Exhausted, I decided to brave it and sleep in our bed. I slept undisturbed. I swore not to mention the incident to Edmund or Mom.

Our marriage vow, "Till Death Do Us Part," took on new meaning.

Chapter 26

Montreal

On December 3rd, six months into our marriage, Edmund was transferred to Montreal and had to report to work by January 5th.

I was devastated. Time with Mom and Alan, lunchtime laughter with friends, dance school, and Art Students League would vanish. My gut pulled me to stay in New York and wait. My heart tugged me to join Edmund. I was his wife, and I loved him. It was an hour away by plane.

Mom reminded me I could always come home, as she would be there. We would write and talk on the phone. Edmund had security issues, but he loved me.

We spent Christmas with Mom and Alan, sharing the full resplendence of our Holiday tree, meals, and present exchanges.

Alan was dating a young woman named Fiona. She was of Philippine descent and lived with her father. She was an accountant. I liked this new development.

Neither Roy with his brood nor Nancy and her family joined us. I was upset because their visit would have distracted us from my imminent departure.

On December 26th, after a tearful au revoir, I settled in the passenger seat of Edmund's car, deciding to make this an adventure. Our stopover at a Lake Placid Inn was fleetingly blissful. Edmund's attitude was changing. Using the knowledge of my dyslexia as ammunition, he yelled about my slowness in reading the map and mimicked my stutter.

This meanness crumbled my fragile spirit. I wanted my familiar New York City streets to walk to tiredness, yet feel refreshed. I could have called Mom, but I'd worry her. I would not waste Azrael's time.

At daybreak on December 29th, we were on the road again. Before the car started, he said he had me all to himself now. The hairs on my neck stood up.

Arriving at the U.S./Canadian border, my passport was stamped *Landed Immigrant*. Shocked, I frantically babbled, "Sir, what does Landed Immigrant status mean in Canada? Aren't my rights and freedoms the same as in the United States?"

The Mountie and Edmund laughed.

We entered Montreal at midday. I observed a stark gray skyscape with construction sites and snow-covered cranes. The Montreal Summer Olympics were to start on July 17th.

We continued to a modern residential building at the top of Côte de Neiges. Our moving truck had arrived. Unpacking distracted Edmund from my tears of homesickness and feeling trapped.

Over coffee on December 31, Edmund suggested we ice skate on Mont-Royal. The walk will be less than an hour. Edmund had taught me to skate well. Our skates were hung on the coat hooks next to our coats.

"I'm game, but first, let's call Mom to let her know we've arrived safe and sound," I respond.

"We'll find a phone booth on the way," Edmund said.

"Silly, our phone has a dial tone," I offered, holding the receiver in my hand. "You are wrong. We'll call Mom later," Edmund insisted.

I didn't want to pursue this, so I dressed in long johns and layers of warm clothing. Our brisk walk to the top was challenging as I was unaccustomed to this frigid climate. The inside of my nose hurt when I inhaled, but I stayed focused on the adventure.

"Where's the skating rink?" I asked when we arrived at the top of Mount Royal.

"You're so pampered. We skate on the frozen grass," Edmund said.

We sat on a log to put on our skates. My frozen fingers throbbed as I maneuvered them back into the mittens.

"Keep me in your sight," Edmund said as he skated off with ice flying in my face. "Sure thing," I said, paying no attention.

I removed my red scarf and wrapped it around the tree beside me. I skated back and forth to my marker. The clumps of grass beneath the ice made my body quiver. Just as my teeth joined in, Edmund reappeared. Grabbing my red scarf from the tree and twisting it around my neck, he reached for my hand. I hesitated.

"Give me your hand," he insisted.

His grip was firm. I felt confident and eventually relaxed as we glided hand in hand, beautifully cross-stepping in sync over the bumpy terrain. I swelled with love for my mysterious husband.

We quietly celebrated New Year's Eve in our new apartment. However, after wishing Mom a Happy New Year, I felt lost.

January 5th arrived, and Edmund drove me to my new job. I never expected a fair job transfer from New York, but Mr. Fontaine helped me secure a temporary position in their Canadian office at Rue Ste Catherine.

Edmund handed me Canadian currency for a taxi home, adding that we would figure out public transportation that night.

"Where are your offices?" I naturally inquired.

"You don't need to know yet," Edmund said dismissively, closing his car door.

I repressed Edmund's secrecy and rushed into the building with trepidation about my new job.

Five hours later, I was waiting for my taxi. I considered it my chariot, whisking me away from a painful workday. My Montreal boss told me he was angry that I'd been hired without even a telephone interview between us. He had someone in mind. Nevertheless, I was determined to work hard to prove him wrong.

Edmund was sent to different cities in Canada during the week and home on weekends. Edmund's away time was a godsend as his controlling actions increased. He would surprise me at my office without calling. Then spent the evening asking me who the guy was to whom I said goodbye. Jean, a French Canadian, was my height with dark hair and eyes. Our friendship was immediate, laced with dry humor and curiosity about the existence of angels. Jean was not a threat like Edmund jealously imagined, but he was becoming my confidant.

Edmund opened my letters from Mom. I retrieved the delicate pink linen notes from his hands and re-read Mom's beautiful script. Then, I would follow recipes like her Königsberger Klopse, letting the aroma of cinnamon and nutmeg return me to her kitchen.

Edmund's comment that he gets the phone bills had me counseling him on trust. I shared how I witnessed my foster brothers and sisters with similar issues. He said I had a problem.

I wondered why I was a warrior for others but not for myself. Should one have to be a warrior with a new husband?

Where is Azrael? Don't tell me my Archangel could not cross the Canadian border. No, just a busy angel.

My winter workday routine began in my warm kitchen, enjoying my espresso and listening to the local news. My two points of interest: (a) was the temperature outside below zero, and (b) was there a new known terror attack planned by the separatist political movement to attain independence from Canada?

When the temperature was frigid, police offered frozen folks shivering at bus stops rides down Côte de Neiges to avoid frostbite. I shamelessly befriended local officers of the Sûreté du Québec and adhered to their accustomed schedule.

If I were lucky enough to arrive at work with my frozen ears intact, my only concern was where the next possible attack from the Parti Québécois would strike. The dangers of blowing up state government buildings or causing traffic turmoil in downtown Montreal, where I worked, were newsworthy.

March had arrived, and the temperature was above zero, a relative heatwave. I walked to work down Parque Mont-Royal. Giggling, my co-workers told me that when the spring thaw arrived, I would see I had been walking on top of benches as the snow had reached 51 inches that year.

During most lunch hours, I joined Jean in a service at the nearby Catholic Chapel. I watched Jean perform the ritual of making the sign of the cross from his forehead to his chest to his shoulders. I liked it and started doing the same when I entered and exited the chapel. Jean laughed at my irreverence to a particular religion. I said they were all good, I guess.

I learned Parisian fashions landed in Montreal before New York, and today was their arrival. No known terrorist trouble was brewing in downtown Montreal, so Jean and I planned to shop our lunch hour away.

March 7th marked my 28th birthday. I convinced Edmund to gift me a weekend visit to Mom over the U.S. Mother's Day in May.

I buckled my seatbelt as the excitement of heading home swept over me. Then, Azrael's wing landed on my shoulders. I debated whether the aircraft was safe or whether Mom and Alan were okay. Funny, I never considered Edmund to be the target.

I wondered if witchcraft separated Edmund from me, from love. What if his family were clever with coven skills? In the articles I read at the library, I recalled that a coven wanted family members to marry into their clan. Could I fight back, or was this my imagination excusing Edmund's controlling behavior?

The plane landed at La Guardia Airport; I taxied to Brooklyn.

"Surprise," I exclaimed as Alan stepped from Dr. Greenberg's office. "A taxi awaits you, dear brother," I continued.

I learned Alan was still dating Fiona. The long weekend passed with Mom and I weeding the flower bed, shopping, and laughing. The time was packed with Mom reminiscing about singing in her teenage years and adoring Marion Harris, a famous singer in the early 1900s.

"Wait, Mom," I sputtered, "Did you name me after your favorite singer, not Montana?"

"I thought I'd kill two birds with one stone. Give you my singing idol's name and make Tana feel better about your birth," Mom admitted.

"Why haven't you told me? I'm taking Molly for a walk," I barked.

Mom was in bed when I returned.

I kissed her forehead and said, "Ah, I don't care."

Then, I tickled her to ensure she heard me.

Mom's hand reached from beneath her blanket and slapped my butt.

On the return flight to Montreal, I wore Mom's gift, a sand-colored sweater. I remembered this fine wool in her knitting basket years ago, the day of her first heart attack. I knew I'd wear it often.

I gazed out the window on the short flight to Montreal. I was not looking for Dad. I was reflecting on the possibility of leaving Edmund. My joie de vivre was dissolving as Edmund belittled and confused me, insisting his screaming was my fault. I discussed this with Mom. She said the decision had to be mine alone.

I learned I was fired. My boss said he hired a French Canadian, but my gut felt Edmund got to him. I would never know.

"My next audit is in Ottawa. Now you can join me," Edmund announced, removing his eyeglasses and staring into my eyes.

Without flinching, I responded, "Yes. Are we driving?"

For the following five weeks, I was glued to Edmund. Our being together 24/7 almost freed Edmund of his wild insecurities. He drove himself to the daily audits instead of letting me drop him off. I spent my days as a prisoner reading in the hotel room or circling the hotel in a secluded wooded area. Even then, Edmund called me or returned to have lunch together. He insisted it was customary to want me with him constantly, and my suggestion for therapy was crazy. I journaled my thoughts, as always, in stenography. I struggled to determine if I loved him or felt sorry for him.

Back in Montreal, free of Edmund during his work hours, I inhaled frankincense as I entered the Catholic Chapel for its lunchtime service. The stained glass windows splashed rainbows across the interior. Jean, head bowed, was in his usual pew. I made the sign of the cross, thankful. I was beginning to search for my beliefs beyond Archangels. Jean took my hand. I shared my fears about Edmund. We faced the altar to focus on prayer. I heard a loud sigh echo throughout the chapel. Jean glanced at me. He heard it, too. The altar evaporated as Archangel Azrael solidified, encompassing the chancel. My eyes were wide open. Like the ocean, Azrael's wings were filled with rich shades of blue. I did not see millions of eyes as written in books. The figure felt eagle-like. My fear was not of my Azrael but of why he appeared.

Another louder sigh surrounded us as He faded.

Jean became frightened of me. I knew this would be our last encounter.

I called Mom the second I walked into my apartment. She said she was writing me and that all was okay at home. I told her Edmund and I would visit his family on the Canadian west coast in July. There was a plane change in Calgary. I planned to somehow head to New York alone. If I missed that opportunity, I would try on my return flight.

On July 21st, we were on a flight to Vancouver. I was terrified that it was a witches' gathering. Azrael was firmly planted on my shoulder. I tried to ensure my protection by wearing a gold crucifix on my neck, the charm bracelet with another crucifix among many happy charms, and my magical gold bracelet.

As we landed at Calgary Airport to change planes, the flight attendant made an announcement.

"Passengers, please remain seated. Would Marion Hoffman come forward to the captain's chamber?"

My body became rigid as I gasped for air. I met the flight attendant's eyes with terror.

Next, somehow, I was in front of the cockpit. Taking my shoulders, the captain whispered, "I am sorry to tell you that your Mother, Florence Hoffman, passed away an hour ago."

I screamed, over and over, "No, this is a trick. You're lying."

Edmund tried to comfort me, but I ripped my arm from his grip. My nostrils flared in a mix of agony and anger. We were escorted to a plane bound for New York City. Archangel Azrael wrapped me in His wings. My favorite welcoming skyline tortured me that day, reminding me why I had arrived.

Chapter 27

My Mom, My Everything

Entering the administration desk at the Manhattan hospital, I robotically said, "Florence Hoffman passed away in your Emergency Room. She was two months from her 72nd birthday. She had a donor card and wanted to donate her eyes and organs. Was this satisfied? May I see her?"

Edmund balked at my request. I frowned at him. The nurse suggested waiting until Florence Hoffman was laid out in the funeral home. Poking the nurse's chest, I ground out the words she was my Mom.

In the hospital mortuary, I placed my cheek on Mom's and pretended she was not gone.

We can fix this. You promised to be here for me. We kept our promises. I don't know how long I stayed, but as I walked out of the hospital, I wanted to run and pound walls until my knuckles bled and scream until I had no voice. It was still light out, infuriating me as I couldn't cry openly, hidden in the night. Edmund offered a taxi. I knew the subway was faster. We weaved down the subway stairs, anxiously awaiting the Number Six train to Throgg's Neck. Alan was home alone. I knew he desperately needed me.

Mayflower Avenue looked unfamiliar. Or had it dimmed with the loss of Mom's light?

I snuck into my home's alleyway. My hand shook as I inserted the key into the back door lock. Aware of Edmund's love for Mom, I allowed his hand to steady mine as I did for him on our strange wedding night.

Alan was scrunched in Mom's spot on the couch. Feeling guilty about having Edmund's support, I dropped his hand and rushed to Alan. Edmund entered Mom's bedroom.

Alan began, "I held Mom's hand in the hospital. It was still warm. There was blood all over her dress from the Emergency Team trying to save her," Alan confided, weeping.

"Where was Mom when she had the heart attack?" I asked. "Macy's," Alan uttered.

For a split second, I felt better as Mom was happy there.

Nancy arrived and headed straight to my husband in Mom's bedroom as they ransacked Mom's closet. The two lovelies ascended, holding colossal glass jars of coins and a piece of luggage. My flash of faith in Edmund's support vanished. Roy arrived and instructed us to gather around the kitchen table.

I asked Alan, "Has Molly been walked?"

Alan mumbled, "No. Good call."

"Molly, Molly," I sang, searching. I found her shaking under Mom's bed. I invited Edmund. He mumbled he'd listen for me. I didn't care. He awkwardly sat at the kitchen table with Nancy and Roy. Grief did not fool Alan and me into joining them.

That night, Alan went to bed early. Unnerved, I opened his door without knocking. I inspected his room for glasses of water.

Turning his head from being buried in his pillow, Alan whispered, "You trust me, don't you, Sis?"

Without conviction, I answered, "You're my brother, aren't you? Goodnight."

Edmund and I had barely spoken since we disembarked the plane. We stood in my old bedroom as I made up the single bed for him. He tried to hold me. I walked to the doorway.

"I'm lost. I have no space in my body to focus on anything but Mom and Alan," I said.

I entered Mom's bedroom and closed the door behind me. I noticed romance magazines beside her Bible. That was Mom, spiritual with a dollop of sexy wit. I crawled between the white sheets she slept in the night before, breathing in the perfume she spritzed on her pillow. I lifted myself from the edge of the bed, opened Mom's L'Air du Temps perfume bottle with the exquisite dove top, and touched my wrists with its fragrance. Mom used to say the Ad was right in that the scent gave her optimism.

"No, Azrael, the longer I'm awake, the longer I'm with Mom," I whispered, wrestling with sleep. Sitting up, I spun my arms, punching the air in every direction. Who was I hitting? I rocked back and forth. I crouched to the floor on my knees and prayed for help. I believed I could not live without Mom.

The following morning, Edmund stayed with Alan. They were going to mow the lawn and spruce up Mom's garden. Roy and I went to the Funeral Home to choose Mom's casket. After 40 minutes of wandering in circles, we decided on the one with the peach-colored satin pillow.

Then, sitting in his car, I goaded, "Why aren't you placing an obituary in The Daily News? The neighborhood loved Mom."

I had no energy to argue with Roy's lack of response.

"Let me out here," I insisted. He pulled up to Jimmy's grocery store.

"Have you heard?" I asked.

Jim came from behind the counter and hugged me. "Sherry from the bakery told me. Your Mom always had a smile and a wisecrack, even with all her troubles. I loved her," Jimmy said, bowing his head to hide his tears.

He continued, "We are letting everyone know. If it is okay with you, we want to place a tribute to Florence in our store windows."

We held hands.

I whispered, "Perfect. Thanks. Do you have any bones for Molly?" I continued, "She's not eating."

I left with a brown bag of bones, trusting that this gossip grapevine would operate like the Daily News.

"Marion," Jimmy shouted after me, "We'll take care of Mom's wake."

All the coaxing and cuddling did not revive Molly's appetite. She died of a broken heart two days after Mom. We interred Molly's body in Montana's backyard, the burial ground for eight dogs and eleven cats, last count. Tana did not express her sorrow for losing Mom. At least not in front of me. I accepted her way. We laid Molly to rest.

The funeral parlor opened at noon, but I arrived at 8 AM. The funeral director humorously said I wasn't disturbing anyone. I wondered if families still took their children to see dead loved ones. I questioned if they knew the eternal nightmares caused by this act of respect for the departed.

Sitting beside Mom's casket, I fussed with her hair, applied fresh Revlon red lipstick to her lifeless lips, and chatted. I told her that holidays gathered as a family would be buried with her, but I promised to keep Christmas and Easter alive. I said everyone missed her and that returning would be okay. Nothing happened. I placed my hand on Mom's chest, but it remained as hard as Dad's was in his casket. Then I threw a sizzler to wake her.

"Mom, I'm pregnant," I whispered, touching my belly. You need to wake up, Mom, please. I didn't want this new life to be already touched by death. No reaction. I pulled my compact mirror from my purse, placing it under Mom's nose, hoping it would fog up.

Uncle Fred, 75, removed my hand, snapping my compact closed. This jovial storyteller did not utter a word and chose to sit in the back of the somber room. Uncle Frank, in his 60s, arrived every evening.

Squeezing my thigh as hard as I could, I repressed that these brothers of Uncle John had never visited him at Harlem State. Uncle Henry had joined Mom many times.

Was I the chosen one to tell Uncle John that Mom was dead? I jumped out of my body, mentally running from this reckoning. My mind played tricks on me. I pretended to take care of business but hovered above my body when these unbearable thoughts arose.

My siblings joined me in the evenings. Roy and Nancy chatted politely with visitors, accepting their condolences. I did not talk. Alan bravely deflected everyone from me, as his eight-year-old self protected me from hysterical adults when Dad was pronounced dead.

Azrael's earthy fragrance overwhelmed me no matter how much perfume I spritzed on my black knit dress. I surrendered now and then, allowing peace to enter my soul. This made me feel guilty. Mom just died. I didn't deserve peace.

I kept my husband at a distance. I was not blaming him for Mom's death, but I resented losing months with her.

For three days, the funeral parlor had a steady stream of folks from all corners of New York City to pay their respects. Shady from Harlem, the Benjamins from the Fordham section of the Bronx, the McManns from Brooklyn, and every Throggs Neck local one could imagine.

Some shared how their mothers taught them sewing and cooking, a pittance to my Mom's teachings. I learned courage, kindness, and laughter from her.

I regretted not inviting Joey Bastone, as he adored his Mrs. H, and his respectful Italian upbringing would demand his attendance. Seeing Joey might add to my confusion. I was in a fragile place.

On the final evening of Mom's funeral, Mrs. Garibaldi, who had attended every night, elbowed me and whispered,

"Guarda, segno di Dio per Firenze, your Mama," pointing to the nuns kibitzing with Rabbi Harris.

I agreed this camaraderie was a sign from God that Florence's love would live on.

Our Presbyterian pastor gave the primary eulogy. While Alan understood my request for a second eulogy by Rabbi Harris, my other siblings were furious.

Mom babysat Rabbi Harris's three-year-old, Schlomo. They were over the moon when their son ran to Mom's arms upon her arrival.

Mom regularly took Schlomo to a nearby Convent as the Nuns adored this renegade Presbyterian who taught them about soil, planting vegetables, and pruning fruit trees. The gardens were exquisite. The Nuns ran and skipped with Schlomo, holding their tunics above their feet with their veils flying. Then, they would lie sprawled on the grass in piles of laughter as Schlomo ran circles around them.

One evening, Schlomo handed his parents a bouquet that the Nuns had gifted him.

"Daddy, look what the Nuns gave me," exclaimed Schlomo.

Rabbi Harris's eyebrows initially shot up in surprise, but a hearty laugh followed. He was never vexed with Mom.

The Rabbi shook the Reverend's hand and, with sparkling eyes, spoke for a full 20 minutes. His anecdotes about Mom had everyone crying and laughing.

It was my turn to say goodbye formally. Standing next to Mom's coffin, one hand firmly on it, I began:

"I'd like to read you a p-p-poem.

"Deep in Childhood's f-f-fragile boundary
Hours gather from time dissolved.
I see myself on F-February days.
And your f-face stitched against the mind.
Hair—white, smooth as ice rivers,
Eyes warmer than my breath,
Soft body in a f-flowered dress
Hugs into mine, and with a deep caress
I am the heir to all she left with age,
Healing the wound of time.
"Stay," I w-whisper to the dark,
Without you, my loneliness grows steep.
Your arms around me bring me the stark
Reality of home...."
But time is fixed in position,
I am a beggar in my house.
My eyes open to the sky—
A f-f-flock of starlings f-f-f-flies

I paused and debated smacking my head, wondering why I chose a poem with so many 'fs.'

My mother's portrait,
In her white f-frilled blouse,
Closes the childhood's f-fragile boundary."

Sweating, I sat down between Alan and Nancy.

Nancy leaned in and said, "Mom never wore a white blouse."

Stunned, I almost laughed.

The tradition of sealing the casket arrived after the immediate family bid farewell. The funeral director called Alan to the coffin, and together, they removed Mom's pearl necklace. As Alan brought it to me, according to Mom's last wish, Nancy grabbed it. Pearls rolled a thousand directions over the stone floor like scarabs scrambling in an Egyptian tomb. We left Nancy and the director groveling, collecting the glistening nuggets. Alan and I departed for the Long Island National Cemetery.

Mom's coffin was lowered halfway into the freshly dug cavity in front of my Dad's gravestone. It was my turn to drop a rose onto Mom's casket. I couldn't let it go. I saw my husband waving his arm, signaling me to drop it as though I was embarrassing him. Standing on my left, Nancy whispered, "Drop it." Alan stepped up and cast his rose.

Archangel Azrael's weight shifted as He led me to Mom's graveside. My rose floated slowly, releasing petals on the way.

It took great strength for me to leave my mother's graveside. I imagined how sweet it would be to lie beside the fresh earth and talk with her.

Edmund caught up and stared at me with intense pain. He asked, "See you at home?"

I did not answer. I retained no memory of the limousine ride home. Guests streamed in and out, sharing stories of the grand lady, my Mom.

"I need to talk with you, and my ride home is hurrying me," whispered Aunt Augusta.

"Okay," I agreed, entwining my arm in hers and walking out to the garden.

"I suspect you will be the one to go to John to give him this terrible news," Augusta said.

Flustered, she whispered, "I want to join you. It's a long story. This isn't the place."

I stared at her strained face and said, "I know about your love story with Uncle John. I understand."

I agonizingly knew how love entered uninvited.

"I'm going tomorrow," I said to Aunt Augusta's wobbly rear end.

Edmund and Alan helped clear the aftermath of Mom's wake. Suddenly, I felt confined. I dragged them to the back porch.

Pulling items off Mom's clothesline before sitting, I wondered if this fragrance of fresh laundry would ever be duplicated. Then, wedged between Alan and Edmund on the stoop, I felt safe, forgetting I was the strongest of the trio.

"What is that saying about happy is the corpse?" Alan reflected. "Happy is the corpse the rain falls on, right? Well, looks like rain is on its way," he said.

We perused the late evening sky, filled with dark rain clouds.

Staring into Mom's cherished garden, I whispered, "Mom hated that Elm. I remember she asked Tony to chop it down."

Silence swept over us as night closed in. Then, the rain came, bringing its distinctive smell. Alan stood up, stretching, and said, "Petrichor, coined by Australian scientists in 1964 to describe the unique fragrance associated with rain. The word was constructed from Ancient Greek and means the ethereal fluid that is the blood of the gods in Greek mythology."

I beamed at him as we went in.

Standing at the large kitchen sink with Alan, I mused, "Like old times, I wash you dry."

A massive flash of lightning shot through the house. Edmund ran to us from the front room. We ran into the pouring rain.

I stood between Alan and my husband at the edge of the slate path to Mom's garden.

Holding each other's hands tightly, we gasped at the phenomenon. Lightning had struck only the Elm tree. Its split trunk and branches were scattered across the slate path into the vegetable patch, clearing the fruit and pine trees by inches.

Dancing and getting soaked, we sang to Mom,

"Do you believe in magic in a young girl's heart
How the music can free her whenever it starts
And it's magic if the music is groovy.
It makes you feel happy, like an old-time movie.
I'll tell you about the magic, and it'll free your soul.
But it's like trying to tell a stranger 'bout rock and roll."

Our Mom knew how to say Au Revoir.

Chapter 28

Strong Heart

The next day, Alan said it was too soon for me to go through another tragic encounter. I shared that time was never going to make it easier. I also feared Roy might call to alert the institution's authorities, and I'd never forgive myself for not helping Uncle John through this. I headed to the Port Authority Bus Terminal.

Aunt Augusta stood in line at the Harlem Valley State Hospital bus stop. I spotted Maggie, the faithful husband visitor for 25 years.

"Maggie, how are you?" I politely asked.

"Hi. Where's Florence?" Maggie asked.

I didn't answer, afraid of tears and worn from the apparent response. Maggie hugged me.

I introduced Maggie to Aunt Augusta.

"Marion, I've known Augusta as long as I've known your Mother," Maggie said.

"Of course," I muttered.

Settled in our seats on this bus to hell, Aunt Augusta started fidgeting with her purse. I took the bag and snapped it shut. Squirming in her seat, she shared how her love for Uncle John never wavered over those torturous years. I returned her purse. She rhythmically clicked it open and shut, distracting herself from the pain and driving me bananas.

I leaned back, accepting the familiar nausea bus rides imparted, realizing we were two women who valued love, sorrow included. No further conversation was necessary.

We disembarked and stood beside the path, brushing the creases from our clothing. I thanked Aunt Augusta for enlisting in this heartbreak. Instead of repressing memories of walking this path with Mom, I leaned into them for courage. Azrael caressed my shoulders. We three entered.

The all-too-familiar metal door creaked open.

"Hi, Harry," I whispered to the security guard.

"Where's Florence?" he asked, instantly knowing the answer. Squeezing his arm, we connected in grief and fear.

"This is going to be a terrible blow for John. I'll stand by," Harry, the rare kind guard, offered.

"I spoke with his doctor yesterday to arrange for extra sedatives over the next few days," I said.

"I'll find the doc," Harry mumbled.

My Uncle John laboriously limped across the room. I waved the brown paper parcel. Our eyes met, and he quickened his pace as though I was bringing him happiness.

John's eyes went to Augusta. They tenderly held each other. "I decided to join Marion this time, sweetheart," said Augusta.

John looked back and forth at Augusta and me, and became agitated.

"You don't match," imparted John.

"Let's get the cigs out, Unkie," I suggested.

He stared at me, puffing through a whole unfiltered Camel cigarette in one drag. "Is my Flo sick?"

I considered lying that she'd be here next time. However, my delayed response triggered John to grab my wrist.

"Please let go. Let's hold hands instead," I falteringly suggested. "Your Florence, my Mom, passed on. I'm sure she is in heaven and watching over us," I bargained to lessen his pain.

John stood up and opened his arms wide, appearing like an eagle on a mountain cliff.

John's chortling screams chilled my bones.

Aunt Augusta rushed to the door.

I signaled the guards to maintain their distance.

Standing as tall as I could to meet John's pain, I said, "I'm here."

I kept pace with John, circling the room's vast perimeter, not knowing if I could protect him or others. We maintained this stride for about 20 minutes when a doctor arrived.

"John, I'm so sorry," I said, weeping with him.

Uncle John whispered, "I better go. Florence is with us, Marion. I see her."

"Yes, Uncle John. Mom will always be with us. Azrael, too," I responded. I saw a spark in John's soaking wet eyes.

I turned to the doctor and begged, "Please let me be with him while you give him the sedative. I need to be sure."

Doc nervously replied, "That's impossible, but I promise we will give it to him the second we return him to his room."

"You all suck," I defiantly declared.

Drained, leaving the building, Aunt Augusta and I moped to the bus. We agreed to call one another after future visits to Uncle John. Augusta admitted her daughter was unaware of this intrigue. I promised to take her secret to my grave. Again, oddly, intimately, following my Mom's footsteps.

My Uncle John was forced to live and suffer the death of his Strong Heart. It would appear to the average onlooker that he had always wanted to die. I learned by knowing him that it was an incorrect conclusion. In his chatter about current events, exquisite drawings, love of chocolate and nature, and gentle ways, I saw his immense love for life. His full-bodied laugh was contagious. During our visits, if a fellow patient screeched, Uncle John would stroke their shoulder. The one hurting would calm down. This act endeared Uncle John to me and embedded the importance of touch.

He may have appreciated life more than we passersby. He and thousands like him were only killing the pain their illness bestowed on them.

Chapter 29

Taking Over for Mom

Mom's Will was about to be disrespectfully read four days after her burial. Alan retreated to his room. Mom's remaining children gathered around the coffin table in her home. I tried to opt out, but my attendance was required. Roy and Nancy salivated, wanting to know what more they might receive.

Bernie began, "I, Florence Morse Hoffman, hereby bequeath the house on Mayflower Avenue to my daughter, Marion, and my son, Alan."

"Of course," Nancy complained.

I retorted, "Mom thought Alan might need to remain here indefinitely. She knew I'd protect him. Mom gifted you lump sums when you married."

Within weeks, those two greedy bystanders contested the Will, and Mom's wishes were cast aside like her pearls. The house was to be sold, and monies divided unfairly. That action was not the demise of a family but the death of a farce. Bernie helped me delay the sale until I found a solution for Alan, agreeing to keep this from him.

Edmund was on his way to Montreal to request a transfer to New York. He knew the wrongs families inflicted and that I would remain with Alan. He unthinkingly said Alan could live with us, forgetting our marriage was in tatters. Edmund hid from this fact as a little boy would.

On the first morning with Alan, I watched him slug down his medicinal concoction and head to his accounting job, maintaining oceanography as a hobby. Dr. Greenberg, the Brooklyn Psychiatric wizard, had become my demigod. Who would have thought that?

I sat in Mom's rocking chair, stroking the worn edges of its wooden arms caused by Mom pushing off a million times to fix us a meal, comfort a foster child, or open the locked door with a stern face when I arrived late from a date. This is where she pretended to knit, waiting for the police to call when Alan was missing. It had cradled an honorable woman.

Strewn across the coffin table were three photo albums. I was the designated keeper of the family flicker. Some say memories are more potent than relying on photographs. What does that mean for those of us who have holes in our memories?

I started dusting to sweep away a traumatic recollection that haunted me, leaving me guilty that I had ever feared my brother.

Alan, around 19 at the time, sat at the kitchen table between 1 and 3 AM, blasting his radio for over a month. Mom told me not to open my bedroom door, no matter what. A couple of years later, I learned that Alan turned up the music to drown out the voices in his head. So, this was a perfectly sensible action. If only I had known.

I jumped out of those thoughts with the ringing of the green monster, the telephone. "Sure, have fun at the movies. You have your dose of evening meds, right?" I inquired. "Nah, I'll take them when I get home," Alan sheepishly said.

Fiona got on the phone and snarled, "Alan is fine."

Annoyed at Fiona's gall, I pulled on my sweater and walked to Waterbury Avenue Playground. The park had not changed. The rubber swings on long heavy chains, the shallow pool with six fountains, the sandbox, and my old favorite, the monkey bars. I swung my legs around a cold bar. Resting upside down, I remembered the day Dad built a monkey bar in our backyard. I was three. He ascended the basement to our garden with three hefty pipes and a bucket of cement. An hour later, we stared at the sparse metal sculpture.

Mom declared, "Let's try it."

My hands did not fit around the cold metal tube. Alan swung his skinny legs over it, giggling, upside down. Then, Mom tucked her dress into her apron's belt and swung her well-shaped legs around the monkey bar. Her head barely cleared the grass. Mom made the simplest moments sunnier.

I walked home warmed by this memory.

Alan arrived home at noon the following day.

"Hi, Sis," Alan said as his shaking hands lined up his pills.

I gave him a disapproving stare and poured juice for him.

A week later, Alan's 30th Birthday arrived. I baked a chocolate cake following Mom's recipe, expecting this to be the last celebration in our childhood home. As we ate enormous chunks of cake, he announced he had proposed to Fiona. I had heard about men rushing to marry soon after their mothers' deaths. I was glad he did not know that Mom's Will was broken and that there was a need to settle him elsewhere. Maybe this was fate, and I could stop worrying.

I lay awake that night, mulling over Alan's surprising declaration. I did not expect help from Azrael as this wasn't his expertise. Was it my position to bless Alan's marriage like a parent? I hardly knew Fiona. Her opposition to Alan's medication was distressing. I had no right to share his mental health history to convince her. I vaguely recalled Alan talking about having a vasectomy, too, but was any of this my business?

Fiona refused my repeated dinner invitations. I offered Mom's diamond ring to her as an engagement ring. She declined it, wanting a new one.

The following Saturday, Alan asked for my blessing on his marriage. So much for mulling. I said he seemed happy. Was that so? He said they could iron out their differences and enjoyed many of the same things. I kissed his cheek. His eyes shaped into crescent moons as he grinned broadly.

I touched my lips, realizing kissing his cheek had disturbed me. Since Alan's first suicide attempt, my wanting to hold him and yet not wanting to touch him hung over me.

Somehow, Fiona wrangled a wedding at St. Patrick's Cathedral chapel during Christmas week. Alan did not invite our siblings, remembering how they abandoned us. I liked that he asked Montana to attend. In Tana's weird way, she was there for us.

Fiona looked angelically determined in her white wedding gown of many layers of tulle.

Alan and my husband, the Best Man, were striking in their tuxedos. I wore an Yves Saint Laurent Rive Gauche gray suit.

I asked a stranger at the bottom of St. Patrick's steps to snap photos of our little group.

The spectacular Rockefeller Center Christmas Tree was across Fifth Avenue from St. Patrick's Cathedral. The Channel Gardens, lined with twelve luminous angels, added a touch of splendor. As I photographed the wedding party posing among the angel sculptures, I imagined Azrael flitting around them.

This holy wedding and my growing belly sent me down a fantasy-laden, sentimental path toward my husband. Edmund moved into the apartment we found in a handsome, Art Deco-style, pre-war building on East 79th Street.

Alan lived with me for a few weeks, and Fiona lived with her father while the newlyweds readied their Manhattan apartment. I agreed he could take whatever furniture he wanted. I hoped that one chair, a familiar painting, would remind him to stay on course with his necessary medicine and therapy appointments.

Upon Alan's departure from our childhood home, I hugged him. I was thrilled; it felt normal, free from fear. I wanted to test kissing his cheek, but his body stiffened, alerting me that he was troubled.

"Fiona put a down payment on a Long Island townhouse. I don't know why she insisted we paint the apartment, as we'll probably leave in a few months. Her father will live with us," Alan sputtered.

Hiding a selfish pang, I said, "Her Dad seems like a kind man."

"Yeah, that's okay," Alan slurred.

Squinting at him, I said, "You are taking your meds regularly and keeping your therapy sessions, aren't you?"

"Listen, Fiona says our sex life is better when I take less," Alan sheepishly replied.

I responded furiously, "You know the meds are not an option."

"Still my Toughie Maroono. Have to go. Fiona is waiting," Alan whispered.

On the third frosty Monday night in January, I rushed into my childhood home, shaking the new-fallen snow off my camel hair swing coat. I was the lone caretaker until the new owners moved in. Then, pulling the string for the light over the now-missing kitchen table, I gazed into the living room. I saw the faded red linoleum around the perimeter of a crisp red rectangle where our Persian rug once lay. Mom's rocker was pushed to one corner. The green monster telephone was on the floor. I was stunned.

I mumbled to myself, "You told Alan whatever."

Glancing into Mom's bedroom, I noticed Mom's bed and dresser remained. On her bed was the tiny Samsonite ivory luggage with a tag tied to the leather handle bearing my name. I opened it as wads of white tissue paper sprang forth. I unpacked knitted baby booties and sweaters with matching hats. Did Mom know?

February arrived, and with it, the closing of Mom's house. I noticed the buyers appeared strained. The husband was happy, but the wife was not, reminiscent of my parents. Mom found the suburbs lonely, whereas Dad was enamored with the fresh air. Could this feeling be suspended in the ether? Could the house be haunted? I chalked these silly thoughts off to my imminent departure.

I left the house I grew up in with my belongings, pressed leaves from Mom's garden, and the no longer mysterious luggage. I was relieved. Death had chased me there. Peace rarely seasoned the atmosphere. But no one was to blame. There was no abuse or neglect. Everyone did their best. There were simply circumstances.

Chapter 30

Parallels

I moved into 240 East 79th Street. This is where I would raise my child. Edmund purchased expensive baby clothing and bedding from Saks Fifth Avenue, creating a juxtaposition to his frequenting local bars instead of coming home after work. I met my fears about his behavior by journaling.

My birthday arrived without celebration as I was too tired to go out, and Edmund would not stay in. I went into labor around 5 AM on March 8th. Edmund was excited. I didn't mention his behavior to keep focused on the wonder of this birth. We walked to New York Hospital, a few blocks away. Walking continued to strengthen me.

March 9th, 6:51 PM, my daughter, Erica, was born.

UNESCO (United Nations Educational, Scientific, and Cultural Organization) declared 1979, Erica's birth year, as the International Year of the Child, giving her birth an extra dollop of oomph.

My hand stretched over Erica's swaddled body, sleeping peacefully in my arms. If a desire to protect my daughter at all costs meant we were bonding, it was so.

As evening approached, Edmund called to say he was unable to visit. I heard loud music in the background. To me, he had already disappointed his daughter. We had no visitors.

Edmund had accomplished isolating me. Had Fiona isolated Alan? He did not call or visit me before his move to Long Island. He did not leave a forwarding address or telephone number. Montana said Alan had not even told her he was moving. I believed if he could visit, he would.

Staring at Erica's pink face, circled with a full head of black hair, I promised I would welcome her friends along the way. No isolation for her.

The citrusy side of Frankincense tickled my nose. My best friend didn't desert me. Azrael contained his body at the side of my bed. I felt his eyes, not those of the world. I was sure he was smiling, although his face was not visible. His sigh cradled us. This tender visit allowed my tired eyes to close.

Three days later, I introduced Erica to Mom's rocker and the sock doll Edmund had waiting for her at home. I slipped the knitted yellow booties on her perfect feet. Mom was near. Like Peter Rabbit in the first book I read to Erica, I was euphoric.

Edmund continued to arrive home after bedtime most nights. He said I was boring. There was no arm around my shoulder, little to no conversation. Months passed, with Edmund traveling much of the time. My marriage was not working, as highlighted by a call to our home from a tittering woman asking me to tell Edmund she had an exciting time.

I realized Alan was about to turn 33. I ramped up calls to find him. I called his last job and was told he was on a long-term leave of absence. More frightened than ever, I called Dr. Greenberg. Alan had not kept his appointments for the last three months. Dr. Greenberg called Nassau County hospitals, giving them our telephone numbers in case Alan's name came up.

I lost my battle to stay in New York for Christmas. On December 20, we headed to Saskatoon to celebrate the Holy Birth with his family, still unknown if a coven of witches. I hung my gold crucifix on Erica's neck, tucked beneath her dress. I donned the charm bracelet with a crucifix and my magical gold bracelet. I packed Holy Water.

We stayed with one of Edmund's sisters. The house was cluttered and dirty. Black candles burned to the wick sat openly on the dresser in our room. Mumbling what a decorative touch, I hid them in a drawer and sprinkled Erica with Holy Water. The backyard was unkempt, with an equally unclean chicken coop.

Edmund was uneasy and paced most of the visit. He warned me never to let Erica out of our sight. I saw his figure sitting on the edge of the bed during the night, keeping vigil. My desire to comfort him was dead. By the third morning, he had dark rings under his eyes.

On the fourth night, Edmund faced our daughter, sleeping peacefully between us, and passed out. I was restless. I sat up, deciding to take my turn at watchfulness.

We returned to New York on the afternoon of December 27. Edmund headed to his Manhattan friends. I rushed to Tana, needing the old neighborhood.

I sat on the Naugahyde-covered couch, pulling Christmas presents from my suitcase.

"Come on, open them," I encouraged.

Tana had tears in her eyes. I knew something terrible had happened as I never saw her cry, not even at Mom's wake. Tana showed no interest in my beautiful daughter. She lowered herself into her designated chair, staring at me.

"Marion, Alan killed himself," Tana abruptly said.

I halted peeling off Erica's pink snowsuit, and squeezed her so tight she yelped. I deposited her next to me.

I hid my face in my hands. Did I hear correctly?

"Are you sure?" I asked.

Tana whispered, "Yes."

My greatest fear had happened. I became furious.

"Why didn't anyone call me?" I growled. "I didn't have your number," said Tana.

"You refused to take my number," I harshly reminded her.

I knew my letters to Roy and Nancy listed my telephone number.

"When?" I asked.

"The 21st," said Tana. Then whispered, "Nancy believed you failed Alan by being away."

"What? I was only away for a few days. They were not around for twenty years." I screamed.

I hated myself. My succumbing to Edmund's wishes and traveling westward killed my Mom, and now my brother. No, ridiculous. This is my fault. I was weak compared to my old feisty self. Nancy was right.

Tana did not move to hold me or my daughter. She refused to share Alan's cemetery location, saying Nancy asked her to deny me this crucial information.

I placed Erica in her stroller, wrapped in a velvet quilt. I headed to my old place of solace, St. Raymond's Cemetery. The air smelled like snow. I walked among the white tombstones and marble angels. I knelt at a random grave, but prayer didn't come. Azrael arrived. I stood up and ran out of the cemetery, away from my best friend's love. I did not deserve to be comforted.

I called Dr. Greenberg and fled to him.

In the taxi, I cried. What am I supposed to do with this death? I lay my head back as Erica touched my tear-stained cheek. I'm failing my daughter, having promised to fill her life with happy adventures. But life and death were warring in front of me. I saw that both won. It depended on which direction I looked.

Dr. Greenberg was waiting as the taxi pulled up. He swept Erica into his arms and reached for my hand. I refused it. I could not handle touch.

He placed a tired Erica into a wooden crib in his office, explaining that he treated young mothers with post-partum depression.

"I'm glad you came to me," whispered Dr. Greenberg.

My eyes focused on the slightly worn paths in the printed blue and orange rug created by years of his patients' pacing.

"Are we sure Alan's dead?" I asked, jumping from the chair.

I began pacing perpendicular to the carpet's worn path. Alan was not just anyone. He was my brother. My

Eeyore. I was his Piglet. I was supposed to be there for him. I marched harder, faster, up and down. My mind mushroomed with memories of convincing Alan to come out from under his bed, rooting for him in Little League until I lost my voice, fetching his muddy shotput, his breakaway grin, and the smell of his splattered blood.

The present and future broke through. Alan will never see my daughter; I'll never try kissing his cheek again, and I'll never be able to ask forgiveness for not being near.

Dr. Greenberg sat me down and gave me water. He believed I was ready. It must be so.

He explained that a Nassau hospital informed him of Alan's suicide. He said my fear about Fiona was correct. She convinced Alan to stop the medication in May or June. Alan broke his elbow running after someone or something in July. We were not sure how this happened. His boss granted him a leave of absence.

I whispered that his boss had taken my number in August but would not give me Alan's.

Doc continued that he learned Alan's boss called him on Monday, December 17, informing him they were letting him go.

Dr. Greenberg rose from sitting on the edge of his desk and walked to Erica. His emotions overwhelmed him. After all, he had known Alan for ten years. He moved to his worn leather desk chair, fumbling with papers on his messy desk.

Staring at the notes, he resumed, "Somehow, Alan got hold of a gun. Astounding, considering his recorded mental health history. Friday, December 21, Alan's wife and Father-in-law left for work. Around 9:30 AM, Alan called his boss. Sitting on the interior townhouse stairs, saying goodbye to his boss, he cocked the gun and shot himself in the mouth. I believe that was an act of rage toward his boss and wife. He knew what she would come home to."

"The hospital had no information as to Alan's burial. I'm sorry," whispered Dr. Greenberg.

Dr. G. had called my childhood home number, which was out of service. He left messages on my apartment number from December 21 through that day. I had gone directly to Tana from the airport.

"Marion, we've been through a lot together. We're family," offered Dr. Greenberg.

"Family. We're better than that," I said.

Dr. Greenberg cradled me as I sobbed.

"Alan used to call you the infinite soldier. He said he was surprised you didn't scare the disease away," Dr. Greenberg said.

"My sister feels it was my fault for being out of town," I whispered.

"It is not your fault, Marion, no more than mine. I suppose it is not Fiona's fault either, as most do not understand," he added.

"More important, what do you believe?" he asked.

I did not know if I had failed Alan. I wanted to see Alan's grave. Suddenly, almost vomiting, I sobbed, unleashing my body's pain.

Sometime later, I shared how I ran away from Archangel Azrael's comfort at St. Raymond's.

Dr. Greenberg offered, "You are blessed to have Azrael in your life. I was taught that His responsibility was to help the departing soul detach from the physical body and cross over to the next phase of life in the hereafter. He assists dying souls through seven heavenly halls. He also helps those grieving the loss of a loved one pull their lives together. As far as I can see, you are blessed to have him in your life."

"You are the fourth scholar to say that," I murmured.

I stood by the crib as Erica woke up, giggling. I floated above us. I saw her face reflected in my eyes. I compressed back into my body. My love for Erica superseded my fear. I had to accept my splintered warrior's heart, but how?

Dr. Greenberg helped me with my coat. I kissed his cheek.

"You are a rare human," I said.

Outside, a snowstorm had begun. I knelt by the stroller and removed Erica's mittens to introduce her to snowflakes. She kicked her feet and automatically stuck out her tongue to catch more snow. I laughed. I choked it back. I roared, letting tears and laughter break through.

I walked faster and faster along the busy Brooklyn streets. Azrael's feathers were strewn across every mug I passed. Encouraged by this vision, my Samurai Warrior mode kicked in as I hailed a cab to 79th Street.

What must my next step be?

Chapter 31

Terror

Home was deathly quiet. Edmund respected my pain, although he did not console me. I accepted his psyche's scar tissue from his damaged childhood. I saw his inconsistent attempts to arrive home directly from work as unspoken support. But anxiety tore through me nightly, waiting to hear the key in the door as the clock ticked 6 PM. Maybe Edmund turned over a new leaf for Erica. I would search for my old joie de vivre.

I decided to write Nancy and Roy to forgive them, but it would be a lie. I'd write something. Was Nancy and Roy's guilt for years of neglecting Alan vanquished by punishing me? I remained repulsed by their cowardice.

On nights I woke up pouring sweat, reliving Alan's death, I would grab my worn *Winnie-the-Pooh* book and read to my cradled Erica. I whispered how her Uncle Alan was like Eeyore. And perhaps he'll watch over her. Sometimes, this brought relief.

One harrowing night, I recognized that finding Alan's grave site remained prominent in my thoughts. I recalled how folks with missing loved ones said they could not rest without the body. Families with soldiers missing in action shared the same. Maybe this was a detour requiring correction. Perhaps I needed to feel Alan beyond the physical body. I also had to accept that I may be incapable of that tall order. I was still trying to find my deceased Dad. What is death? I still had no idea.

On March 9th, as Erica turned one, I introduced her to her first ice cream soda at our local diner. Edmund left birthday presents on our sofa for Erica and me. No cards, no well wishes.

As the world dared to rebloom in late March, Edmund bounded into our apartment, announcing he had been promoted to Regional Auditor for Ontario and that we would move to Toronto in May.

I was numb from loss, and I had no particular humans remaining in New York City to nurture. I would rise to the joys and challenges of Erica, my blessing. I accepted the relocation.

My spirit was temporarily lifted as we entered the luxurious apartment complex in High Park, Toronto. The new rotund building encircled a lush courtyard. Our apartment was internally bordered by a curved terrace and a glass wall exposing our living room.

This move to Edmund's native country did not improve our relationship. There were no hello kisses, laughter over dinner, and planning our future intermittently tangled with Edmund's rages. Instead, our only communication was his rage and my soft response, hoping to calm him.

My health was declining, with bouts of fever. Finally, in late June, I was placed on antibiotics for a uterine infection. I began to heal.

In July, Edmund's company sent us to Puerto Rico for a few months while he trained the new Caribbean Auditor.

I looked forward to the beachfront Isla Verde Condominiums, an American enclave, the company letter listed. As we settled into the rented car at the San Juan airport, Edmund said we would stay at a house in Borinquen Gardens instead. While recognizing the isolation he was creating, I shared a New York Times article in which President Jimmy Carter commuted Oscar Collazo's sentence to time served. Mr. Collazo and Lolita LeBron, Puerto Rican militants of the Nationalist Party, would be arriving on September 6 to receive a hero's welcome. Borinquen Gardens was their destination.

"I know," said Edmund.

"Then why endanger us by moving near them?" I asked.

His jaw ground. I hit on a secret. My demise here would mean he could return to Canada alone and with everyone's sympathy. Was I crazy, imagining such a dramatic event? Azrael's constant nearness exhausted me, but frighteningly, validated my suspicion.

A local, Bertha, was assigned as my welcomer by the company. She was in her late 60s, elegant and warm. We hit it off immediately. I insisted that she and her husband, Isador, dine with us on our second night. Edmund was rude. Bertha expressed worry for me. I risked sharing my fear that my life may be in danger. She jumped on this, saying she felt it, too.

We spiritual women decided to have Erica baptized at the Second Union Church of San Juan in Guaynabo, which accepts all denominations. Erica's christening went off without a hitch on a late September Sunday. I walked Bertha and Isador to their car. With a Cheshire grin, Isador handed me the car keys, their Christening present. A pink taxi whisked them away. Edmund was furious.

Two weeks later, Bertha called to say Isador was ill and could I please visit. I headed to our pool, where Edmund was lounging. I was prepared for an argument.

"Sure. I'll run the car over to the garage this afternoon and fill her up for you," Edmund answered, his eyes hidden behind aviator sunglasses. His change of heart surprised me, but my focus was getting to Bertha as soon as possible.

The following day, at 7:30 AM, Edmund left for the office. The sun was crossing our carport. I rolled down the car windows to cool the car and locked Erica's car seat.

"Please stop jumping on my shoulders, sweet Azrael. I promise I will drive carefully," I sang to my best friend.

Snapping Erica's seatbelt, I walked to the driver's seat. I turned the ignition key. The car stalled. I tried again. The car started. Sparks shot from the gear shift box between Erica and me. I lifted Erica high over the sparking box, pressed her to my body, and ran from the car. The vehicle exploded, bursting into flames. I landed on a patch of grass with Erica in my arms. She was screaming. I searched Erica's body under her clothes for injuries. None. Thank God. I rocked her to calmness.

Carmen, my Cuban neighbor, rushed to us. "I've called the fire department. No, don't move," placing her hand on my shoulder. Then, gasping, she whispered, "You have angels near."

Bright yellow fire trucks arrived, followed by the Chief of Police and his entourage. After the medics checked

Erica and me and cleaned my minor wounds, the heavily decorated Chief of Police knelt by me and introduced himself as Chief Alberto. He asked me if I knew who the Indepentistas were. Was I sympathetic toward them?

He helped me into my house. I had to trust him. When I finished sharing my fears about my husband, he stood with me while I wiped gray soot off Erica's face with shaking hands.

"How can I help?" asked Chief Alberto.

I wrote Bertha's telephone number on Mom's leftover pink linen notepaper. Chief Alberto opened his uniform jacket, placed the note carefully in his shirt's breast pocket, and buttoned it.

Chief Alberto said, "I will call Bertha and Isador. I give you my word."

The police combed through the wreckage. Edmund appeared and was questioned.

Chief Alberto and his entourage escorted Erica and me to the airport to return to Toronto.

He told Edmund to remain in Puerto Rico until the investigation was complete.

Being on my own in Toronto, I felt empowered, not lonely. Instead of the car explosion weakening me, it strengthened me. Was this post-shock? Whatever it was, I planned to keep this new gut power. This was the death of a marriage.

At 31, I had found the courage to save my daughter and myself, but not the way.

Edmund arrived in early December and acted as if nothing had happened. In the past, my loneliness drove me to believe in this phony, happily-ever-after phase. My playing along this time was to gain time. I became a good wife.

Chapter 32

The Escape

I became observant of prying eyes across the courtyard into our living room. I connected Edmund's nightly review of my movements in and out of the building with one particular doorman.

One day, as I pushed Erica in her stroller through a mall I frequented, I stared at the sausages hanging on hooks above a clinically clean white metal counter and started bawling.

"Why are you crying at my sausages?" asked a striking-looking woman with large, deep brown eyes beneath thick eyebrows and long, light-brown hair. Her thin body didn't give away her strength, but, like Mom, her well-formed biceps did. Her Italian accent was enchanting.

Wiping my eyes, I said, "No, not your sausages. This display reminds me of my childhood grocery store. A contented place for me."

"I'm Maria. You come have espresso with me," invited the woman.

Then, not waiting for my answer, she took the stroller with Erica and led us through two large metal doors.

"This is my husband, Angelo," Maria introduced.

Angelo touched my shoulder and said, "We've noticed your sadness. Talk to my wife."

Maria guided me to a tiny office decorated with classic white and gold Italian sofas and chairs. Maria gave Erica an anisette biscuit as we sipped espressos from exquisite navy blue and gold porcelain cups. Nearly two hours later, after I had spilled my guts to Maria, Angelo joined us and nodded to his wife.

"If you choose to leave your husband and start a new life with your daughter in New York, we'll help," said Maria.

"That's it," added Angelo.

Walking home, I repeated, "That's it." Laughing at the warmth and resolution of my new friends and co-conspirators.

Plotting my escape melded my spirit of freedom with the sadness of love lost.

I remembered a friend, Diane, at the chemical company in New York. I called her on a public phone. Diane was tired of living with her parents on Long Island. She placed a deposit on an affordable Manhattan penthouse to share with Erica and me. I laughed at her panache. The 24-hour concierge service would provide a layer of protection.

I began buying replacements for Erica's favorite stuffed toys. I periodically dropped them off at Angelo's Deli. I did the same with precious items like Mom's silver and photo albums.

Anything I could hide in Erica's stroller without being missed. My childhood Christmas decorations and other belongings were stored in the building's basement. Angelo filled his car with them the day before my planned escape.

D-Day arrived on a clear, crisp February day.

"Come on, let me drive you to the office today," I suggested, snuggling Edmund. "My therapist is doing wonders for me," I whispered.

"Then you admit this has been your fault," snarled Edmund, smirking.

"Well, almost all," I teased, kissing his neck. I controlled my palpable fear by resorting to my old habit of squeezing my nails into the palms of my hands.

"No, not this time," he said.

Edmund left for the office at noon instead of his usual 9 AM, delaying my getaway. I suspected my co-conspirators were nervously waiting, wondering if our plans had gone awry.

I learned that my neighbor, Kathryn, the she-devil across the courtyard, had accepted money from Edmund to spy on me. That day, Kathryn had positioned herself on her balcony to peer at my every move.

Upon his departure, to satisfy the she-devil, I performed the routine of an average shopping day, handing Erica a little red jacket and hat for her *Winnie-the-Pooh*. While Erica sat on our handmade Persian rug to dress her bear, I slid into our luxurious Bassett leather dining room chair to sip coffee and doodle a fake grocery list.

Our green marble dining room table reminded me of Edmund's stony green eyes. Yes, green couch, expensive green furnishings everywhere to soothe his obsession with himself. He thought I had baby-shit brown eyes. Other suitors had called them Tiger eyes. My cub had tiger eyes, too.

Guilt and sorrow ravaged me as all this was either given to us as presents from my Mom or stolen from my tiny inheritance.

My head raced over the necessary steps to escape. In the kitchen pantry, hidden in my shopping bags, I unearthed a duplicate purse to my usual purse. This contained my passport and a $500 Canadian and American cash mix. I risked this placement a few weeks ago, as Edmund frequently rummaged through my clothes closet.

I slipped Erica into her favorite red Miss Piggy sweater and bundled her in a snowsuit. I donned the camel-hair swing coat from Mom as armor. I closed the heavy door to the luxurious apartment, determined never to see it again.

Edmund was no longer my snake charmer.

I forced a smile in the elevator before landing in the lobby.

"Good morning, Gary," I casually said, passing our doorman.

"Where are you headed, Mrs. K?" asked Gary.

"To the mall. I hope you're here later to help me with my packages," I replied.

"Sure, Mrs. K," assured Gary.

As if I didn't know he would be on the phone with Edmund before I turned the corner.

Count your money, dear Gar, 'cause you won't gain from my terror soon.

I descended the bus steps, piggybacking Erica, and walked directly into the food square.

Shoving Erica's folded red stroller into a store cart, we headed to Angelo's Delicatessen.

A relieved Angelo winked and said, "I've got the best meatloaf mix today, but first, can you help me with a kitten we're feeding in the back?"

"Sure," I agreed.

He led us through the metal doors and onto the employee parking lot, mumbling that Maria was kneeling in their office, praying, worried you were found out. As Angelo handed me the car keys, he kissed Erica and made the cross sign on his chest. I reached into my purse, donned my magic gold bracelet, and placed the crucifix around Erica's neck.

"I'm afraid. What if at the border...." I imparted.

"You'll arrive before Edmund knows you are missing. My son, Johnnie, is waiting in the parking lot downtown where your husband parks. He will remove and pocket the spark plugs from his Volvo. Johnnie will meet you in New York to pick up this car in about a month," responded Angelo.

"Go," he sang, "When the moon hits the sky like a bigga pizza pie, that's Amore."

I knew the dashboard well, as Angelo had reviewed its details several times. My hands shook as I turned the ignition key, and nothing happened.

Angelo shouted, "Again, just cold."

I jumped as the engine turned over. I looked at Angelo.

"I'll call you. Kiss Maria for me. Thank you." I mouthed through the window.

Freddie Flintstone, Erica's favorite bottle, was empty in 15 minutes with two hours left to The Rainbow Bridge. I pulled over at the next stop to change clothes.

The back seat was littered with parcels of apple juice, a thermos of coffee, clothing, and a container of antipasto. Maria had stuck notes on many.

I had never worn a bright orange sweater and a man's oversized olive-green trench coat. Erica was now in a navy blue snowsuit. I thought she'd hate trading her pink one, but she helped me! She snuggled into the front seat with her bottle of apple juice and the car's engine full of petrol. I stuffed Marie's note of encouragement into my pocket and jammed the packaging into a trash can. I took off.

My heart palpitated approximately 20 minutes from the Canadian/United States boundary. I pulled into the last gas station before the border patrol. I needed to calm down. Can I do this? I could still go back.

A knock on my car window shocked me.

"AHHHHHHHH!" I screeched.

The man tapping jumped back and sheepishly gave me the peace sign. I held my chest, and Erica wailed.

I shrugged my shoulders and mouthed, "What?"

Angelo said to trust no one. I scrutinized the man. He wore biker clothes and sported a full beard. The knuckles on his left hand were tattooed H. E. L. L. I did not need to view the other hand. He smiled. I inhaled. Dare I trust him? He held up one finger, gesturing for a minute, and rushed away.

I snapped Erica out of her seatbelt, and she crawled onto my lap. Her little bum touched the steering wheel, and the horn blasted. I screeched again and turned off the car.

"Where is Dog?" declared Erica.

She dove into her oversized, beige, stuffed toy named Dog in the back seat, making me laugh. My retreats into laughter with her balanced my bizarre existence. Existence, not life. Will I ever retrieve my joie de vivre?

Erica tossed the giant stuffed toy at me and returned to her front seat. We were interrupted by a tap on the window. Knuckles held a sign: *I need a lift. My bike broke down, and my group had already doubled up. Destination: Lake Placid for a conference.*

I rolled down the window.

"Group? Conference?" I questioned, chuckling.

I made a rash decision. Having a second adult in the car might throw off bulletins that may have started coming through.

I lifted my face to this outsider and forewarned, "I must cross the border without incident.

Your group will stay far away until we are in New York State."

He ran to the bikers a block away. After a brief exchange, they all raised their hands with the peace sign. Like the notes in a song, my courage rose a few bars. I placed Erica in her children's safety chair in the back seat. She piled her stuffed toys all over her from toe to neck.

Knuckles slumped into the passenger seat, raised his eyebrows, slapped his legs, and said, "Let's go."

"Not until you fasten your seat belt," I instructed.

He grinned and clicked it into place. The engine purred on.

My last vision of Erica was her long lashes and pink cheeks resting on Dog as I coasted down the highway. Arriving at the Canadian/United States border sent me into a fit of hyperventilating and jabbering.

"Miss, miss, breathe," my passenger commanded as he inhaled and exhaled demonstratively.

I squeezed my nails into my palms, allowing the pain to force me to refocus on this endeavor.

"We must not fail," I shrieked at a terrified Knuckles.

"You're scaring me, lady," he yelped.

We were in line on the Canadian side of the Rainbow Bridge. Even in the middle of the week, there was a line. I removed my passport and wallet from my glove compartment and placed them securely on my lap.

I turned to my passenger, "You have your passport, don't you?"

"Hmmm, do I?" he joked.

"Oh God, don't do this to us. We must make it this t-t-time," I stuttered.

"Sorry, just kidding. Wow, you're wound tight," said Knuckles.

I shook my head in disbelief as we moved up to the window. Knuckles had distracted me by accident or perhaps with clever intent.

"Your passport, please," demanded the fierce-looking Royal Canadian Mounted Policeman.

I imagined him as Dudley Do-Right from the comics to stay calm.

"Yes, sir," I whispered.

"I see a toddler in this photo. Is Erica with you?" asked the Mountie.

"Yes, she is asleep behind me," I responded.

The Mountie shone his flashlight on Erica's face. Her lashes fluttered as she reached for Freddy and shoved the bottle back into her mouth without opening her eyes.

"Check," said the Mountie.

Shifting his eyes to my passenger, he signaled for his passport. My passenger handed it over, ensuring his jacket hid most of his hand.

"How do you know one another?" inquired the Mountie.

Aargh! I hadn't considered this. Turning to Knuckles, I gave him my death-ray stare to shut up.

I turned to the Mountie, faking calm, and replied, "He is a neighbor in High Park. He's never seen New York City, so he offered to share driving and gas."

Dusk drifted in early, streaking billowy lavender and pink clouds behind the Mountie's silhouette. He stepped away with our passports.

A gasp escaped my mouth. He turned back.

Knuckles said, "God bless you. That was quite a sneeze."

My knuckles were blue, squeezing the steering wheel. My passenger sat rigidly still.

A commotion started several cars behind us. Motorcycles revved. Cycles moved forward and circled back and forth. Whistles were being blown from every direction.

The Mountie stood near the hood of my car and stamped our passports. He tossed them at us through my open window as he rushed to assist other Mounties with the raucous.

I needed air. I stood and stretched outside the car. I started the engine when I saw the Mountie pick up something from the ground. It was Maria's note. The Mountie began waving his arm over his head, shouting stop toward me.

I frantically looked at Knuckles. He whispered Go. The Rainbow Bridge was 1450' to freedom. I cried uncontrollably as we edged off the bridge onto the U.S. side.

Knuckles tossed his head back and grumbled, "Women."

I drove below the speed limit, barely seeing the road's white lines through tears.

I mumbled, "Bernard, is your real name?"

He nodded, handing me a dirty handkerchief. I wiped my eyes with it as laughter broke through.

"Bear right on I-90. It's only about 30 minutes if someone else were driving," quipped Knuckles, giving me directions to a Hell's Angels Safehouse in Buffalo, New York.

I laughingly said, "Sarcasm, Knuckles, when you are at my mercy? Really?"

Knuckles stared at me and said, "You are braver than you think."

The screaming sounds of Brrrrrm, Brrrrrm surrounded us.

"Ah, your conference buddies," I exclaimed.

Erica peered out the window and asked, "Mommy, who?"

"They are our friends, honey," I said.

Finally noticing Knuckles, she shouted, "Who?"

"I'm Knuckles. Pleased to meet you," he said, reaching between the seats and shaking Erica's round hand.

I followed the extraordinarily enormous gentleman on his Harley. His arms were like tree trunks lumbering up and down, giving clear signals.

250

"How did he find a helmet big enough to fit his noggin?" I asked.

Knuckles shook his head in disbelief and said, "I wouldn't ask him."

Pulling the car in front of a shack, I turned off the engine.

Knuckles and I stared at one another with tenderness, realizing we would disintegrate into being strangers again. I drank in this moment of intimacy.

I retrieved my almost two-year-old bundle of joy from the back seat. Erica pulled her hand from mine, ran to the 'Big Guy,' and wrapped herself around his knee. What is she doing?

Erica raced back to the car, "Mommy, open!"

She shuffled through her toys, pulled out a pink squirrel, and ran to Knuckles. She handed over Cherry. He gently lifted this gift from her hand, looking at me to confirm it was okay. I nodded my head affirmatively.

"This little guy will ride with me from now on. Erica, can I name him after you?" asked Knuckles.

"No, Cherry," stated Erica.

Everyone taunted him, "Knuckles has a cherry."

"Okay, okay, so I do," said Knuckles, turning red. Darkness surrounded us.

While moving Erica's safety seat to the front and Erica rearranging her 'friends' in the back seat, a woman from the group approached. She handed me a scrap of paper with directions back to I-90, mumbling, "These guys can't write. I've been there. Wish ya luck."

We awkwardly hugged.

Except for comfort stops, I stayed on the road. Then, finally, I saw the rectangular green sign with white writing, *New York City*, along the highway. My road time was 6 hours and 20 minutes. Knuckles, alias Bernard, would have been proud of this feat.

I steered the car into the circular driveway of the East 90s' new Douglas Elliman building. A uniformed doorman met us. He buzzed 30B, but there was no answer.

Then, Diane ran out of the darkness, screeching, and whisked Erica into her arms. Stretching my legs, I sniffed the grime and listened to the joyous sounds of taxis honking, loud voices, and trucks screeching to a stop.

New York, I'm back.

Chapter 33

The Evolving Door

Our new home on the 30th floor was stark, with west-facing, expansive windows across bright white walls. Diane's wealthy parents had co-signed the apartment and provided furniture. Her mother asked me to encourage Diane to be self-sufficient in return. I agreed. I owed her a great deal.

I stared out the massive window, mesmerized by my twinkling city. The New Moon was nowhere to be seen, but she and I would begin to fill ourselves with light.

My bedroom consisted of a single bed with a high tufted fuchsia headboard and a crib connected by a plush cherry pink rug. My bed was outfitted with a pink sheet set and a polka-dot hot pink duvet. It reminded me of my childhood bedroom. I took a deep breath and decided to take a no-nonsense approach, allowing this pink to fortify me.

I tucked Erica into the pale pink crib with three blue and gold cherubs on the curved headboard. My daughter snuggled her toy Dog, falling fast asleep.

As I rested on my bed, sadness for Edmund arose. A swish of feathers against my head reminded me to let go. Love takes us to places we don't want to go, but when we return, we've often grown.

I glanced at my daughter. Like me, she will discover good human men to trust, like Doc Greenberg, the clergymen, and the professors who touched my life with wisdom and kindness. If necessary, she will be saved as I was by Angelo and the most unusual, Knuckles. While Azrael, my cherished best friend, repeatedly saved my life and mind, I believed he would agree it would be grand if Erica did not require his companionship.

Life sped up in New York, just as I had hoped. I practiced a fire drill, holding Erica and walking down the 30 flights. I researched nursery schools while Diane found agencies offering secretarial jobs.

I called Maria and Angelo. Our conversation was filled with relief and love. Their son, Johnnie, would pick up the car in late March. I had already purchased T-shirts with the NYC logo for them.

I dressed Erica in her maroon velvet coat and matching hat and donned my heather gray suit as we headed to the nearby well-respected *House of Little People Nursery*. We would celebrate her second birthday that night. Turning 31 did not thrill me.

"Fingers crossed for you. I know Erica will knock them out," shouted Diane, laughing.

Erica made the cut. My favorite nursery features included daily music lessons and a small room with six potty-training seats. Mom would have laughed.

Caroline, the nursery's director, understood I was the only one to fetch Erica. If that changed, I would call ahead even if I was bleeding. I hadn't yet trusted Diane to be an alternate. Caroline said I was not the only mother in this predicament and suggested I get a restraining order. My gut churned at the surreal thought that I needed one. I was embarrassed. I shared this with Diane. She said she was looking for something to do.

That evening, Diane dressed Erica in a red sweater and beret to match her flaming red coat. I wore Angelo's oversized trench coat, trusting it would cocoon me when dealing with the police as it did with the Canadian Mountie.

Diane swooshed her sexiest swagger as she pushed Erica's stroller into the police precinct. While I inquired how to obtain a restraining order, Diane flirted with the cute officers.

The Desk Sergeant looked me up and down and asked why I wanted one. When I explained, he said it was insufficient. He said good night and resumed looking at papers on his desk. I was dismissed. I gripped the stroller with one hand, dragging Diane from her uniformed, drooling men, and stormed out of the precinct.

From that day on, I became acutely aware of my surroundings outside 30 B. Men whose backs resembled Edmund's height or hair color made me jumpy.

I forged ahead, utilizing the nursery's part-time hours to acclimate Erica while I signed with administrative agencies, bringing Diane along.

The first time I left Erica at the nursery, she became hysterical. Her tiny, round hands opened and closed, reaching for me. How could I make her understand? I rushed to a nearby phone booth and called the nursery, ready to return and take Erica. Caroline answered the phone and assured me that most children reacted that way when their parents left the first few times.

She added that it was a healthy sign for the child to be lovingly attached to the parent. I reminded myself that Dr. Spock wrote that nursery schools were beneficial for only children.

Caroline soothed me, "Erica is seated at the piano with John, our pianist, touching the keys. Can you hear the tinkling?"

I listened. Still unsatisfied, I returned to the nursery and peered through the window. I saw Erica on the piano seat and vowed to hurry back. I remembered my foster siblings. Did they scream in terror, leaving the Hoffman house?

Diane moaned while we filled out the agencies' forms, making me laugh and easing my anxiety for Erica.

A few hours later, at the nursery, Erica raced to me and said, "Mommy, look," pointing to a little boy. Caroline said they held hands while singing. I hugged Caroline and the piano player for too long before rushing out with Erica in my arms, not in the stroller.

I honed my administrative skills in temporary jobs for several months. In September, I spread the word to agencies that I was ready for a permanent position.

I headed to a job interview on a crisp October morning. Erica curled up on our couch with Diane. I repeated instructions to avoid letting anyone in and not to venture outside the apartment with Erica. Diane became annoyed, placing her hand over her heart and swearing to God.

My interview was on the Upper East Side in The Manhattan House, Penthouse One. I was to meet with John, Archivist for Benjamin David Goodman, the legendary American clarinetist and bandleader known as the "King of Swing." My hands sweat knowing I had an embellished resume and a celebrity was reading it.

"I dig your hat," said a smooth-voiced, distinguished gentleman in a claret red silk quilted smoking jacket over perfectly pleated black trousers. His black velvet slippers had gold tassels.

A mature woman in a maid's uniform approached me, "I'm Margaret," taking my camel hair coat. I kept my antique forest-green cloche on.

I looked at a huge oil painting in the plush living room and realized I was talking with Benny Goodman. I mentioned my interview was to be with John. Mr. Goodman asked if I was disappointed. I blushed, wanting to run out. Then, Mr. Goodman laughed and led me to a chair.

Our interview was filled with delightful chatter, without a smidgen about my skills. In addition to being a famous jazz musician, Mr. Goodman, now in his later years, explained that he was reigniting his classical music roots. He explained that years ago, he commissioned leading composers to write new works for the clarinet. Among them were Aaron Copland, Bela Bartok, and Paul Hindemith.

Mr. Goodman escorted me to his second-floor office. Benny put his arm around my shoulder and led me to a desk. I was to start work as his Assistant the following Monday.

I ran home, stunned by my good fortune. My job was 30 minutes walking distance from my home and Erica's nursery. Mom would have jumped for joy at this opportunity with Benny Goodman. Sorrow blanketed me as Alan's trumpet-playing days sprang to mind. Battle on.

I found Diane finishing a manicure for Erica, complete with red nail polish. I apologized for my over-protective lecture.

Within weeks, Mr. Goodman asked me to call him Benny. I was honored.

Benny preferred working in NYC to touring, easing my fear of how to handle my single-parenting situation. He frequently performed at the 92nd Street Y, New York City's world-class cultural and community center, where people connect through culture, arts, entertainment, and conversation. By December, I understood my duties as an Advance Person. Days or weeks before the band and crew arrived, I would quality-check facilities, accommodations, and promotional material to my maestro's standard. Goodman played 2 1/2 strength reeds, and I ensured I had a hand-picked batch. I would triple-check that a second line of instruments was in place on the night of the performance. I learned hard lessons about the musicians' fragile egos as they frequently complained that the spare instruments were not up to par. I had to trust the piano tuner because I was tone-deaf. I pampered him.

Forced to become a people person, interacting and negotiating were surprisingly easy. My stutter went unremarked. The creative world was more accepting than the general public, seeing a fault as unique.

I was a paid worker. I had learned that Benny paid his musicians poorly, claiming they should be honored to perform with him. I understood that my poor salary fell in line, but it was mine.

My feet danced in place during a rehearsal, absorbing the music. Benny stared at me long enough for me to cringe and stand still. I wondered if this stare was "The Ray" musicians warned me about. Instead of screaming at a musician unprepared at rehearsal, Benny would stop the program and stare until the musician cracked and apologized.

March rolled around, and I turned 32. At 8:30 AM, I entered Mr. Goodman's office and found 12 long-stemmed white roses with a note. I panicked as Edmund used to give me white roses.

I jumped as the phone rang. Benny called to say Happy Birthday. I stammered.

My daily schedule with Mr. Goodman began with a briefing in his penthouse at 9 AM sharp. That day, he instructed, "Out with it. Why did you sound nervous on the phone? We can't have that."

I told my tale of woe due to hubby Edmund as briefly as possible. "We need to change a few things around here," Mr. Goodman said. Had I said too much? Was I going to be fired?

"Let's have Sammy take you to Erica around 4. Now, work. Get me the Carnegie Hall gig. I want Spanky for that," said Mr. Goodman.

Benny Goodman quickly became my second angel.

I introduced Sammy to Caroline at the nursery, handing in his photo. She was impressed that he was bonded. From that day on, he brought Erica to my office for hugs on their way to Penthouse One. Mr. Goodman and Erica chatted over milk and cookies on the evenings he was not preparing for a performance. Margaret was happy with this development, hinting that Benny did not see his grandchildren as often as he wished.

On March 9, Erica turned three. Sammy took her and six friends to a nearby McDonald's for her birthday party. We Moms met the limousine outside the fast food shop. Sammy arrived frazzled as the automatic car windows swished up and down, and the music on the radio changed stations rapidly. All orchestrated by a few pairs of sticky hands.

That night, fortified by the silly fun, I gathered the courage to call Edmund to give him the opportunity to wish Erica a Happy Birthday. Maybe he won't answer. I nearly hung up upon hearing his voice. Holding the receiver for Erica, I watched her face for clues that all was well. Erica pushed the receiver away and buried her head in my lap. Trusting Edmund would not harm his baby daughter, I apologized she rushed off. He chortled and said he told her she had a bad Mommy. I hung up, realizing that future communication must be through the courts. Push on, Marion.

I arrived at Penthouse One promptly at 9 AM the following day. Margaret shushed me and led me to Benny's dining room table. Benny was not waiting for me as usual. I glanced through the nine-foot-high arch into the living room. Seventy-one-year-old Benny, wearing a sapphire-blue quilted morning jacket, was laughing and kibbitzing with 64-year-old Yehudi Menuhin, violinist extraordinaire.

In contrast, Yehudi wore an ill-fitting cardigan complete with elbow patches. Benny introduced me from afar, grinning proudly. Then, they bowed their heads as though in prayer for a moment of silence.

They began to play Bela Bartok's "Contrasts for Violin, Clarinet, and Piano."

I inhaled the magnificent music filling the penthouse. Then I giggled. Margaret frowned. I was free from my 26-year search for my deceased Dad. I believed my Dad had unearthed a path to say he loved me through Yehudi Menuhin's violin performance. Benny winked at me. I suspected he felt the music moved me to this explosion of joy. I would do nothing to destroy that belief.

The next couple of months passed in a peaceful routine. Diane took temporary secretarial jobs but fought against a permanent one. This strained her contribution to our rent. Her parents picked up the slack.

In late May, Diane dropped out of our apartment share and moved back to her parents' home on Long Island. She couldn't bear the taste of financial responsibility and wanted to hang out at the beach. I was aware of her immaturity as it was part of her charm. I never did add her name to fetch Erica at nursery school, but I had much to thank her for.

I maintained the high rent for a few months while searching for a less expensive apartment.

In early June, Benny surprised me in the office. He was elegantly dressed in a gray linen suit. I wore a red linen sheath dress. Benny hummed, "Lady In Red." He tested a Compact Disc Player about the size of a record player on its side. Sony gave this to Benny to obtain his opinion of the sound. He played it over and over, taking excessive notes. I knew I was witnessing a historic moment.

Beaming proudly, he invited me to Michael's Jazz Pub on East 56th Street for Woody Allen's Monday night clarinet performance. Margaret babysat Erica in his apartment.

Walking into Michael's on Benny's arm gave me a taste of power as we were guided to a front table pulled from nowhere. Benny sauntered toward Woody, nonchalantly interrupting the segment.

Woody jumped and excitedly announced, "Hey, everyone, it's Benny Goodman."

Round of applause.

Woody sat down to continue playing, but Benny whispered to him.

Woody handed Benny his clarinet as though in a trance. Benny removed Woody's reed and started sucking on a reed pulled from the pocket of his silk shirt, eventually inserting it into Woody's clarinet.

Benny played *These Foolish Things (Remind Me of You)*.

Benny returned the clarinet to Woody. Mr. Allen muttered something, visibly disgusted as he was germophobic. He did not play further that night.

A man in the audience confiscated Benny's saliva-dripping reed. Wrapping the wet reed into his handkerchief, he stopped at my table, whispering he was an amateur clarinetist and believed this reed might make him play better.

Benny captured me. I was enamored. An unconventional friendship was forming between us. I clung to his fatherly affection, yet wondered if I could be romantically involved when he sang to me. He was a big flirt. I reviewed possible engagements with him in his penthouse some evenings, and his girlfriend would arrive and wait. She was a beautiful, stylish, mature woman. I liked her.

Chapter 34

The Call

I was busy booking musicians early that July. Benny hand-picked them for each gig. The massively talented instrumentalists rehearsed before Benny joined them. Benny sent me to ensure they practiced. Those interludes from office work were pure merriment for me. Leroy Eliot "Slam" Stewart, a well-loved and respected double-bass player long before working with Benny, was one of my favorites. Slam made his bass talk to me and said my stuttering lent well to scatting. Ronald J. "Spanky" Davis was a young, talented trumpet player. According to Benny, Spanky didn't practice enough to send his music to heaven. His musician buddies and much of the jazz world thought differently. John Paul "Bucky" Pizzarelli, jazz guitarist, was a quiet gentleman. He escorted me home from rehearsals even when I protested. Fear of Edmund's threatening appearance dissolved.

Back at the office, catching up with concert invitations, the busy phone rang.

"Hello, Benny Goodman's office. How may I help you?" I asked. "Hello. This is Frank Sinatra," said a voice.

"Spanky, is that you? Stop the jokes. I'm busy, but I will hire you when Benny needs a horn," I giggled.

"Miss. What is your name?" asked the caller.

I gulped, thinking this voice might belong to Mr. Sinatra.

"Marion, sir," I mumbled.

"Please give the following message to Mr. Goodman. Frank Sinatra asks a favor to play at the Whitehouse on November 2nd for The King and Queen of Jordan during their visit," stated the voice. "You got that?" asked the voice. "Here's my number," Mr. Sinatra offered.

"Yes, Mr. Sinatra," I replied.

Then, I immediately called the number. Mr. Sinatra answered on the first ring and growled that it was the correct number.

I gave Benny the message.

Mr. Goodman thundered that he would not play for a Republican President and never in hell as a favor to Sinatra.

Mr. Sinatra, personally, persisted with daily calls for almost three weeks, knowing I had to give Benny every message. By the end of the second week, we skipped polite chatter. As the third week stretched, he became agitated and asked my opinion about Benny agreeing. I declined a response, and he slammed down the phone. Yet, he called the next day.

I dialed Frank's number on the fifth day of the third week with Benny's definitive answer. "Hello, Mr. Sinatra. Benny will play at the White House on November 2. Please excuse me, but I have been instructed to quote his message verbatim: "I am playing to honor our country in welcoming The King and Queen of Jordan, not as a favor to you, Frankie. End quote," I said, stifling laughter.

Frank laughed and asked, "Do you know who his musicians will be?"

"Yes, sir, I do," I responded.

"Well?" Frank asked, irritated.

"I can't tell you, sir," I whimpered.

Frank ended our conversation, "You've been terrific, Marion. Get a new dress. Your invitation is on its way."

Chapter 35

Moving and More

Entering the New York Family Court that September was intimidating. Faking confidence, I marched through the vast lobby and past multiple security guards. My knees weakened as I pulled the highly polished courtroom door open. The space was sparsely furnished, with two substantial wooden desks miles apart. In front of the room was a raised wooden podium, the judge's bench. That position gave the judge control of the room. His staff sat close by so they could communicate quietly.

A figure waved to me to join him. I had a brown envelope with a few documents and felt unprepared. I pulled out a photo of my daughter to remain strong during this first round of achieving custody. The presiding judge yawned while stating I must compile police reports, acceptable witnesses, that sort of thing, as proof of domestic violence. I was to retrieve the particular police report from Puerto Rico, and photos, if possible.

"You mean, beyond the journals I handed in, I have to find solid witnesses willing to give written testimony to my being emotionally tortured or, better still, hit?" I asked.

The judge stared at me.

I took a few minutes, head down, to retrieve composure. I apologized for my outburst and agreed with the judge's decision to offer Edmund visits under two conditions. I was to remain during his visits with Erica, and he was to show proof that he had begun therapy.

The judge continued that Ontario would be informed of the ruling. I was instructed to record Mr. Koenig's visits until I returned to court in three months and to make an appointment on my way out. I thanked the judge, noting how inconsequential the experience made me feel. I started shoving the papers into my now-ripped brown envelope. My legal aid stopped me.

"The good news is you have temporary custody," said the bored judge.

I sat, stunned. The legal aid smiled at me. The world was suddenly a better place.

I asked Caroline for advice on how to help Erica understand that her Dad would no longer live with us. She had none. It was personal. Caroline said my relationship with my daughter appeared well-adjusted, shown through Erica's drawings, her questions, and her daily running to me, giggling.

Erica had not asked about her Dad. Edmund's being away on business trips and staying out after work made our life without him less noticeable.

Over a dish of chocolate ice cream, I showed Erica a photo of Edmund holding her as a baby. She asked for her blue bunny and began crying. I was shocked. During one of Edmund's last rages in Toronto, he tore the blue bunny from Erica and tossed it over the terrace. I swallowed my prepared speech, comparing Edmund's sickness with her sniffles. Erica jumped from her chair onto my lap. Stroking her hair, I told her the blue bunny would return. I bit my lip, realizing the shopping task I had just sworn to. She asked for her Flintstone bottle. Snuggling, we napped on the couch together as the bowls of ice cream melted.

In October, we moved into a walk-up building on East 34th Street. Our new address had the earmarks of what we New Yorkers call interesting.

Our renovated one-bedroom apartment was on the third floor. I painted the white bedroom a pale blue, leaving white spaces resembling clouds. Erica's crib was traded for a wooden children's bed with guard rails. I set my bed in the living room and created a North African-style space with colorful cushions from a local Moroccan store. I filled the decorative fireplace with candles and piled my books beside and on the mantle. I had an antique loveseat recovered in a sturdy slate-blue fabric used on British Rail seats.

On the first morning, as I scrambled eggs, operatic singing filled our new apartment. I threw open the living room windows. A tenor was singing O Sole Mio. I swelled with joy as I heard fellow tenants opening their windows. Saturday mornings, my neighbor, Vinnie, a WW II Veteran with piercing grey eyes, a severe limp, and a reasonably constant hangover, rolled his washing machine from his apartment directly across the hall into my kitchen. I moved it back when I finished my laundry, including a thank-you lunch.

Richard and Emily, a British couple in the movie business, resided one floor below. They showed me their current project, creating a film picture book, *Watership Down*.

A homeless woman nicknamed the Fire Lady sometimes rested in the building's vestibule. Our young superintendent alerted me that she occasionally threw lit matches at passing folks. As a result, the police periodically took her to Bellevue Hospital, where she was released back to these streets within days.

I bought a Cadillac of a bicycle and had a deluxe children's bike seat welded on the back.

Erica and my matching safety helmets completed the picture. I strapped Erica into her bike's safety seat and peddled everywhere.

Life was creating new, happier memories. Would they demolish the lingering frightening ones? Were they supposed to, or were they to crash in and out like the tide?

I missed Azrael. After all, he was my only lasting friend for 26 years. I began praying for my Archangel's well-being. Life was full of surprises.

October 31 arrived. The only decorating I did for that Halloween was to stick a pumpkin in our apartment fireplace. I took Erica and her oversized "Dog" to Benny's penthouse for a sleepover with Margaret. The blue bunny was still at large.

Confident in Erica's safety, I headed to Washington, D.C., to prepare for the November 2nd White House gig. As this was a spectacular engagement, a 24-hour vigil was expected of me. I was relieved that Benny chose Spanky to be my Co-Advance Person. We were two compatible Pisces.

Benny Goodman's Quartet consisted of Milt Hinton on bass, Hank Jones on piano, Bucky Pizzarelli on guitar, and Buddy Rich on drums.

Spanky was responsible for the White House piano being tuned to Benny's specifications, and a second and third batch of instruments were in place. I kept a secret box of Benny's reeds in my hotel room.

I ensured the musicians showed up, pampered them, and monitored them around the clock. Noting my nerves, the bassist woke me at 2 AM the night before the gig, saying he didn't feel well. Wrapped in my black floral kimono, I rushed to his room with the hotel doctor, only to find the three musicians grinning as they serenaded me with *Take The A Train*. I bowed and kissed each one on the cheek, sending them to their rooms feeling like Snow White.

On the day of the event, I had just returned to my hotel room after supervising the placement of the programs on the State Dining Room table, which was precisely 1 inch to the right of the wine glasses. Someone frantically knocked on my door as I wiggled into my slinky royal-blue Chinese mandarin-collared gown.

Spanky burst in and informed me that Buddy Rich refused to leave his hotel room unless his name was above Benny's on the White House Program.

"Good luck," said Spanky, laughing.

"Very funny," I moaned.

With two hours to show time, I ran to Buddy Rich's hotel room with my legs zig-zagging due to my tight-fitting gown. I told myself not to stutter, as it would lessen my authority. Then, taking a deep breath, I entered Buddy's room.

"Mr. Rich, you look dapper in your trousers. May I help get your shirt and tuxedo on?" I asked.

Buddy stretched out on the bed, his hands folded casually behind his head, and asked, "Have you placed my name above Benny's on the program?"

"The offi-f-ficial program was placed on the State Room dining table, including the King and Queen of Jordan's setting, hours ago," I responded.

"I can offer that Benny announces you f-first and gives you a longer spiel than the other musicians," I compromised.

"I hope your stutter is real because it's softening me," replied Buddy Rich. I smiled demurely. Buddy didn't move. Time ticked by.

Finally, Buddy said, "Okay, you've got a deal."

"May I help you finish dressing and escort you?" I requested.

"Scared, kid?" laughed Buddy.

"Yes, sir," I replied.

"You should be because we both know you have to convince Benny," said Buddy, unable to contain his laughter.

Benny announced Buddy Rich as requested. Three standing ovations followed the legendary performance. Benny looked straight at the King and Queen of Jordan and bowed. Security men led Benny to their Majesty's side. I swelled with pride.

Later, I stood with Benny, swaying to the music provided by the four musicians for the guests to dance. I adjusted Benny's bow tie as he ascended the stage for an impromptu solo.

An unmistakable voice whispered, "I believe you owe me a dance."

I became rigid. The Voice touched my arm. I almost walked away. I told myself not to miss that moment. I faced Frank Sinatra, my head lowered. He tenderly wrapped his arm around my waist. A manly fragrance broke through his cologne, making me shake. I looked up. We smiled. He pressed his cheek against mine as we floated on the dance floor.

"I'm sorry," I whispered.

"What for?" Frank softly asked.

"Shaking," I mumbled.

Frank pulled me closer.

"Relax, kid," he whispered.

"Marion, like in Robin Hood, right?" asked Frank. Relaxing, we giggled about Benny giving us the *Ray*.

Frank still had his arm around my waist when the dreamy dance ended.

Benny grumbled, "The musicians are waiting for you, Marion."

Frank whispered he would see me in New York.

Chapter 36

Acceleration

Back in New York, I rushed to Penthouse One, excited to pick up my daughter. I swung Erica into my arms and smelled Benny's girlfriend's perfume saturated on her dress. Margaret laughingly said Erica was too fast for her. Erica pulled me to her coloring book, and I helped her sign her work. This was new. Margaret explained that Erica had walked to all the paintings and asked why scribbling was at the bottom.

The memory of Frank's tender touch was still with me. Phew. Margaret and I giggled about Benny's annoyance with my Frank Sinatra dance. Margaret wondered if he would fire me. Benny did not fire me, but I did not receive an annual raise. I was unsure if it was his retaliation or his cheapness. I adored working for Benny, but New Year's Eve rolled around without a holiday bonus.

As a single parent, I began job interviews in mid-January. I ended with a position doubling my salary.

Mr. Goodman accepted my resignation. This was a painful parting as our relationship had rolled into a friendship. I was frustrated as we worked well together, and he could afford my salary increase. I worried that Erica would be upset, too.

Margaret called. She overheard Mr. Sinatra bugging Benny for my telephone number and asked if I wanted her to give it to him. Frank was thirty years older than I and married to a lovely socialite and a fellow Pisces. I fantasized about meeting him at one of his New York City hangouts, Rao's, and sharing espresso kisses. I chose to decline future complicated clandestine dates. I accepted that I would have moments of regret, like most women.

In early March, I reported to the president of an international shipping company. I had a nursery school staff member bring Erica to my job on Friday evenings to make her feel secure about my whereabouts. Enamored with Erica, secretaries offered crayons, jelly beans, and stuffed toys. She adjusted well. I missed Benny.

The evening before my April court date, Edmund rang. I was disheartened as he had not visited Erica or started therapy. He told me he was remarrying as soon as our divorce was final. Snake-charmer shamelessly shared that he had bought a custom-fit beige suit for the occasion, having not sent my belongings or a dime for child support. He wanted me to say hello to his new wife. Shocked, I agreed, hoping to warn her. The newbie ignored my words and said I was jealous. Edmund met my attempt to help his next victim with wild threats. I faced how sneakily his abusive behavior had entered my life. I also felt guilty for losing Mom's gifts. This was the web Dr. Greenberg explained I needed to climb through.

Staring at the phone, imagining it to be the dragline of a spider web, I smacked it. I was determined to step out of this phase. I would make up for those losses. I grew up as a survivor. I am a worker and a happy single parent.

The next day, I stood tall, facing the Judge. "Good day, Mrs. Koenig," began the Judge.

"Hello, sir," I boldly responded.

"I have a new ruling from the Ontario Court and will read it aloud for the Clerk to record," the Judge continued.

I wrapped my hands around the edge of the desk to steady myself as my knees wobbled.

"A good Samaritan came forward on your behalf. His sworn statement confirmed significant incidents of abuse. His apartment was catacorner to your apartment in High Park. This elderly gentleman had reported two incidents to the police, who claimed they did not intervene in domestic issues.

A bald gentleman with a gray mustache flashed through my mind. He had stopped me in our lobby and whispered that I could knock on his door anytime. My independent attitude didn't always serve me well. Or was I only able to cower during Edmund's tirades?

The judge continued that Edmund had surrendered his right to shared custody.

Furthermore, the Ontario judge stated that you chose to reside in the most expensive city in America, disregarding that it is your hometown. He lowered child support from $1, 800 to $1, 000 per month. Therefore, I can only read this as punishment," stated the Judge.

"Please note, New York does not have a reciprocal law with Ontario. We cannot demand these funds from your husband," said the judge.

"I see. He didn't respond to the court order to return all he stole. I can raise Erica without fear. Thank you," I mumbled.

"Edmund sounds unstable. I advise you to stay alert," the judge added almost warmly.

I brushed the judge's comment off, determined to ignite the courage Mom had ingrained in me.

May blossomed, briefly bringing romance. An elegant man with graying hair, wearing a navy-blue suit, sauntered to my office, flirtatiously introducing himself as Mitchell, VP of Finance.

I viewed dating as a huge step, so I declined his initial requests. We flirted and laughed at the office. Our first dinner date ended with a front-door kiss. He bent down, and I stroked his hair. My fingers became entangled in his heavily hair-sprayed locks. To lighten the moment, I asked if I had broken his hair. Unfortunately, Mitchell did not share my sense of humor. We remained friends.

The company's President, my boss, drank heavily while gambling large stakes at Mah Jongg most nights. I stayed the course into late autumn. One disgusting day, he tossed his briefcase on my desk, insisting I open it. It was crammed with porn magazines. I closed it and lied that I could not unlock it. He removed the chair facing his desk, forcing me to take shorthand standing. Time to move on.

Chapter 37

Unplanned Progress

Days before Christmas, I received a single mother's holiday miracle. I landed what appeared to be a calmer administrative position, maintaining my salary. I was to report to Anthony Walters, Head of Sales at the newly opened St. James Condominium Towers in Sutton Place.

Anthony had a massive head of wavy hair, making his head appear too big for his average build. He was a few years younger than I and had an upper-crust British accent. Our interview was not in line with New York State employment regulations. Mr. Walters said my resumé made him comfortable. He asked about my marital status and daughter, whispering that there should be little to no overtime. I suspected this was Mr. Walters' first executive position due to his awkward questions and fidgety stance. I believed my brush with powerful sorts would allow me to teach him the ropes, endearing me to him. As I departed, Mr. Walters said to call him Anthony, and he'd see me in the New Year.

I skipped up the steps of St. Patrick's Cathedral to light candles and share the good news with Mom and Alan. The main entrance's nine-ton bronze doors gave me pause. The 26-foot Rose Window above the main doors gave me courage. I performed the sign of the cross, remembering my friend, Jean. Acknowledging right or wrong, rituals gave me hope. So, I, the Presbyterian, lit candles for all in front of the Sacred Heart figure.

I told Mom about Erica's cheeky personality juxtaposed with the fragileness I saw. I shared that her granddaughter seemed to be a shoe-loving woman like herself, constantly wearing her red Kermit boots indoors or out. I whispered how I cradled Erica in her rocker.

I bundled the foster children into a mental ball of soft, colorful yarn, seeing them playing and warm. I sent them kisses. Yet, I did not find peace.

I told Alan to be patient about finding his grave, reminding him I had unearthed him in Times Square. I asked if he had an ocean in heaven to study. I told him I was not angry with him for taking his life. Then guilt sent me down a dark corridor. On my knees before the Sacred Heart, I blanked out. A bystander tapped my shoulder, asking me to move. I was disappointed that Azrael didn't show. Walking along the now-dark city streets, I accepted that grieving had no time limits and no boundaries. It may ride alongside my new life. It was okay.

The next day, I took Erica to the Metropolitan Museum of Art. We entered the Medieval Sculpture Hall. The twenty-foot blue spruce was decorated with lifelike angels over an eighteenth-century Neapolitan Nativity scene. Erica sat cross-legged at the tree's base, captivated by the creche figurines. I searched for Archangel Azrael in the porcelain-faced angels. My loneliness for him frightened me. Would my wish for his return create more deaths around me? Would he return? Does his presence have to be connected to death? Wasn't our friendship beyond that?

Erica's hand reached for mine, reminding me where my heart and soul belonged. Ashamed, I swept my daughter into my arms. We left, humming, "Oh, Christmas Tree."

I began my new job at St. James's Tower the following Monday. I learned Anthony's half-brother and co-developer was Peter de Savary, the eccentric, cigar-smoking Englishman with a personality consisting of high energy. It was rumored he only slept two to three hours a night. Mr. de Savary and his executive staff temporarily resided in Rhode Island, preparing to participate in the American Yacht Race.

The St. James's salesforce comprised bright, young, good-looking men with first-class British accents. I snickered, thinking who could say no to these guys?

My days sped by interpreting New York potential clients' comments to the salesmen as each returned from a showing with distraught faces. They insinuated that the customers were rude, didn't know a marble surface from a granite one, and how dare they arrive wearing filthy shoes and chewing gum? I could barely believe I was being paid for this fun position.

A call interrupted my fifth working week. Caroline said that Erica was holding her ear and not eating.

Anthony offered his car. The Pediatrician prescribed antibiotics. On the third day, nursing Erica at home, I called my friend, Carol, as Erica was not improving. She was vomiting. Carol suggested we take her to Louise, her Psychic friend. I reminded Carol that she was a nurse, and that sounded nuts. She softly replied that she had seen unexplained miracles in the hospital. That is where she met Louise. My Erica was hurting, so off we went.

We arrived at Louise's building in New Jersey with a swaddled Erica. We were guided into a room painted a blinding bubblegum pink. Am I supposed to learn something from pink rooms? Yes, even the curtains, chairs, and rug. Being inside a well-chewed stick of Hubba-Bubba gum was somehow uplifting. A large, carved wooden altar lined the far wall. Lit candles surrounded the statue of St. Jude in his emerald green robe, symbolizing spring and renewal.

I whispered, "Carol, sometimes altars are for sacrifice, not worship." Carol replied, "Get a grip. I know Louise. She has healing powers."

I bugged Carol, "I wonder if they rotate the saints depending on who Louise is assisting."

Carol pinched my arm.

Louise lifted Erica from my arms and gently touched Erica's ear. Let it be known that neither Carol nor I mentioned Erica's illness to Louise. Carol and I were designated to a far corner of the room.

"I sense an old man hanging on her with an ear problem," Louise purred.

Considering Azrael was my longtime best friend, it was far from me to poo-poo this announcement. I remembered Mom's magic as I touched the gold bracelet encircling my wrist.

Louise started chanting loudly. Unfortunately, the words were in Latin, so I could not translate other than the comforting phrase, *Amor de Dios*. Her voice was unpleasantly high-pitched, not what I expected. Fifteen minutes later, Louise thankfully stopped. I kept my eyes on Erica and noted that she did not seem phased. Louise pointed to the center of the room near the altar and asked Erica to stand there. Erica nodded agreeably.

"Now, sweet one, I want you to put your arms out to your sides and slowly turn three times in a circle. While you turn, I will spit perfume into the air above you. It will feel like raindrops. You won't be afraid, will you?" Louise softly engaged Erica.

Poking Carol in the ribs, I whispered, "What have you got us into? You are such a banana. I should have known better."

I was ready to grab Erica and run.

Carol said, "Shut up."

Erica smiled at me for the first time in a week and began spinning with outstretched arms as though she understood the ritual. Louise clapped her hands together and fell to her knees.

Erica ran to Louise and hugged her, then to me. I half-heartedly thanked Louise as I wandered out to the taxi.

The following morning, Erica charged into the kitchen, saying she was hungry. Did the antibiotics do the trick, or was it Louise's magic?

I returned to the office Monday morning, thankful to Anthony for the paid time off. I wanted to get to know him better. Anthony rarely chatted with anyone. He had a melancholy way about him. I did witness a slight smile when he listened to my tips on how to deal with clients from Brooklyn.

One day, an aristocratic voice said, "Anthony thinks you are marvelous."

I looked up, ready to smirk at this blatant attempt to flirt. A young man with a pale face above a pale linen suit and a winning smile stood before me.

"How would you know, sir?" I asked.

The confident man offered, "Shall we go in together and ask Anthony?"

I replied, "I'm busy," dismissing him, flustered.

The following morning, Anthony called me into his office. The pale man was already in the office.

Anthony said, "This is Terence Blake, my friend."

Anthony continued, "This is Marion. Now, both of you, get out of my office."

Guiding me to my desk, Terence insisted I have dinner with him. While an office romance could be fatal to my pleasant job, I noted that everyone seemed to date everyone in this sales atmosphere. I accepted.

That evening, I tucked Erica in at Richard and Emily's apartment before Terry's arrival.

His swoon-filled eyes and boyish charm were what I needed, nothing serious. As we nibbled dinner, our humor and similar tastes in music created a bond. Our goodnight kiss was delicious.

Our love affair grew faster than I wanted and more profound than we realized. I fought my shadow self to avoid presenting this new love with obstacles. I wondered how a human could live up to the love and trust my Archangel had showered me with.

I turned 33 on March 7, and Erica four on March 9. I baked the Hoffman special chocolate cake and dressed us in our best party clothes for the night's celebration. Our neighbors, Vinnie, Richard, and Emily, joined Terry in the living room, chatting about Merry Old England. Erica was on Terry's knee. With a lit cake in hand, I observed the group. So here I am in Manhattan, surrounded by three Brits. Let's not forget the British Rail fabric on my loveseat.

Our classic New York love affair consisted of lovers' walks through Central Park's Avenue of cherry blossoms and munching hot dogs outside the United Nations Gardens during brief lunch breaks at work.

Our passion was other-worldly, spiritual, as though our bodies had met before over many lifetimes, and we couldn't quench our fire. When spent, we curled in a deep sleep in each other's arms.

Weekend jaunts completed this picture-perfect relationship: A day at the Bronx Zoo with Erica and Terry talking 'monkey talk' to the chimps or visiting my friend Donald and his new wife in Connecticut. Donald and I laughed, remembering how we perched on a branch together, watching the sunrise many moons ago. A visit to Erica's Ramapo Day Camp to see the children perform in their production of *Annie* led us to rush to Macy's as a homage to my Mom and to buy the red signature *Annie* dress from the recent film. That became Erica's favorite dress. I hand-washed it nightly for its repeat performance.

Terry was several years younger than I and had a carefree life. His communication with Erica was more of an equal, fun-filled friend than a father. Yet, Terry and I did not argue over where to go, what to eat, or anything else. He had casually revealed his love for Erica and me on several occasions. Unfortunately, I did not respond in kind. Was I impervious to loving a man at this point or ever? Was Terry's love the right kind required to be Erica's father? I concealed these uncertainties from Terry. I reserved this time to float above the clouds of decisions.

Just after Memorial Day, Terry and I were wrapped tightly under my blue floral quilt, aware of the pain to come as he must soon return to his beloved England. He sat up, cupped my face in his warm hands, and confronted me, "We seem perfect for each other. I don't think we should let this end. At least not yet."

I whispered, "We are, but don't you have reservations? I do."

Terry persisted, "I do. But we deserve time together."

"Come to England with me," suggested Terry.

Terry continued, "I've chatted with my friend, Olly, and my sister, Vanessa. You could take a break and live in the English countryside while I pursue my career in London. I would visit on weekends. Vanessa said you would be near her, and there was a proper country school for Erica."

I was stunned. This friendship approval ritual was foreign to me. The idea of being in a strange country with a lover as my sole connection made me wonder if I was creating a pattern that had started with Edmund. His mentioning his sister frightened me. I canceled the weekend with Terry.

I entered my workplace on Monday morning to find Terry sprawled on my office couch.

He stared at me without a word as I shuffled papers. I thought of his audacity to not give me space. Then he smiled. I melted.

The point of my affair with Terry was to attempt dating. His love of a sport called Cricket, his wandering the globe, and his pure joy in living awakened an adventurous side in me that I barely recognized.

I was aware of the thick stone towers my psyche created against intimacy. Intellectually, protecting myself against the warmth of love was absurd. Yet, it was so. My daughter, Erica, was the only human I let in completely since my Mom. The pain Edmund caused me repressed my love for a man beyond lustful desire. Of course, I always had Azrael somewhere in my ether. I wondered if this was enough.

Chapter 38

To Go Or Not To Go

I decided to visit Dr. Greenberg. He let me know our discussion would be a professional therapy session. I felt uneasy. I saw his casual advice over the years as friendly banter.

Past experiences surged to the forefront of my mind. I spoke of my intolerance for violence. Once, I jumped off a bus to intervene in a street fight. My tactic was to scream at the top of my lungs, startling the combatants and freezing the scene like a camera frame. This impulse caused me to leave movies before the end and turn off TV shows if the slightest savagery began. Secondly, there was my squashing the love of a man beyond lust. Thirdly, the exhausting reoccurrence of waking at 3 AM in response, I supposed, to Alan's dead-of-the-night suicide attempts. Fourth, the holes in my memory. My most profound concern was that my fears would harm my innocent daughter's growth.

A wide-eyed Dr. Greenberg said, "Your self-knowledge is a positive result of your painful youth. That and your curiosity are a winning combination for your mental health. Let's focus on your fear of moving out of your safe zone physically and emotionally."

He said reactions to years of losing close loved ones at an early age manifested in multiple ways. Memory loss is one way our brains defend us from traumatic shocks. Repeated suffering can lead to Post-Traumatic Stress Disorder (PTSD). Symptoms may include nightmares, heightened reactions, anxiety, or depressed mood. We can work on finding the triggers and lessening their burden. However, putting yourself in danger will not bring anyone back. Keep journaling. Lean into your spirituality.

After an hour of intense work, we took a break, sipping colas. Then, grabbing our sweaters, we took a walk. I was proud to be seen walking with him. My belief that my Dad visited me through Yehudi's violin music did not change the fact that I periodically appreciated father figures along the way.

Settled back in the office, Dr. Greenberg presented his rationale for my moving to England. He asked if my remaining confused family had begun to communicate. I relayed that my latest letters to Nancy and Roy remained unanswered. Time and space away from old wounds may help me find solutions. He would give me a couple of books. Erica and I could explore the English countryside with its quaint villages and historic sites. And New York City wasn't going anywhere. He added that while Terry's life had been easy, perhaps he needed the depth I possessed. He saw Terry's offer as a gift.

Putting up his finger to momentarily stop my response, he said, "My only practical concern is that you have enough money."

I nodded in agreement, knowing I could support myself for two years, since the US dollar was more substantial than the British Pound.

Content in my chair, I whispered, "So, this is therapy. Everyone should have this chance. Important, I think."

I left Dr. Greenberg's office fortified that this move had much to offer Erica and me.

Just as I was about to announce my move to the world, a new pang of guilt claimed my heart. Would my leaving New York City of my own accord mean I was deserting the foster children, now adults, in passing faces on the bustling streets? If I recognized one, would I bravely approach them? Would they love me or hate me, including me in their abandonment?

Instead, would our eyes shock each other without stopping? Would the relentless question of whether they are safe be extinguished abroad? Sometimes, if I stood perfectly still on a perfectly still day, I heard children moaning. Fast-paced walking was my solace.

I visited Dad and Mom's grave, searching for a definitive answer. The rain had stopped minutes before my arrival. I detected the rain's appealing fragrance. The arrival of Alan's spirit made me excited and apprehensive. Was he buried nearby? Shut up, Marion. He's here at this moment. Kneeling, I smiled at the bright yellow dandelions flush against my parents' tombstone. Are they gardening in the beyond? I recognized that when I share family stories and secrets with my daughter, all must be prefaced with your deceased, dead, passed on, in heaven relative. Our family reunions would be in cemeteries like today. I didn't know if I would burden Erica with the living family cowards.

Not finding an answer, I walked the quiet path, heading for the cemetery's exit. Spotting a worm washed onto the sidewalk, I returned it to the earth. I was going to help Life win.

Chapter 39

Life Was Winning

After dinner, a few days later, I asked, "Terry, can I bring my bike?"

He stared at me, taking forever to answer. Was my remark too casual? Then he said, "Perfect for your country adventure."

Summer quickly rolled along. I was thankful Terry enjoyed taking photos, as I wanted masses of them to relive those carefree moments. Our sunny days at Jones Beach and our trip to Fire Island in early September were captured forever in photographs. Erica gained platinum streaks in her hair, a strong body, and a fast-growing vocabulary.

In late September, Anthony organized a farewell party for Terry in an empty loft. I painted silhouettes of palm trees while Erica drew her version with chalk on the floor. I was thankful the night's festive event lightened the looming separation. Terry left for the airport after the party. Erica and I were supposed to fly with him, but the crucial custody documents had not arrived.

The night after Terry's departure, I experienced an astral projection. This wasn't my first experience, but the most vivid one. I dreamt that Azrael taught me how to fly. I flew out my third-floor window, but was going so fast that I bumped into buildings without harm. I was giddy. Azrael soared above and around me, showing off his skills. I captured one ocean blue feather in the midst. Back in bed, half asleep, I invited Azrael to explain. My best friend did not appear. Will I ever learn that one does not invoke an Archangel?

I awoke with a jolt. Was this dream flight to be the crescendo of our twenty-seven-year bond? Unlike human friendships, there would be no farewell party or lingering kiss. I felt this momentous ending deserved more.

That day, I took Erica for our last bike ride to Washington Square Park and on to a sports store to dismantle my Cadillac bicycle for shipment.

While questioning my artistic talent, I made an appointment at The Art Students League for advice. I entered, breathing in the bitter smell of linseed oil. I reverently presented my portfolio, asking the League's administrator if a grant program was available. The administrator explained that because I had not attended for a couple of years, they could not help. However, he offered to call City & Guilds of London Art School because he found my portfolio promising.

I left the League's building on West 57th Street and jaywalked its rushing traffic lanes. I felt invincible.

A Sanitation Truck swerved and screeched to a halt inches from me.

My thousand-winged friend appeared before the truck, expanding across the double-wide, four-lane street. He reached five stories in height. The face of a gorilla with black, intense eyes looked back at me. Azrael was mocking King Kong.

Suddenly, the earth trembled beneath my feet as a wind encircled me. I closed my eyes and lifted my face. Scents of my Dad's vegetable patch, Mom's *L'Air du Temps* perfume, and Alan's boyhood well-oiled baseball mitt wafted up to me. Archangel Azrael was bidding me au revoir. He had other folks to help accept the passing of their loved ones. He had new souls to tenderize for the beyond.

With both hands, I blew him a kiss, shouting and crying, "Thanks for the surprise ending, my dearest friend!"

The Sanitation workers continued cursing as I dashed eastward to pick up Erica from nursery school one last time.

With new clarity, I donated my violin to the Manhattan School of Music in Harlem, keeping my promise to Shady. The Family Court continued its battle with the Canadian system for my move to England with Erica. My neighbor, Richard Adams, gave Erica a hard-covered copy of his film picture book, *Watership Down*, as a parting gift.

My last day in New York City began at 5 AM. Holding my unpacked espresso cup full of steamy coffee, I opened the living room windows to hear the chorus of traffic. I was glad there was no opera singing. By 8 AM, Erica was curled up in the living room, dipping her toast fingers into her soft-boiled egg. Her favorite TV show, *Dogtanian and the Three Muskehounds*, was on. She had a crush on Dogtanian.

The downstairs buzzer sounded, and I cheerfully invited, "Come to the third floor."

I heard, "Shit, three floors, Mac," before my finger lifted from the buzzer.

The brawny movers tossed my five heavily packed boxes onto a dolly within seconds. I pointed to the two boxes marked FRAGILE, reaching for the tiny top one.

I whispered, "Maybe I should put Mom's crystal vase in my suitcase."

Mover One's gigantic, calloused mitt removed my hand from the box and shook it.

He declared, "Don't worry, lady, ya packed real good. They'll be on the ship heading for England before midnight tonight."

I tipped them, closed my door, and covered my ears, trying not to hear the dolly slamming stair to stair.

Almost immediately, there was a knock on my door. Vinnie, wearing a fresh shirt and Paco Rabanne cologne, grabbed me, said goodbye, and rushed down the stairs.

My building's super appeared at my door asking if he could take some stuff. I refused.

Watching my furniture be removed would hurt too much. I had lost so much with my moves. We agreed I'd leave the door unlocked and the key on the table.

Erica and I returned from our last ice cream soda at the corner shop around 7 PM. She headed for her room, yawning and commanding, "Tuck me in."

Tenderly making circles around her closed eyes, my daughter drifted off. Stretching, I tiptoed out and finished packing. I wrapped Uncle Henry's oil painting of a ship rocking in a rough sea with my heavy sweaters and closed one suitcase. Our traveling outfits were laid out on the antique loveseat.

Around 9 PM, I cheerfully answered the phone, expecting Diane to wish me bon voyage and ask how soon she could visit me in England.

"How did you get my number?" I stuttered, collapsing onto my bed.

Edmund chortled, "I convinced a court official I had to say goodbye to Erica and that you wouldn't mind. Are you there?"

Edmund continued. "Fine, don't answer. I'm thinking of seeing you off at the airport tomorrow. I know Erica is better with you, but I want to see you panic one last time as I snatch her just for a moment."

I hung up.

Chapter 40

Stand by Whom?

I settled into the yellow Checker Cab on that crisp October morning. I wore my pale yellow jumpsuit secured at the waist by my tan leather obi belt and running shoes. Erica wore her *Annie* dress and red Kermit boots. I secured my diamond stud earrings, gold chain with a Pisces symbol coin, and the magic gold bracelet. I fastened my gold cross around Erica's neck. All from Mom. I looked forward to sharing stories of her Grandmother Extraordinaire's magic.

Wide-awake, Erica, strands of her braided hair unraveling in the wind, gazed out the taxi window, asking what that was, and that, and that, giving me little pause to be sentimental about departing my New York City. The familiar skyline broke through the sunrise haze, reminding me how, on my past journeys, it had welcomed me home. I reminded myself that I could always return.

The rare times I had taken taxis rolled in. Mom and I, as we headed to Pocatello to raise hell or my surprising Alan in front of Dr. Greenberg's office. Important events were reserved for taxis.

CHAPTER 40: STAND BY WHOM?

We arrived curbside at John F. Kennedy International Airport. I paid the driver and piled my belongings into the sturdy, burgundy stroller. Suddenly anxious, I froze outside the airport's glass doors. I recalled how Mom and Alan died when I dared to be on planes. I gripped Erica's hand, repeating a mantra to stay in the present, and marched in.

The airport was packed with droves of people. I kept Edmund's threat paramount. The expensive restraining order continued to prove useless. But, on the other hand, maybe he was bluffing.

My adrenaline pumped fiercely as I scoured every face and movement around me. I slugged down an espresso. Semi-settled in the airport's orange plastic seats, I cuddled Erica.

My MRK monogrammed, beige, and navy-blue canvas tote was stuffed with sandwiches, ensuring Erica's favorite peanut butter and jelly on white bread led the food charge. A quart of espresso for moi, water, apple slices, a plastic bag with a wet washcloth, and extra empty baby bottles in the shape of animals, although Erica preferred her Freddie Flintstone-shaped bottle. I had packed her Little Golden Book Collection and my new journal for my soon-to-be incredibly tranquil life.

Erica was an independent four-year-old. She undid her braids, letting her masses of long, untamed, auburn tresses tumble around her shoulders. Her grandmother would have said she looked like a banshee.

"I want to sleep there," Erica declared, pointing to my suitcase.

"I don't think that's a good idea, honey," I whispered.

She broke free of my arms, placed hands on her hips with the worn pink blanket with faded blue piglets dangling from one hand, and stared. I unlocked the suitcase, and she curled onto the stacks of rolled clothing, immediately falling asleep. Unfortunately, this shift created problems guaranteeing Erica's safety.

I locked the stroller in front of the luggage. Then, I wrapped Terry's oversized olive-green trench coat around me and squeezed into a tiny spot between the window and the suitcase.

This was the second man's coat to wrap me in a protective cocoon. My arms confidently entwined around Erica.

Too highly caffeinated to doze off, I retreated into the mélange of my life and struggled to remember a visit from my sister Nancy and her two daughters in Toronto.

According to the court documents, Nancy and her daughters, Donna and Deena, 19 and 16 years of age, respectively, visited Edmund, Erica, and me in Toronto. I could not recall their visit. Nancy showed me photographs of her black Labrador. I told her I did not remember their dog. Nancy thought I was on drugs. Had she forgotten my healthy practices following Adelle Davis, a vitamin guru? Did she consider that Edmund might have drugged me and that my baby daughter and I needed rescuing? I struggled to evoke their visit. I was appalled that my sister had left me there!

Erica's movements pulled me from this past reckoning. Over the next ten hours, we intermittently ate, took walks, and read and re-read nursery books. During the hours

Erica slept, I fought to remain awake. Flipping through my purse, ensuring essential documents were in place, I came across the present Terry had left with me, asking me to open it at the airport. Was this request made doubting my departure? Probably. Under the beautifully wrapped gift paper was a worn jewelry box. The antique ring had a delicate white gold band with a small emerald and two diamond baguettes. It fit my ring finger perfectly. This new symbol of love strengthened my resolve to board the plane to England.

Finally, sixteen hours after arrival, we were accepted as standby passengers. An airport announcement that my flight would start boarding in approximately one hour grabbed my attention. I settled Erica on my hip and lined up behind a slew of cheery folks excited about their upcoming adventures. I spotted Edmund in the distance.

With Erica's legs wrapped around my waist and my right arm snuggly around her, I politely asked fellow travelers on the line in front of me if I could please skip ahead as my daughter was getting heavy.

As I progressed up the ramp's entrance to the plane, one person at a time, Edmund loomed larger, closer. Then I heard his footsteps as his leather soles snapped against the airport's marble flooring. I impolitely maneuvered ahead of people without asking. I was in front of the flight attendant.

Edmund, jaw locked, glared at me.

I shifted Erica to my left hip, away from him.

Aargh, the Flintstone bottle was lying on the orange plastic seat! I can't risk running for it, so I repressed the possible consequences of seven hours without it on the plane.

I felt Edmund's breath on my neck as he whispered, "Hello."

I stared at the flight attendant.

She reacted with a wink and took my ticket. She placed her hand on my shoulder, directing me forward. I heard Edmund ask the nearby desk attendant if any seats were available on my flight.

As I entered the plane's ramp, I watched him race to buy a ticket. I boarded the plane with Erica safely in my arms.

I sat tentatively as Erica pulled her blankey out of the bag. She faced me, grabbing my yellow jumpsuit shoulder pads to help settle on my lap. Her legs, in their now twisted white tights, knelt on either side of my thighs.

Erica asked, "When can we walk because I want to say hello to people?"

"You know people on this airplane?" I asked, frantically hoping she would say no.

"No, silly, but they are smiling at me, so that's only right," said Erica.

Blowing kisses on my daughter's hands, I prayed to stay strong. Think! If he boards, then what?

I looked down, hiding in my mind. Then, finally, an announcement was made that the doors were closing for takeoff. Dare I relax?

A Flight Attendant stood over me, handing me the Fred Flintstone bottle.

"This kind gentleman saw you leave this," said the attendant.

I screamed in my head, "No, dear God, no."

I looked up with defiance.

An older gentleman looked at Erica with an endearing smile.

"She reminds me of my grandchild, full of chatter. Bless her," he kindly said. I squeaked out, "Thank you," barely holding myself together.

The other attendant approached and whispered, "He didn't make this flight. May I fill the bottle?"

I nodded affirmatively, turned off the overhead light, and let tears run freely from my weary eyes. We could rest. Erica and I had seven glorious hours safely away from daily strife.

Chapter 41

Made It!

Our plane landed on time at Heathrow Airport. Feeling safe from Edmund, I let Erica walk beside me instead of carrying her.

The Customs Officer I was assigned looked grumpy. I shook off this silly thought, aware of my nerves. I would muddle through this interrogation procedure and continue to the other side of the door.

Holding her *Winnie-the-Pooh* stuffed bear to the officer's face, Erica asked, "Does my friend need a passport?"

Laughing, the officer replied, "No, not if he's your friend, young lady."

The ice was broken.

The officer questioned me about the length of my stay, the reason for my visit, and where I would reside.

I responded calmly, "My name is Marion, like in Robinhood. My Visa allows me one year. I will be living in Wiltshire."

I was pleased I referenced an English tale. A further 30 minutes was spent filling out a stack of documents.

The Customs Officer looked into my eyes to ensure he had my undivided attention and said, "If you don't renew your Visa on time, I promise Scotland Yard will be at your door. Understand?"

"Yes, Officer, I understand," I answered loudly.

The Customs Officer stamped my passport and Visa and said, "Welcome to England, ladies," winking at Erica.

Piggybacking Erica, I whispered, "Eri, we are going to *Winnie-the-Pooh* country."

My daughter bounced, squeezing her legs around my waist with her bear dangling from her hand. I took a moment to attach Winnie securely to her wrist with the bear's red bow tie.

The automatic door opened to Heathrow Airport's vast, bright reception room, buzzing with strangers yelling welcome to folks rushing through with us. Spotting a sign above the crowd, *Maid Marion*, I walked confidently forward.

May Archangel Azrael ease everyone's crossing.

The End

Acknowledgements

Exposing my story was frightening. But the opportunity to inspire one soul to hang on for tomorrow and the inevitable laughter and peace that awaits, won over my fear.

Seeking professional help is part of the "Deal to Heal."

It brings a smile to my face to look at this page of people tough enough to question my drafts yet kind enough to support me through my self-doubt.

Linda Langton, Book Agent Extraordinaire, who believed in my story in its roughest stage. Linda welcomed each improving draft with encouragement.

Phyllis Melhado, Author (*The Spa At Lavender Lane*), Mentor, and dear friend. Phyllis introduced me to Langton International Agency and continuously cheered me on. Phyllis is an exceptionally eloquent, kind human, a rare treasure.

Jacqueline Gay Walley, my tireless Coach and Editor, put up with my balking at her calm, consistent corrections.

Regina McBride, my Developmental Editor, presented lengthy, detailed notes that delivered an intensive course on writing skills. She gave me the confidence to trust my story.

Dr. Lisa Licht Hirsch, Ph.D., Licensed Clinical Psychologist and my therapist, continues to strengthen me through painful Post Traumatic Stress Disorder (PTSD) passages. Her listening skills hear beyond the words.

Dr. Rob Jacklosky, Professor of English, University of Mount Saint Vincent, invited me to a Mini Writing Workshop on campus grounds. Rob's enthusiasm for my writing caused me to trust my words. My lifetime experience with teachers was filled with feelings of failure. Thank you, Dr. Rob "The Amazing Professor" Jacklosky.

Ralph E. Gomory, Winner of the National Medal of Science, graciously allowed me time and space for my personal creativity when I was Chief of Staff during his presidency of the Alfred P. Sloan Foundation. I had a wild, sometimes hilarious experience balancing a manuscript between Ralph and his co-author, William J. Baumol (*Global Trade and Conflicting National Interests*). Our 25-year bond epitomizes the depth of friendship.

Jellybean and **Happy,** my feline muses, who landed on my desk most mornings, signaling me to begin writing.

Enjoy Connecting,
Dear Readers

My dad, Charlie

Uncle Bill & Aunt Augusta's wedding

Uncle Henry with Limo

Uncle John

Alan's childhood

My upside down world

Dedicated to the foster children

My painting, Pocatello

Mom's little book to me

Alan, grown up

Edmund & Marion's wedding

Mom and me at my wedding

Baby Erica & me

Baby Erica & her Dad

Possible car bomb

Erica in Benny Goodman's Limo

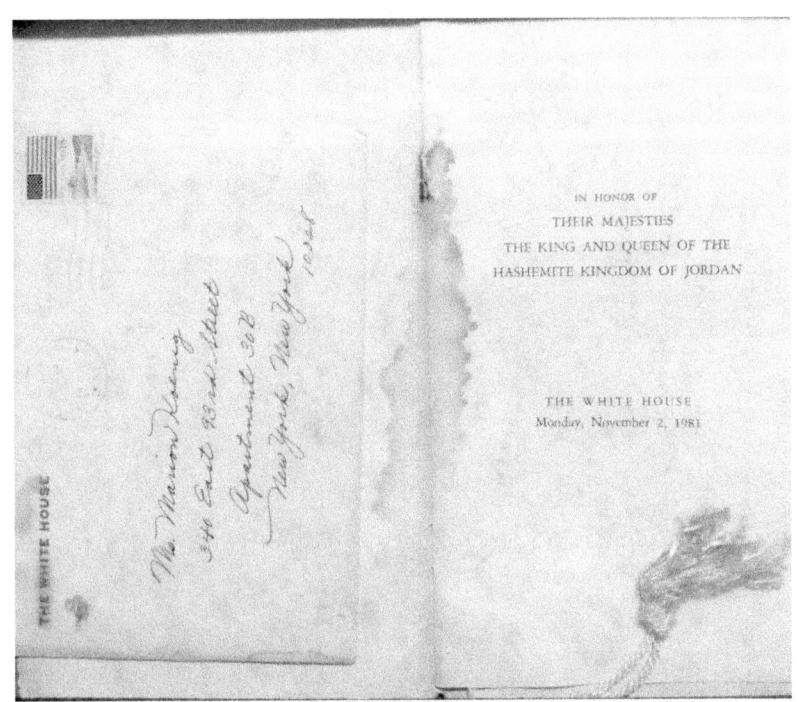

The President and Mrs. Reagan
request the pleasure of the company of
Ms. Koenig
on Monday evening
November 2, 1981
at 9:30 o'clock

Music   *Black Tie*

White House Invitation

Four-year-old Erica